**THE
ARMED FORCES
OF CANADA,
1867-1967**

NOTE

The inferences drawn and the opinions expressed in this book are those of the editor, and the Department of National Defence is in no way responsible for his presentation of the facts.

THE
ARMED FORCES
OF CANADA
1867-1967

A CENTURY OF ACHIEVEMENT

edited by
Lieutenant-Colonel D. J. Goodspeed, C.D.

DIRECTORATE OF HISTORY
CANADIAN FORCES HEADQUARTERS
OTTAWA 1967

Contents

Foreword

It is appropriate that as part of the celebration of the centennial of Canadian Confederation a volume should be written summarizing what the Armed Forces of Canada have done for their country, the Commonwealth and the world during the hundred years that have passed since the Dominion of Canada was created.

The Dominion came into being amid the menacing stir of the Fenian troubles, which helped to convince the provinces of British North America that they should act on the aphorism that union is strength. The perils of that day also served to suggest to statesmen and citizens that the colonial dependence on Britain in matters of defence which they had practised for generations was not altogether worthy of a community that aspired to be a nation. The process thus begun was long and gradual. In the nineteenth century the armed forces of Canada consisted entirely of a homespun militia of limited military value, whose continued existence in peaceful times was probably due in great part to the fact that it had a certain political importance. (It is worth remembering that at least five of the militia colonels who commanded units in the North-West Campaign of 1885 were also Members of Parliament.) Yet this force which Canada always discovered and turned to in emergency was the heir and the embodiment of a very old and honourable native military tradition in which both French-speaking and English-speaking Canadians were sharers. It was in fact one of the most valuable items in the outfit of the new nation.

This book tells something of the evolution that changed a colonial militia into a national army, and brought national naval and air services into existence beside it. It describes what these forces did in two World Wars and in more recent crises. Of their influence on their country's position in the world it says less; but today it may be fair to assume that every Canadian appreciates how much of Canada's status as an independent power was won for her on the battlefield. The men who fought at Vimy and Falaise, who helped to keep the Atlantic sea lanes open, who flew the Sopwiths of one war and the Lancasters of another, deserve to be counted among the founding fathers of modern Canada. And I hope that the reader of this volume will not cavil at another point which it seeks to make: that it has been mainly through her armed forces that Canada has made her influence felt in the world at large. In recent years they have exerted that influence in the interests of peace in a variety of operations around the globe. These activities, chiefly undertaken under the authority of the United Nations, are described in some detail in this book.

The story ends with the integration of the command structure of the Canadian Forces in 1964-66, not the least interesting episode in the volume. The book itself is the first production of an integrated Directorate of History which the present writer was invited to inaugurate in 1965. It has been the work of many hands. Lt.-Col. D. J. Goodspeed, the Senior Historian, was the prime mover and carried the main planning and editorial responsibility. Portions of the book were drafted by the following members of the Directorate: Mr. C. H. Brown, Mr. P. A. C. Chaplin, Mr. R. V. Dodds, Lieutenant J. L. Granatstein, Flight Lieutenant H. A. Halliday, Mr. F. J. Hatch, Dr. J. M. Hitsman, Mr. J. D. F. Kealy, Mr. M. K. MacLeod, Captain J. A. Swettenham (who also collected the illustrations) and Mr. T. Thorgrimsson, who also gave invaluable editorial assistance, prepared the index and helped immeasurably with problems of production. The maps were produced by Mr. E. H. Ellwand with the assistance of Corporal W. R. Constable. The Director held a general watching brief and contributed an occasional paragraph. Mr. E. C. Russell, the Executive Officer, helped in many ways. Much gratitude is due to Major R. F. Wodehouse of the National Gallery of Canada and to Mr. G. W. Hilborn of the Historical Division, Department of External Affairs, for generous assistance and advice; to W.O. 1 D. F. Boudreau of the Directorate of Photo Services for his unfailing cooperation, and to Staff Sergeant A. Brazeau of that Directorate for fine photographic work. Thanks are also due to Mr. C. P. Clark, Director, C.F.H.Q. Graphic Arts; to his Deputy, Mr. D. W. Baker; and to Mrs. M. G. Lise Moreau of his staff, who together with Mr. Ellwand, prepared the general layout of the book.

C. P. STACEY
Director of History

May, 1966

A FIGHTING HERITAGE

Canadians have never been a military people, but their history has echoed with the clash of arms. War has played a decisive part in shaping their destiny. Today, a century has passed since a foreign invader has set foot on Canadian soil; but the earlier history of the country is largely the story of desperate defence, bold counter-attack and gallant fighting against odds. The first buildings erected in Canada by white men were crude forts, and thereafter the inhabitants of Canada had continually to defend themselves, as the Iroquois, the New England colonists, the British and finally the troops of the American republic invaded the country in turn.

Under the Lilies

From 1609, when Samuel de Champlain joined a Huron-Algonquin war party and killed two Iroquois braves with one shot from his harquebus, until about 1700, the colony of New France was in constant danger from the savage warriors of the Five Nations who lived in the north-western part of what is now New York State. Iroquois war parties raided farms, burned missions, all but annihilated the Frenchmen's Indian allies and on occasion even threatened larger settlements such as Ville Marie and Trois-Rivières.

In these circumstances, no farmer went to plough without a loaded musket ready to hand or attended mass unarmed. Every able-bodied male in the colony was potentially a soldier with the obligation of bearing arms, and a document which has come down to us from 1651 shows that the men of Trois-Rivières were required by law to possess weapons, drill and do guard duty. Doubtless other settlements had similar regulations.

The Iroquois planned to invade the colony in force and eliminate it in the summer of 1660 but were halted by 16 gallant Frenchmen and some friendly Indians under Adam Dollard at the Long Sault. Although Dol-

lard's little band was overwhelmed after eight days' hard fighting, the grateful colonists of New France believed that the resistance at the Long Sault had caused the invaders to abandon their bloodthirsty plans for the summer. The respite did not last for long, for the Iroquois continued to press in around the French settlements, constricting movement, hampering development and constituting an ever-present peril. In 1665, in response to repeated appeals, King Louis XIV sent the colony 24 companies of regular infantry, mostly belonging to the Carignan-Salières Regiment, and the following year the Marquis de Tracy led an expedition into Iroquois territory and forced the Indians to sue for peace. Their task apparently accomplished, most of the regular soldiers were returned to France during the next two years, not to be replaced until 1755.

In 1669 King Louis instructed the Governor of New France to organize a proper militia. The task was not difficult, for the principle of compulsory military service had always been recognized in the colony and the Canadians knew that with the departure of the regular troops their salvation depended upon themselves. By 1673 Count Frontenac had militia companies in every parish, and some of the larger parishes had more than one. The local captains of militia were important personages with civilian as well as military functions, although in time of crisis their companies usually provided drafts of men rather than fighting as formed units. Some time after the withdrawal of most regular soldiers in 1667 and 1668, those who remained behind, together with subsequent reinforcements, were permanently localized in the colony and administered by the French Minister of Marine who was responsible for the colonial empire. From 1691 about 28 companies of these *troupes de la marine* were usually stationed in New France. As time went by, most officers and a proportion of the men of the *troupes de la marine* came to be recruited in the colony, so that these "Colonial Regulars" became, in a sense, Canada's first permanent force. Most *troupes de la marine* were infantry, but an artillery company was organized in 1750 and a second one followed in 1756. Three years later, in 1759, the French Commander-in-Chief, the Marquis de Montcalm, established a volunteer force of 200 cavalrymen. As with most European armies at this time, the military forces in New France were supplied and administered by a civilian organization under an Intendant, a system that permitted both inefficiency and venality.

Encouraged by the New England colonists, the Iroquois again went on the warpath in the 1680s, and for the next 15 years their terrible war-cry was a familiar and dreaded sound about the smaller Canadian settlements. Some temporary respite was gained when the Marquis de Denonville led a large expedition against the Iroquois Confederacy in 1687, but two years later, after the village of Lachine was overrun and its inhabitants massacred, the fiery old Count Frontenac was

sent back as Governor to end the Iroquois menace once and for all.

That year "King William's War" broke out in Europe, and this sharpened and gave point to the traditional hostility between French and British colonists in North America. Knowing that the Iroquois were acting as allies of the New Englanders, Frontenac struck at both foes impartially. In 1690 he sent raiding parties against Schenectady, New York, Salmon Falls, New Hampshire and Portland, Maine. In retaliation, a New England naval expedition, commanded by Sir William Phips, attempted to capture Quebec in October, but Frontenac boldly replied to Phips' summons to surrender that he would answer only with the mouths of his cannon. The invaders were repulsed when they landed; and the ships' bombardment was effectively answered by the Quebec guns. The regular troops were not needed; the Canadian militia did the fighting, and the hero of the defence was a native-born Canadian, the Sieur de Sainte-Hélène, one of the famous Le Moyne brothers. (Pierre Le Moyne, the Sieur d'Iberville, harried

(Courtesy J. M. Gray, Esq., M.B.E.)

DÉFENSE DE QUÉBEC PAR M. DE FRONTENAC, 1690

Though it is pretty evident that the artists had never seen Quebec, this engraving of Frontenac's cannon engaging Sir William Phips' ships seems to catch the spirit of the episode. Engraving by the brothers Rouargue, Emile and Adolphe, of Paris, period 1836-56.

2

Boats from the British fleet attack and burn the *Prudent* and capture the *Bienfaisant* during the siege of Louisbourg in 1758.

the British throughout the length of North America but is best remembered for his five adventurous expeditions to Hudson Bay between 1685 and 1697, in the last of which he captured three British vessels and took York Factory.)

Iroquois raids continued during the next few years despite Frontenac's attempts to reach a settlement with the Indians, and in 1696 the old Governor — he was then in his 75th year — personally led an expedition against the Oneida and Onondaga villages of the Confederacy. In the following year Britain and France suspended hostilities by signing the Treaty of Ryswick, and in 1701 at a "great congress" in Montreal the Iroquois formally smoked the pipe of peace with the French and their Indian allies. The pledge of peace was not kept, for the savages could not long resist the temptation of intercepting the French fur trade or of continuing that irregular warfare which was their pride and their delight. Yet although the lure of the forest ambush, the tomahawk and the scalping knife called them back insistently to the warpath, never again were the Iroquois to be the principal threat to New France — but only because a more formidable foe was soon to attack the little colony.

Between 1702 and 1713 Britain and France again opposed each other in the War of the Spanish Succession. In North America the first eight years of the conflict were marked only by border raids and massacres, a type of warfare that provided congenial employment to adventurous young men on both sides but could never achieve a decisive result. In 1710 a more serious English attack captured Port Royal, and three years later, when the Treaty of Utrecht brought the war to a close, France, because of defeats in Europe, relinquished to Britain Newfoundland, what is now mainland Nova Scotia, and the area bordering Hudson Bay.

A troubled peace prevailed for a generation, until the outbreak of King George's War in 1744. That year the French unsuccessfully attacked Port Royal (which had been renamed Annapolis Royal), and in 1745 William Pepperrell, with a force raised in New England, took Louisbourg. When the war ended in 1748, all conquests were returned; but the next year Britain founded what was to be a great naval and military station at Halifax. The peace that followed was only a breathing spell, an interlude for gathering strength, and even this lull was broken when a French force under Coulon de Villiers sharply defeated a band of Virginians led by Lt.-Col. George Washington at Fort Necessity in 1754.

3

Both Britain and France sensed that their ancient colonial rivalry in North America was reaching a climax and both sent reinforcements. In 1755 four battalions of regulars arrived in New France and two in Louisbourg. These troops, later reinforced by another four battalions, were to be the mainstay of the French military effort in North America, although they were greatly aided by the colonial regulars and the Canadian militia. War was not declared until the following year, but this technicality did not prevent Lt.-Col. Robert Monckton from landing 2300 men in Acadia in June 1755. He captured Forts Beauséjour and Gaspereau and later that summer deported most of the French inhabitants to the American colonies. The French had their revenge when a British force under Major-General Edward Braddock was routed near Fort Duquesne by 254 Canadians and about 630 Indians under Captain Claude de Contrecoeur. Braddock himself was mortally wounded and 1400 of his 1900 men became casualties, although Indian and French losses amounted to no more than 25. However, the British could take some satisfaction from the repulse and capture of the commander-in-chief of the French troops, Baron Dieskau, during an attack on an encampment of American provincials at Lake George. During 1756 and 1757 Oswego and Fort William Henry fell to the French, now led by the Marquis de Montcalm, and a British expedition to capture Louisbourg proved abortive, but next year the fortunes of war began to turn. The three million inhabitants of the Thirteen Colonies powerfully overmatched the 60,000 Canadians of New France; scarlet-coated British regular regiments were appearing in increasing numbers; and the Royal Navy controlled the Atlantic. Montcalm was able to defeat the incompetent Major-General James Abercromby when he attempted to storm Fort Ticonderoga on Lake Champlain, but the British under Major-General Jeffrey Amherst captured Louisbourg, and in August Fort Frontenac fell to a force commanded by Lt.-Col. John Bradstreet.

Nevertheless, the fate of New France was not to be decided by these outlying skirmishes but by a direct assault on Quebec. In late June 1759, Major-General James Wolfe landed some 8500 splendidly trained British regulars on the Isle of Orleans, less than four miles away from Quebec. Montcalm had nearly 16,000 men under arms, but of these only five understrength battalions were regulars, some 2600 were *troupes de la marine* and the remainder were partially trained militiamen. Worse still, Montcalm and the Governor of the colony, the Marquis de Vaudreuil, were bitter enemies; there was more than a little antagonism between the colonists and the soldiers from France, and

the fortifications of the town were inadequate and badly designed. Nevertheless, the British operation at first proceeded slowly, and an attempt to capture the Montmorency Heights at the end of July was sharply repulsed and had to be abandoned. The first hint of autumn was already in the air, bringing new hope to the French and causing the British admiral to speak restively of getting his fleet out of the river before the ice came, when Wolfe in desperation made a bold night landing in a little cove above the town on 13 September. By dawn he had placed 4400 troops on the Plains of Abraham. Montcalm sallied forth from his camp with an approximately equal force and advanced spiritedly to the attack, but the deadly volleys of British musketry blew great gaps in his line. In a short, fierce action the French were defeated and both Wolfe and Montcalm were killed.

Quebec held out for five more days before surrendering, while what was left of the French army escaped westward to Montreal under Vaudreuil. Amherst, on the shores of Lake Champlain, moved too slowly to capture Montreal that autumn, and in the spring of 1760 the new French commander, the Chevalier de Lévis, tried to retake Quebec. When Lévis defeated a British force under Brig.-Gen. James Murray at Ste. Foy, it appeared for a time as though France might yet regain all she had lost the previous September, but the first sails to appear on the St. Lawrence in the spring belonged to a British, not a French, fleet. Lévis was forced to raise the siege of Quebec; the relieving French fleet was destroyed in a naval engagement at the mouth of the Restigouche River in July; and that autumn, when Montreal capitulated, the lily flag of the Bourbons was hauled down for the last time in New France. In 1762 the French captured St. John's, Newfoundland, but in the face of overwhelming British sea power were forced to relinquish it again within three months. Next year, with the signing of the Treaty of Paris, the gallant little colony, which for a century and a half had fought courageously against great odds, was ceded to Britain.

Under the Union Jack

Although all the French regulars and a large proportion of the *troupes de la marine* returned to France following the capitulation of Montreal, the British military governors continued the Canadian militia system almost unaltered. The first new militia legislation, passed in 1777, was based on the old concept that every able-bodied male was liable for compulsory military service. The colony of Nova Scotia had passed similar legislation in 1758, and other colonies later did

THE FIGHT AT THE SAULT-AU-MATELOT BARRICADE, 1775

Canada's "old and new defenders", French and British, fought shoulder to shoulder on 31 December 1775 when American forces attacked Quebec's Lower Town. Water colour by C. W. Jefferys.

the same. However, this "Sedentary Militia" existed largely on paper; the men were not armed, uniformed or given training; and as a rule they attended only one muster parade a year.

Even immediately after the conquest, the new British rulers of Canada did not hesitate to employ Canadian militia on active service. In 1764, a year after the Indian tribes of the west under Pontiac had captured Michilimackinac, invested Fort Detroit and attacked Fort Pitt (Duquesne), Colonel John Bradstreet led a relieving force to Detroit. He was accompanied by a French-Canadian militia battalion under the Sieur de Rigauville. As it happened, the Canadians saw no action, but their conduct during the campaign was exemplary, and the episode is significant as being the first of many occasions when French Canadians cam-

paigned side by side with their English-speaking compatriots.

The fall of New France had removed the only menace that had threatened Britain's thirteen American colonies, and the British redcoats, who had been welcomed as defenders in 1759, soon came to be regarded as the burdensome representatives of a distant king. With the outbreak of the American Revolution in 1775, American forces lost no time in attempting the conquest of Canada. Late in the year the British under Guy Carleton, the Governor, were driven back into Quebec. There on 31 December, in a blinding snowstorm, Brig.-Gen. Richard Montgomery and Colonel Benedict Arnold, with about 1800 Americans, launched an attack on the Lower Town but were repulsed with the loss of some 400 prisoners and 100 casualties, in-

5

Cutting of the 30-mile road that became Ontario's Yonge Street was begun on 28 December 1795. Governor John Graves Simcoe of Upper Canada is seen here supervising work being done by the Queen's Rangers. From a drawing by C. W. Jefferys.

cluding Montgomery, who was killed, and Arnold, who was wounded. The following May the arrival of a relieving British fleet forced Arnold to raise the siege and retreat. Later in the summer the Americans, much reduced by smallpox and desertions, abandoned Montreal and left Canada, not to return. That November an abortive revolt of New England colonists in Nova Scotia was easily put down, but in October 1777, Lieut.-General "Gentleman Johnny" Burgoyne, with an army that included about 100 Canadian militiamen, surrendered at Saratoga.

The war dragged on for another six years, marked in the north by a series of British raids against American settlements by Lt.-Col. John Butler's Rangers and Joseph Brant's Indians. In 1783, the Treaty of Paris recognized the independence of the United States but recognized too the separate existence under British rule of the northern portion of the Continent. The long war left behind it unfulfilled ambitions and a continuing hostility, so that for the next hundred years Canadians were to consider the United States the principal military threat to their national identity. To meet this threat Britain maintained a fairly large garrison of regular troops in British North America and later raised some so-called "fencible" regiments which were permanently localized in the colonies in the same manner as the French *troupes de la marine* had been.

The latent American threat became deadly danger when in June of 1812 war broke out between Britain and the United States. Once again American armies invaded Canada. Fortunately, British North America was defended by well-trained British regulars under efficient officers, who were more than a match, at least in the early months of the war, for their numerically superior but inexperienced enemies. In July the American general William Hull invaded Canada on the Detroit frontier but retired soon afterwards to Fort Detroit to capitulate there on 16 August to a significantly smaller force under Major-General Isaac Brock, the British commander in Upper Canada. In the dark morning hours of 13 October that same year an American army under Major-General Van Rensselaer crossed the Niagara River in small boats, drove in the British outposts and massed on the commanding escarpment of Queenston Heights. General Brock had fallen in an initial skirmish, but that afternoon Major-General Roger Sheaffe with a force of British regulars, Canadian militiamen and Indians attacked and decisively defeated the invaders. The victory, a vital one for the future of British North America, was marred by Brock's death, but he had already saved the country. His energy, boldness and strategical insight had prevented the United States from taking advantage of the colony's initial weakness. Thanks very largely to the fact that the Provincial Marine of Upper Canada held a precarious naval superiority on the Great Lakes, the remainder of the year passed with no notable American success.

The next year was similarly indecisive. On 27 April the Americans raided the town of York and a month later took Fort George, but British victories at Stoney Creek and Beaver Dam, and British raids into the United States along the Niagara frontier, redressed the balance. Much more serious was the defeat of the British naval squadron at Put-in Bay on Lake Erie in September, for this meant that Detroit and the western portion of Upper Canada inevitably fell to the Americans. On 5 October, Major-General Henry Procter was defeated by an American army under Brig.-Gen. William Harrison at Moraviantown, and the Indian chief Tecumseh, a gallant ally of the British, was killed. However, two American armies converging on Montreal were both roughly handled; one by a predominantly Canadian force including French-Canadian Voltigeurs under Lt.-Col. Charles de Salaberry at Chateauguay on 26 October, and the other by 600 British regulars under Lt.-Col. Joseph Morrison at Crysler's Farm on 11 November.

Both the British and Americans now began a frantic naval building race on Lake Ontario, but no naval

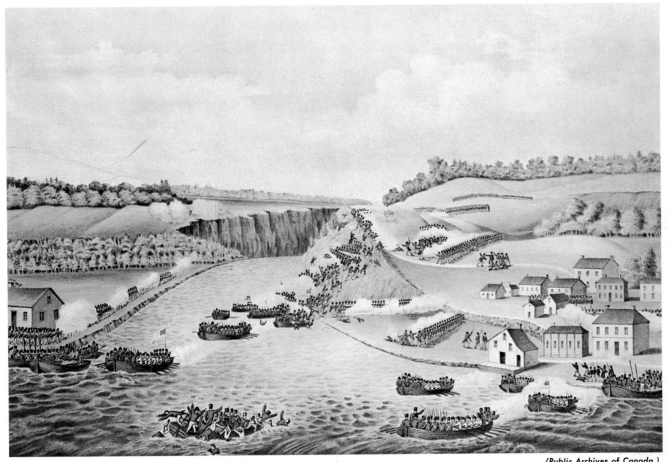

THE BATTLE OF QUEENSTON HEIGHTS, 13 OCTOBER 1812
Engraving by T. Sutherland from a sketch by Major Dennis of the 49th Regiment, who took part in the battle.

battles were fought there in 1814. On 25 July 1814 the fiercest engagement of the war occurred on the Niagara front at Lundy's Lane, when an American force under Major-General Jacob Brown abandoned the field to Lieut.-General Gordon Drummond after prolonged and bloody fighting. In September, as a result of the defeat of the British naval squadron on Lake Champlain, a half-hearted attack on Plattsburg failed, but a force under Sir John Sherbrooke occupied a considerable portion of the District of Maine before the war was brought to a close by the signing of the Treaty of Ghent in December. The Treaty restored to both sides all the territory that had been conquered in three years of fighting.

In spite of the legend that Canada had been saved by her militiamen, the truth is that the successful defence of the country had been primarily due to the British regular regiments and the fencible regiments raised in the colonies, as well as to the Royal Navy's control of the Atlantic. The Canadian militia had done admirable service, but the brunt of the fighting and most of the casualties had been borne by the long-service British units. In the future the reputation of the militia would prove a stimulus to national pride but would also deceive the colonists into believing that little preparation in peacetime was needed to meet the threat of war.

Although the Treaty of Ghent brought peace, it did nothing to eradicate old antagonisms. The Rush-Bagot Agreement of 1817, negotiated on American initiative, almost eliminated the rival navies on the Great Lakes, but the memories of past quarrels, the American dream of a single great republic embracing the whole of the continent, and the remembered injustices cherished by the descendants of the United Empire Loyalists all ensured that relations between the United States and British North America remained uneasy. In the decades that followed 1814 Britain generously spent large sums to construct defences in Canada. Halifax and Quebec were fortified; forts were built at Ile aux

7

Noix on the Richelieu and at Kingston, and — most important of all — the Ottawa and Rideau canal system was constructed at a cost of a million pounds to provide an alternative military route to the vulnerable St. Lawrence waterway between Montreal and Lake Ontario.

In both Upper and Lower Canada political discontent had been simmering for years before it erupted into armed revolt late in 1837. In Montreal in November there was street fighting between the followers of Louis Joseph Papineau, the French-Canadian reformer, and English-speaking "Loyalists" who supported the government; troops had to be used to restore order. By the middle of November considerable numbers of armed rebels had gathered at the villages of St. Charles and St. Denis in St. Hyacinthe County. On the 23rd, a column of soldiers sent against St. Denis by the British Commander of the Forces, Lieut.-General Sir John Colborne, was defeated and forced to withdraw, but two days later a second column dispersed the rebels at St. Charles after a brisk engagement. Papineau, whose agitation had been responsible for the violence, did no fighting but fled to the United States.

The real hero of the rebellion in Lower Canada was Dr. J. O. Chénier, who in December rallied a rebel force at St. Eustache in Two Mountains County. When Colborne attacked with two infantry brigades on the 14th, Chénier bravely resisted until he was killed and his band of habitants put to flight. Although this effectively ended the rising, several rebel leaders sought shelter in the United States, where they proclaimed themselves the government in exile of "The Republic of Lower Canada". In 1838 two minor invasion attempts by this group proved that the rebels had no chance against organized troops. Unfortunately, the political and racial tensions that had caused the rebellion were exacerbated by all too frequent instances of government troops' wantonly burning farm-houses and stealing horses.

The rebellion in Upper Canada broke out somewhat later and was even less formidable. When an armed band led by William Lyon Mackenzie advanced on Toronto on 5 December 1837, it was met by a force of Loyalist militia outside the town. Both sides fired a single volley and fled in opposite directions. The rebels rallied around their headquarters at Montgomery's Tavern and there, two days later, were scattered by the militia under Colonel James FitzGibbon, a veteran of the War of 1812 who was Adjutant General.

Mackenzie escaped to establish a "Provisional Government of the State of Upper Canada" on Navy Island in the Niagara River, but he was driven from

this refuge after a Canadian raiding party destroyed his supply ship, the *Caroline*. During the winter and spring Canadian rebels and American sympathizers made several abortive attempts to invade Canada. A more serious incident occurred in November 1838, when a group of raiders under the command of Nils von Schoultz landed in Canada near Prescott. Regulars and militia forced the invaders to take shelter in a group of buildings on Windmill Point, and there, after four days of fighting, known as "The Battle of the Windmill", they were forced to surrender on 16 November. In December, another party of American adventurers who descended on Windsor was repulsed with ease.

Apart from their political consequences, the rebellions had some significant military results. Interest in the Sedentary Militia was revived; the regular garrison was increased to over 13,000 men in 1838; and several long-service Canadian units were raised at Imperial expense and remained in existence for the next few years, the last of them being disbanded in 1850. In 1840-41 the British Government raised The Royal Canadian Rifle Regiment, a special unit of the British Army which was permanently localized in Canada, to man military posts along the American border. The Royal Canadian Rifles remained in existence until 1870. However, the defence of Canada was beginning to prove very costly to British taxpayers, and from about the middle of the century there were increasing demands from sections of the British public and Liberal politicians to reduce this expenditure, or at least to ensure that the colonists, who had now been granted Responsible Government, bear an equitable share of defence costs. For the most part, Canadians of all political leanings showed little inclination to spend more of their own money on defence.

With the outbreak of the Crimean War in 1854, the regular garrison in North America was drastically reduced, only some 3000 British troops being left in the colonies. However, because patriotic enthusiasm ran high, the Canadian Legislature passed a new Militia Act the following year, establishing a volunteer force of not more than 5000 men who would be uniformed, armed and given annual training. The Militia Act of 1855 was significant in that it marked the beginning of the modern Canadian Army Militia system and foreshadowed the ultimate abandonment of the old principle of universal compulsory service. When the Indian Mutiny broke out in 1857, a number of Canadian volunteer units offered their services but were turned down; however, the following year the British Government raised the 100th Royal Canadian Regiment of Foot in Canada.

The American Civil War, which began in 1861, generated acute tension between Britain and the United States and posed a serious new threat to Canadian independence. British North America was poorly prepared to meet a possible war. There were fewer than 4300 British regulars available; the Province of Canada had only about 5000 volunteers; and Nova Scotia, New Brunswick and Prince Edward Island between them could muster another 5000. Two weeks after the Confederates' guns had opened against Fort Sumter, the British Government began to reinforce the garrison in Canada, chartering the world's largest steamship, the *Great Eastern,* for the purpose. In the autumn of 1861, when the Americans stopped the British steamer *Trent* at sea and war appeared imminent, the imperial Government feverishly prepared a force for Canada, hoping that the transports might reach Rivière du Loup on the St. Lawrence before the river became ice-bound. The troopships lost their race with winter and had to turn back for Halifax, but by the middle of March 6823 British soldiers and 18 guns had been passed into Canada over the "snow road" that ran through New Brunswick. In all, more than 14,000 British officers and men were sent to North America between the summer of 1861 and the spring of 1862. In addition, a number of new volunteer regiments were raised in Canada, some of which are still in existence today. Although early in 1862 the Canadian Parliament rejected a bill which would have provided, by compulsion if necessary, a militia force of 50,000 men, by the summer of 1864 the Canadian volunteers had a strength of 21,700, five times larger than in 1861.

Fortunately, war between Britain and the United States was avoided, but when the American Civil War ended in the spring of 1865, an Irish-American organization known as the Fenian Brotherhood declared its intention of "liberating" Canada from British domination and using it as a counter to obtain Ireland's independence. For a time it looked as though the Fenians might be a real threat, for their society was augmented by large numbers of battle-hardened Irish-American veterans who were ready for further adventures.

Reports that an armed force of Fenians was preparing to invade Canada on St. Patrick's Day, 1866, led John A. Macdonald, the Canadian Minister of Militia, to call out 10,000 men. When the anticipated attack failed to materialize, most of the volunteers were demobilized, and in April a projected Fenian attack on New Brunswick was foiled by a rapid concentration of British

(Courtesy the Public Archives of Canada.)
Well wrapped in blankets, British troops travel through New Brunswick in the winter of 1861, en route to Quebec.

warships and the mobilization of the militias of New Brunswick and Nova Scotia. However, one serious attempt to invade Canada was made in the summer of 1866. On 1 June, a Fenian "Army" under John O'Neill crossed the Niagara near Fort Erie and the following day defeated a small force of Canadian volunteers near Ridgeway. When O'Neill did not receive the reinforcements he was expecting from the United States, he promptly retired from Canada. Fenian threats on the Vermont border resulted in no fighting. Ironically enough, perhaps the most significant result of the Raids was the part they played in fostering the cause of Confederation, for provincial differences were the more easily settled in the atmosphere of excitement and alarm which the Fenians engendered, and the arguments in favour of a unified defence were all but irresistible. In addition, the Fenian threat, which continued until 1871, was responsible for considerably larger defence appropriations and increased the country's interest and pride in its volunteer militia. Many present-day militia regiments had their origin during the Fenian troubles.

On 1 July 1867, Canada, Nova Scotia and New Brunswick came together to found a new nation in

North America. Parades, military reviews, bonfires and fire-works displays marked the birth of the Dominion of Canada. That night, as the lights winked out in the 12 small cities, the hundreds of little towns and villages, and the scattered farmhouses across the land, the citizens went to bed wondering what the unpredictable future held. Their past history had been filled with wars and alarms, but few can have guessed that the years ahead would bring infinitely greater struggles on battle-fields undreamed of in 1867. The Canadians of that time were confident and industrious Victorians. They certainly saw the future in terms of farms, factories and counting-houses rather than of world politics and marching battalions. As the new day came on they rolled up their sleeves and began the gigantic task of building a transcontinental nation in the north.

WIDENING HORIZONS 1867-1914

Early Militia Tasks and Difficulties

The British North America Act, which established the Dominion of Canada, gave the Canadian Parliament exclusive authority over the "Militia, Military and Naval Service, and Defence". The senior French-speaking Father of Confederation, Sir George E. Cartier, became the first Minister of Militia and Defence; but his ill health and the widespread feeling that other legislation was more pressing, delayed the passage of a Militia Act until 22 May 1868. Many sections of this Act had wording almost identical to that of the earlier militia legislation for the Province of Canada. The Sedentary Militia now became a Reserve Militia, in which all physically fit, male, British subjects between the ages of 18 and 60 had a liability to serve unless specifically exempted, but the only actual force would be the existing Volunteer Militia whose personnel were required to re-enrol if they wished to continue serving. Initially in Nova Scotia, where anti-Confederation sentiment was strong, only the Lunenburg Battery of Garrison Artillery re-enrolled, but by the end of 1869 the strength of the Volunteer Militia was 43,541 all ranks: 20,956 in Ontario, 15,066 in Quebec, 3327 in New Brunswick and 4192 in Nova Scotia.

The country was divided into nine military districts, each under a Deputy Adjutant General. Military Districts Nos. 1, 2, 3 and 4 had their respective Headquarters at London, Toronto, Kingston and Brockville. M.D. No. 5 controlled English-speaking units and M.D. No. 6 French-speaking units in the Montreal area. M.D. No. 7 was based on Quebec City; No. 8 was responsible for New Brunswick; and No. 9 for Nova Scotia.

To the consternation of the Canadian public, the British Government announced in 1869 that, in order to effect economies and improve military efficiency, it intended to withdraw all regular troops from Canada during 1870, except for a small garrison at the naval base at Halifax. Many, both in Britain and Canada, believed that this "calling home the legions" presaged the end of the imperial connection; in fact, it had the opposite effect, for once the British taxpayer was relieved of the burden of colonial defence, imperial enthusiasm revived in the Mother Country. In spite of Canadian protests, the last British troops marched out of the Citadel at Quebec on 11 November 1871.

The withdrawal of the British regulars forced the Canadian Government to form two small regular units of garrison artillery to take care of the warlike stores left in Canada by the British Army, to garrison the fortresses at Quebec and Kingston, and to provide gunnery schools for the militia. "A" and "B" Batteries, which were authorized on 20 October 1871, were commanded by former British officers and stiffened by a nucleus of gunners retired to pension from the Royal Artillery.

The British troops would have left sooner had they not been needed for a series of minor crises in 1870. In the spring of that year there was another Fenian scare when invaders crossed into Eastern Canada in two places. At Eccles Hill on the Quebec-Vermont border volunteer militia and home guards had no difficulty in repulsing the 150-200 Fenians who made a half-hearted attack on 25 May 1870. Two days later a Fenian foray into Huntington County of Quebec was easily dispersed at Trout River by British regulars and Canadian militia.

Potentially more serious was the unrest that had developed in the Red River Settlement, a small part of the Northwest Territories which Canada had acquired from the Hudson's Bay Company. The Métis settlers, fearing for their property rights and indignant at the high-handed treatment they had received from

Canadian surveyors, established a Provisional Government at Fort Garry under the leadership of Louis Riel. Since some influential men in the United States were anxious to annex the Northwest Territories, the British Cabinet agreed to the dispatch of a joint Anglo-Canadian military expedition with a strong nucleus of regulars to "convince the United States Government and people that Her Majesty's Government have no intention of abandoning this continent." Command was given to Colonel Garnet Wolseley, an able British officer who was very popular with the Canadian Militia. In addition to the 373 all ranks of the 60th (King's Royal Rifle Corps) and about 70 in other British detachments, 750 Canadian militiamen were recruited in Ontario and Quebec, and a considerable number of teamsters and voyageurs were enrolled.

The troops travelled to the head of the lakes by rail and steamship but from there struck out into the tangled Laurentian forest that stretched to the western plains. The streams up which they made their way in boats were broken with innumerable rapids and waterfalls, and black flies and mosquitoes plagued them by day and night. Yet Wolseley later wrote:

> Our officers carried barrels of pork and other loads on their backs like their men; and the emulation and rivalry between the captains of companies, each being afraid that he should be passed in the race, soon spread to all ranks. You had only to tell a detachment that some other company had done a thing without any great effort, to ensure its prompt execution. There was also called into play the rivalry between regulars and the militia. The latter were determined that, no matter what the former did, they would not be beaten.

Wolseley and his advanced guard reached Fort Garry on the morning of 24 August — exactly 13 weeks after leaving the steamships — to find that Riel and his associates had fled. On 2 September Adams G. Archibald reached Fort Garry and was proclaimed Lieutenant-Governor of the new Province of Manitoba and of the Northwest Territories. Wolseley and his regulars returned to Eastern Canada as soon as they could, but the Ontario and Quebec battalions remained for the winter. A new Military District, No. 10, was created to administer the volunteer militia units formed in Manitoba.

The same John O'Neill who had fought at Ridgeway five years previously led a final Fenian raid into Manitoba on 5 October 1871. The newly-organized Manitoba militia turned out to help the garrison companies from Ontario and Quebec, but the raiders were apprehended by a U.S. Army detachment before they could do any harm.

However, the Canadian Government decided to dispatch a second Red River expedition to Fort Garry across the northern wilderness, and that October and November a force of 212 militia reinforcements and 60 voyageurs under Captain Thomas Scott, of the 42nd "Brockville" Battalion of the militia, made the arduous trip from the East. In 28 days, "during the brief daylight of an almost Arctic winter", Scott's smaller party covered the ground that Wolseley's pioneering force had taken three months to traverse. The "Dominion Force on Service in Manitoba" continued on a dwindling establishment until 1877, when the North-West Mounted Police became wholly responsible for law and order.

In October 1871 the new province of British Columbia became Military District No. 11, and in June 1874 Prince Edward Island became Military District No. 12. Shortly thereafter Major-General Edward Selby Smyth of the British Army was appointed the first General Officer Commanding the Canadian Militia. By now, however, the Treaty of Washington had settled all existing Anglo-American differences, and, the principal threat to Canadian independence being thus removed, many Canadians lost interest in the militia. After the excitement and alarms of the previous few years, peace-

(Public Archives of Canada photo.)
When 400 armed Fenians crossed into Quebec from Malone, New York, on 25 May 1870, the *Canadian Illustrated News* dispatched a "special artist, Mr. Miller" to the front. His sketch appeared on 18 June. At 8 a.m. on 27 May the 69th Regiment (British Army), The Huntingdon (Volunteer) Borderers and the Montreal Garrison Artillery drove the Fenians from prepared positions near Holbrook's Corners.

THE GOVERNOR GENERAL'S BODY GUARD CROSSING LAKE SUPERIOR ON THE ICE, 11 APRIL 1885

Lt.-Col. G. T. Denison, the Commanding Officer, and his adjutant, Cornet W. H. Merritt, are leading. A. H. Hider's water colour hangs in the Officers' Mess of the unit in Toronto.

time soldiering now seemed tame and devoid of purpose; militia strengths declined and some units were disbanded. Since these were also years of financial depression, the militia appropriation was reduced; for 1876-1877 it was only $690,000, the lowest defence budget of post-Confederation history. Limited funds meant limited training and making do with obsolescent stores and threadbare uniforms. Rural units, which customarily did all their training in summer camp, found themselves eligible for camp only every other year. Urban units were better off, for they could muster in the evenings and on weekends, and some of them had wealthy patrons to provide the little extras that attracted recruits.

In 1876 the Royal Military College of Canada was established at Kingston on the site of the former naval dockyard, but there were only 18 cadets in the first class and the college grew slowly. On the other hand, a new Militia Act of 1883 authorized a troop of regular cavalry and three companies of regular infantry to serve as Cavalry and Infantry School Corps (now The Royal Canadian Dragoons and The Royal Canadian Regiment), and the artillery batteries were brigaded as The Regiment of Canadian Artillery. A School of Mounted Infantry was established at Winnipeg in 1885, and in 1887 "C" Battery of artillery was formed at Esquimalt.

General Smyth's recommendation that the Canadian Government manufacture its own small arms ammunition resulted in the foundation of the Government Cartridge Factory at Quebec City in 1882; in 1900 it was renamed the Dominion Arsenal. Another of Smyth's suggestions, that the Canadian Government create a naval reserve, led to the Admiralty's turning over a warship to be used for training. Unfortunately, H.M.S. Charybdis proved to be a worn-out steam corvette that had difficulty in crossing the Atlantic, and after a series of misadventures, culminating in the drowning of two Saint John residents who fell through a rotten gangplank, Charybdis was towed to Halifax in August 1882 and given back to the Royal Navy. More interesting were the attempts of Captain Henry Elsdale, R.E., at Halifax in 1883, to photograph ground defences by cameras mounted in small balloons that were flown like kites. However, his equipment was too cumbersome to be practicable, and the development of aerial

13

Camp Ross, Fredericton, New Brunswick, 1871. Here 1411 officers and men gathered on 29 June for 16 days' training. The Commanding Officer of The New Brunswick Regiment of Yeomanry Cavalry, now the 8th Canadian Hussars (Princess Louise's), Lt.-Col. J. Saunders, is shown reviewing his troops. E. J. Russell's sketch appeared in the *Canadian Illustrated News* of 12 August 1871.

(Public Archives of Canada photo.)

The Canadian Voyageurs on the Nile, 1884. Tracking whaleboats through the first gate of the Second Cataract. (Sketch in the *Illustrated London News*, 29 November 1884.)

photography had to wait for the invention of the aeroplane and the more intricate cameras of the 20th Century.

The Nile Voyageurs

In August 1884 the Canadian Government agreed that Britain might hire boatmen in Canada to help transport up the Nile River the expedition with which General Lord Wolseley — who remembered the voyageurs of 1870 — hoped to rescue "Chinese" Gordon from Khartoum. The Nile voyageurs, except for their officers, who came from the militia, were civilians; nevertheless, the raising of this contingent set an important precedent, for this was the first time that Canada helped Britain in an overseas war. Canadian horizons were widening.

Nearly 400 Canadian boatmen were enrolled under the command of Lt.-Col. Frederick C. Denison, a Toronto alderman and an officer of The Governor General's Body Guard. The expedition was very sensibly and capably organized at short notice by the Governor General's Military Secretary, Major Lord Melgund, who as the fourth Earl of Minto later became Governor General himself; and in September, with typically Victorian *élan,* Denison's party of rough Canadian boatmen set off for a wild and almost inaccessible region infested with savage warriors half the world away. The voyageurs reached Wady Halfa on 26 Oc-

14

tober and pushed expertly up the difficult, cataract-filled course of the Upper Nile, but their perils and hardships were all to be in vain. When the advanced party finally approached Khartoum on 28 January 1885 it discovered that the city had been captured 56 hours earlier and Gordon killed by the dervishes. The expedition was withdrawn and the Canadians went home, having lost 16 men by drowning, disease and other misadventures.

The North-West Campaign

By this time the Métis and Indians in North-West Canada were again in a state of serious unrest. After 1870, many Métis, seeking sanctuary from the encroachment of civilization, had migrated west to the South Saskatchewan River, but now the Government repeated the mistakes it had made 15 years previously. Louis Riel, recalled from the United States, again formed a provisional government, this time at Batoche. On 26 March 1885 at Duck Lake, his supporters clashed with a party of North-West Mounted Police and volunteers and forced it to retreat.

Even before word of the bloodshed at Duck Lake reached Ottawa, an expedition had been authorized under Major-General Frederick D. Middleton, the G.O.C. the Canadian Militia. Apart from Middleton himself and a few staff officers, the force was exclusively Canadian. A total of 3323 all ranks, including 363 regulars, were sent from the East; some 1200 militiamen from Manitoba took the field; and nearly 800 volunteers were recruited in the Northwest Territories. The troops from the East had to travel on foot or by sleigh across four gaps which still existed in the Canadian Pacific Railway line along the rugged north shore of Lake Superior. Snow lay four feet deep and the temperature sometimes dropped to 25 degrees below zero as the hurriedly improvised little army pressed westward. The marches across the wind-swept ice of the great lake were bitter and exhausting, but no men were lost.

General Middleton organized his forces into three independent columns. He was later accused of conducting the campaign with excessive caution, but he had reason to worry about the capabilities of volunteer militiamen, some of whom had "never pulled a trigger" before proceeding west, and his army's administrative arrangements left much to be desired. Middleton's own column, moving against the rebel stronghold of Batoche, was checked for a time by an ambush at Fish Creek but

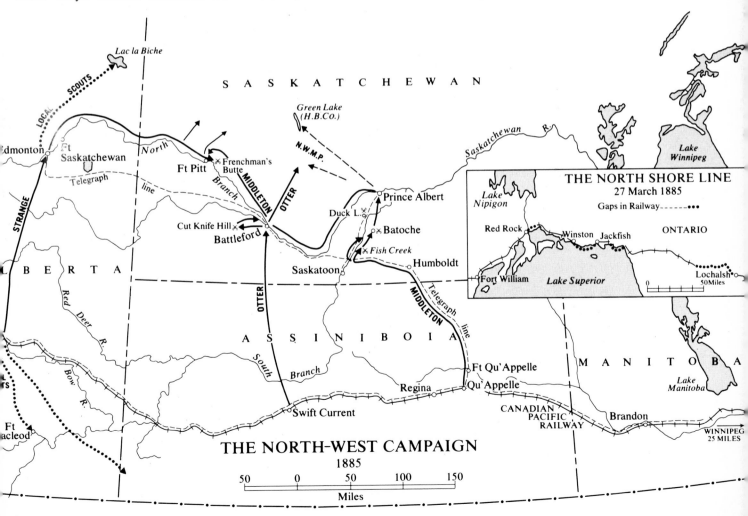

THE NORTH-WEST CAMPAIGN
1885

THE NORTH SHORE LINE
27 March 1885
Gaps in Railway----••••

The York and Simcoe Battalion and Winnipeg Cavalry en route from Fort Qu'Appelle to Humboldt, Saskatchewan, May 1885. The Commanding Officer, Lt.-Col. W. E. O'Brien, M.P., is shown riding near the right front of the foot column.

managed to capture Batoche on 12 May after a confused little battle. A few days later Riel surrendered. A smaller column commanded by Lt.-Col. W. D. Otter of the Infantry School Corps had relieved the settlement of Battleford on 24 April but had subsequently been worsted by Poundmaker's band of Indians at Cut Knife Hill. On 24 May Middleton joined Otter at Battleford. Two days later Poundmaker and his braves surrendered. Meanwhile, Major-General T. B. Strange, a retired regular officer, who is known as "the Father of the R.C.A." and who was then living on a ranch near Calgary, had led the third column north to Edmonton and then east along the North Saskatchewan River. Big Bear's Indians managed to beat off Strange's force at Frenchman's Butte, but shortages of supplies forced them to surrender to the combined pursuing columns on 2 July. Since the prompt military action had dissuaded most of the western Indians from taking up arms, the Canadian militiamen could now return home and leave the North-West Mounted Police in charge of law and order. Militia casualties had been 38 killed and 115 wounded. In this little campaign, the first in history to be fought entirely by Canadian troops, the largely amateur soldiers of the Dominion had acquitted themselves well.

The End of the Century

In contrast to the late 1870s, the years between 1885 and the South African War witnessed a steady growth in the numbers and efficiency of the militia. In 1896, as a result of the Venezuela Boundary Dispute between Britain and the United States, the Canadian Government hurriedly replaced the obsolete, single-shot Snider rifles acquired 30 years earlier with modern Lee-Enfields. A start was also made in re-equipping field artillery batteries with quick-firing guns. In 1896 the appointment of Deputy Adjutant General was replaced across Canada by that of District Officer Commanding. During 1897, for the first time in more than 20 years, practically all the militia received annual training. Of course, the militia was more than ordinarily popular in 1897, for that was the year of Queen Victoria's Diamond Jubilee, a moving and spectacular event filled with all the pomp and circumstance a confident Empire could muster. A Canadian Militia contingent of 36 officers and 141 other ranks went to London to participate in the celebrations.

The discovery of gold in the Klondike brought a horde of prospectors and hangers-on into the Yukon in 1897 and 1898. In all, some 42,500 persons entered

16

(Public Archives of Canada photo.)

Artillery units of the Canadian Militia, stage a demonstration at Barriefield, Ontario, 1891.

The action at Fish Creek, 24 April 1885. Here the Métis leader, Gabriel Dumont, intercepted General Middleton's column advancing on Batoche. The artist shows the militiamen firing from the crest of the hill, trying to dislodge the rebels in the creek bottom. At nightfall Middleton formed an armed camp, and the Métis abandoned their line.

(Public Archives of Canada photo.)

(Courtesy Lt.-Col. C. C. Kruger, C.D.)

"A" Company of The Yukon Field Force on parade in the Yukon. Note the Maxim gun at the rear of the column.

the territory, and the Canadian Government foresaw difficulties in maintaining law and order. The N.W.M.P. detachment in the Yukon was reinforced, and on 21 March 1898 an Order in Council established a Yukon Field Force of 12 officers and 191 men, almost a quarter of the Permanent Militia. The Force left Ottawa on 6 May, travelled to Vancouver by rail, then by steamer to Wrangell in the Alaska Panhandle. Thence the troops moved by steamer up the Stikine River to Glenora and journeyed the last 400 miles to Fort Selkirk with pack mules over the Teslin Trail and in scows and boats down the rivers. Fort Selkirk was reached on 11 September, and in October a detachment of two officers and 50 men went forward to Dawson City. For a year, the Yukon Field Force aided the North-West Mounted Police in guarding banks and gold shipments, fighting

"C" Company of The Royal Canadian Regiment seizing a kopje near Sunnyside, South Africa, 1 January 1900.

(Public Archives of Canada photo.)

fires, building hospitals, and maintaining order. In 1899 the Force was reduced to half strength and the following June began the long journey back.

The South African War

From behind a rocky outcrop on a bare, sun-scorched kopje, a man half rose, raised his Lee-Enfield rifle, and fired upward towards the crest of the hill before him. Immediately the rocks reverberated to other rifle-shots, as "C" Company of The Royal Canadian Regiment engaged the enemy. It was the first day of the 1900s, and here at Sunnyside in Cape Colony, South Africa, a military unit of the Dominion of Canada was in action for the first time in history on a distant continent.

Prime Minister Sir Wilfrid Laurier had not wished to send a Canadian contingent to South Africa and had, indeed, declared that the Government could not do so without parliamentary approval; but by the time war was declared, on 12 October 1899, martial enthusiasm had reached such heights, especially in Ontario, that he felt he could no longer maintain his stand without endangering national unity. Next day the Cabinet arrived at a compromise: Canada would raise, equip and transport to Cape Town a force of 1000 volunteers, who would then be maintained by Britain. The Government insisted that this was no official contingent; it was being raised simply because of "the well-known desire of a great many Canadians" to serve in South Africa. The small financial outlay required was given as the reason for not summoning parliament, and it was asserted that the action "under such circumstances, cannot be regarded as a departure from the well-known principles of constitutional government and Colonial practice, nor construed as a precedent for future action." Yet Laurier had taken a significant step towards active cooperation in imperial defence.

Between the time the Cabinet approved the recruiting of a contingent and the skirmish at Sunnyside, less than three months elapsed. The Militia Department responded to the call to arms with alacrity. The news that volunteers were wanted went out on 14 October; on 30 October the 2nd (Special Service) Battalion of The Royal Canadian Regiment of Infantry embarked in the *Sardinian* and sailed for Cape Town. Almost all this volunteer force was made up of regular soldiers or militiamen. The tiny Permanent Force supplied about 150 of the 1000, and 82 units of the Non-Permanent Active Militia contributed some of their best personnel to make up most of the remainder. Before the troops left, the Government had made an important decision — instead of four independent companies to be incorporated piecemeal into British regiments, Canada would provide a single battalion of eight companies under a Canadian, Lt.-Col. W. D. Otter. This was a precedent Canada's soldiers would remember in later years.

On 29 November the R.C.R. arrived in South Africa where they settled down at Belmont, an outpost camp on the lines of communication, to swelter and freeze and perform the drill, rifle practice and battle exercises designed to turn them into "Soldiers of the Queen". The monotony of life in the "Belmont dust bin" was broken only by the Sunnyside raid, in which "C" Company joined to mop up some Boer irregulars, but at last, on 12 February 1900, the regiment marched. Lord Roberts of Kandahar was massing an army to sweep north and crush the redoubtable General Cronje before Kimberley, and the Canadians joined Major-General Horace Smith-Dorrien's 19th Brigade.

Many men and thousands of draft animals fell by the way on the long, difficult march north, but Cronje's 5000 troops were trapped near Paardeberg on the Modder River by Roberts' 35,000. The Canadians crossed the Modder on 18 February and were immediately thrown into action. Advancing rapidly, they were soon pinned down by Boer fire. At first the day was blazing hot, but by mid-afternoon a cold wind was driving rain across the veldt. Lying shivering in the open, where every movement brought fire from hidden riflemen, the Canadians were almost relieved when a British officer ordered an attack. The Royal Canadian Regiment and The Duke of Cornwall's Light Infantry fixed bayonets and charged together. A few brave men almost reached the enemy rifle-pits before the attack faltered and died under the Boer fire. There was no gain.

However, Cronje's force along the river was sur-

"A" Company of The Royal Regiment of Canadian Infantry, then stationed at Fredericton, New Brunswick, parades on snowshoes in the valley of Garden Creek sometime in the middle 1890's.

(Courtesy New Brunswick Travel Bureau.)

The Royal Canadian Regiment and The 1st Gordon Highlanders fording the Modder River before Paardeberg, 18 February 1900.

rounded, and the besiegers were closing in. By 26 February six companies of The Royal Canadian Regiment were occupying a position 550 yards from the enemy. That night they prepared to make a silent attack, supported by 30 Royal Engineers. The waning moon had not yet risen when the Canadians climbed out of their trenches and moved forward. They got within a hundred yards of the Boers before the alarm was given and deadly fire crashed out; and although the left and centre of the line retired somewhat during the night, dawn found "G" and "H" Companies of the R.C.R., with the Engineers, dug in, commanding the forward Boer positions 65 yards away. The Canadian attack finally persuaded Cronje to surrender his force, and the Battle of Paardeberg was over. Canada's soldiers, at the cost of 34 dead and almost 100 wounded, had fought their first major battle overseas and had established a reputation for Canadian arms.

Paardeberg was the only important engagement the R.C.R. fought in South Africa. With Cronje beaten and Kimberley relieved, Roberts went on to take Bloemfontein and Pretoria, but the loss of their capital cities

meant little to the Boers, who now turned to guerilla warfare. The Canadians marched and fought with Roberts, chasing Boer commandos one week, garrisoning a strong point or guarding a railway the next, resting only occasionally. Skirmishes were frequent, but enteric fever and other diseases took a far heavier toll than the enemy Mausers. By early June the regiment, which had left Canada 1039 strong and in May had received about a hundred reinforcements, numbered only 27 officers and 411 men.

When the Canadians had enlisted they had agreed to serve a minimum of six and a maximum of 12 months. Therefore as autumn drew near, they prepared to go home, confident that the war was as good as over. The first draft left South Africa on 1 October and landed at Halifax on 1 November 1900. Those remaining performed garrison duty for another five weeks, then they too sailed, travelling via England, where they were reviewed by Queen Victoria in one of her last public appearances.

The departure of the R.C.R. did not mean the end of Canadian participation in the South African War. The

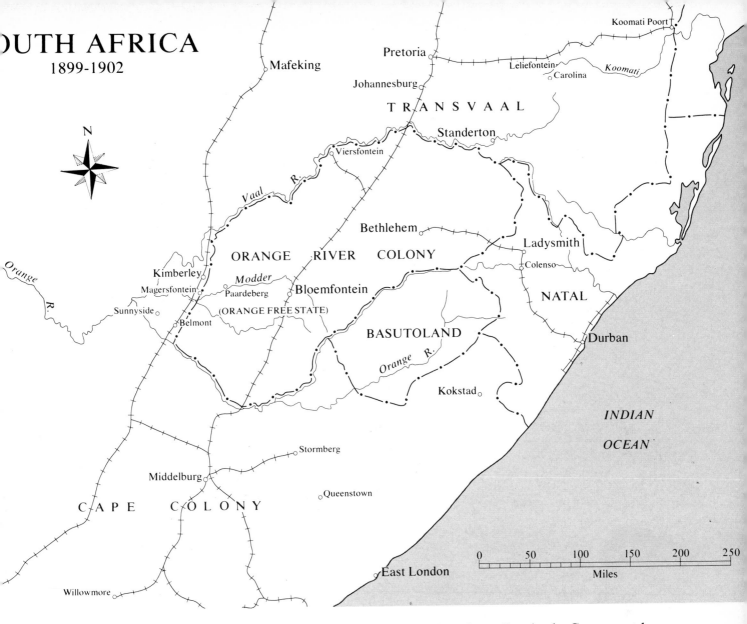

OUTH AFRICA
1899-1902

Government had offered a Second Contingent, and after the bloody defeats at Stormberg, Magersfontein and Colenso in the "Black Week" of 10-15 December 1899, the British were glad to accept. The two regiments making up the bulk of the Second Contingent were the 1st and 2nd Battalions, Canadian Mounted Rifles. Later, in South Africa, the 1st C.M.R. took the name of the Permanent Force unit around which it had been formed, The Royal Canadian Dragoons; and the 2nd C.M.R., formed around a nucleus of North-West Mounted Police, then became The Canadian Mounted Rifles. Three batteries of artillery, from Kingston, Ottawa and Quebec, accompanied the Mounted Rifles; the Permanent Force provided one section of each battery and the remainder came from the militia. The Second Contingent, 1320 strong, had all reached South Africa by 21 March 1900. A 3rd (Special Service) Battalion of the R.C.R. was also raised to replace the British regiment on garrison duty in Halifax. Since the

3rd R.C.R. did not leave Canada, the Government bore its entire cost.

Canada accepted no financial responsibility for several Canadian units raised for service in South Africa. Strathcona's Horse, a mounted regiment, which included many former members of the North-West Mounted Police, was recruited in Manitoba, British Columbia and the Northwest Territories, and was raised and equipped entirely at the expense of Lord Strathcona and Mount Royal, the Canadian High Commissioner in London. The Canadian Government helped to raise but contributed no money for the 2nd, 3rd, 4th, 5th and 6th Battalions of Canadian Mounted Rifles (only the first of which reached South Africa before the war ended), No. 10 Canadian Field Hospital and a contingent of the South African Constabulary. Canada was also well represented in the many irregular units raised in South Africa during the war.

After Paardeberg, regular warfare ceased, but bands

21

of Boer horsemen roamed the land, surprising a small garrison here, ambushing a supply column there — striking hard and then melting into the veldt before a force could be organized to catch them. The British countered with light, mobile columns that could travel as fast as the Boer raiders and, when these tactics brought little success, resorted to vast "round ups" which cleared wide tracts of land of both combatants and non-combatants. Thousands of blockhouses were constructed to defend the British lines of communication and "concentration camps" were built to hold the families of Boers out on commando.

In the fighting the Canadians well upheld the reputation won by the First Contingent. On 5 July 1900, at Wolve Spruit, Sergeant A. H. L. Richardson of Strathcona's Horse earned the first Canadian Victoria Cross of the war when he braved a hail of enemy fire to rescue a wounded companion. The 2nd C.M.R. proved their worth at Boschbult when 22 of them stood off a very superior Boer force, fighting until all but four had been killed or wounded. At Leliefontein, on 7 November 1900, The Royal Canadian Dragoons and the Canadian artillery set the seal on Canadian accomplishments when Lieutenants H. Z. C. Cockburn and R. E. W. Turner and Sergeant E. J. G. Holland all earned the Victoria Cross and Lieutenant E. W. B. Morrison the D.S.O. for a brilliant rearguard action in which two Canadian field guns were saved from capture and a British column from encirclement.

Leliefontein was one of the last engagements of an "official" Canadian unit in South Africa; by the end of 1900 the Dominion troops were all on their way home. Canada's contribution to the war had been small. Only some 8300 men had enlisted, including the battalion for garrison duty and the non-official units, and Canada's financial outlay amounted to less than $3,000,000. The human cost was greater: 89 died by enemy action, another 135 by accident and disease, and 252 were wounded. The Militia units that had made substantial contributions were later awarded the campaign honour "South Africa".

Yet the magnitude of Canada's effort in South Africa was less important than the fact that she had contributed at all. For the first time Canadian soldiers had fought overseas, and the nation had taken pride in their achievements. At the Colonial Conference of 1902, Laurier was noticeably less ready than he had been five years earlier to reject outright British suggestions for imperial unity in foreign policy and defence. He hinted at the possibility of creating a Canadian navy and of paying the cost of the Halifax and Esquimalt defences, and he raised no grave objections to the Canadian

Militia's following British models in organization, training and equipment. Although the British were disappointed in the results of the Conference, an astute observer might have detected that Canada was beginning to show a new interest in defence.

Militia Reform

Between 1900 and 1914 the Canadian Militia was transformed, largely as a result of the lessons learned in South Africa. Reforms had been attempted before, notably by Major-General Ivor Herbert in the early 1890s, but it was not until Dr. (later Sir) Frederick Borden accepted the militia portfolio in 1896 and Major-General E. T. H. Hutton arrived to command the force in 1898 that real progress was made. The militia then consisted of about 35,000 men, of whom some 25,000 received 12 days' annual training. Just enough modern rifles for this force were on hand, but only half the field artillery had modern breech-loading guns and the heavy artillery had no modern guns at all. The supporting arms and services consisted of two companies of engineers. There was no permanent organization above the unit level, although brigades were occasionally formed during summer training camps.

General Hutton wanted a militia with all the essential arms and services, well enough trained and equipped to have something approaching battle-worthiness. He saw to it that almost all units drilled in 1899 and that brigades and divisions were formed at the camps. A Special Staff Course was instituted at the Royal Military College, and several regular officers were sent to Britain for advanced training. The nucleus of a medical corps was established as a first step towards providing essential supporting services. Although Borden sympathized with most of Hutton's plans, the general's uncompromising attitude did not win friends, and after many disagreements with the Government he was asked to resign.

In 1902 Major-General the Earl of Dundonald became G.O.C. and continued Hutton's work. Permanent engineer, army service and ordnance corps units were formed in 1903, and Dundonald's initiative gave the Canadian Militia a signal corps before one existed as an entity in the British Army. An Intelligence Branch was established in Ottawa and a Corps of Guides formed to assist it in the field. The strength of the artillery was increased, some cavalry units were converted into mounted infantry and new mounted infantry units were organized to make a more balanced force. Dundonald pressed for better training facilities and began constructing and improving rifle ranges and building new, more elaborate armouries. His insistence on a large, central training area, where extensive manoeuvres could be held, led to the acquisition of what is now Camp Petawawa. Graduates of the Royal Military College were encouraged to join the Permanent Force, and emphasis was placed on higher professional standards for officers and N.C.Os. To strengthen the "sentimental connection between the great Colonies and the Mother Country and ... between the military forces of the Colonies and the Imperial Army," Dundonald proposed the creation of formal alliances between Canadian and British regiments. An alliance between Toronto's 48th Highlanders and the Gordon Highlanders of the Imperial Army received royal approval in 1904, and by 1914 one cavalry and 15 infantry regiments had formed similar alliances.

Borden supported Dundonald's campaign to modernize the militia, and for several years from 1903 a vote of about $1,300,000 was provided annually to purchase armament and equipment. Dundonald also effected reforms in the headquarters organization at Ottawa, notably the transfer of the engineers and stores branches from civilian to military control. His proposal that five powerful, responsible Higher Commands be superimposed over the existing District Commands was implemented shortly after his departure. The immediate cause of Dundonald's resignation was his dislike of patronage. Also, he shared with Hutton a penchant for trying to accomplish difficult reforms overnight. When in June 1904 he publicly attacked a Cabinet Minister over a question of patronage in militia appointments, the Government removed him.

A new Militia Act, which came into effect on 1 November 1904, raised the Permanent Force establishment to 2000, increased the maximum pay of the Permanent Force private to 75¢ a day after six years' service, and authorized the formation of cadet corps under the authority of District Officers Commanding. The requirement that the G.O.C. be a British regular officer was abolished, and it was left to the discretion of the Government whether there would be a G.O.C. at all. Canadian Militia officers, who had previously been considered junior to British regulars of the same rank, were now given equal status. But the most important provision was one authorizing a Militia Council similar to the Army Council that had been established in Britain that year. The new Militia Council consisted of the Minister of Militia and Defence, the Deputy Minister, the civilian departmental accountant, the heads of the four military branches of General Staff, Adjutant General, Quartermaster General and Master General of the Ordnance, and a Secretary. The Minister regulated Council procedure and stipulated the matters on which he wanted advice, but each member was free to bring any subject before Council. An Inspector General was appointed to keep the Minister-in-Council informed on "the readiness and fitness of the Military forces of Canada for war". The new system worked well. Acrimonious public quarrels between the Minister and his senior military officers ceased, and henceforth what differences arose were settled privately.

Canada Acquires a Navy

The South African War had alarmed Britain. Her leaders were convinced that they must abandon the policy of "splendid isolation", overhaul the army and encourage the self-governing colonies to strengthen their military and naval forces. Although the Canadian Government was reluctant to assume additional defence responsibilities, international events were taking the matter out of its hands. Germany's Navy Laws of 1898 and 1900 and her bellicose attitude were creating the "German threat" that was to dominate imperial defence policy until 1914. Britain felt forced to adopt a policy of concentration, and this led to the withdrawal of British forces from Halifax and Esquimalt. The last British soldiers left Esquimalt on 22 May 1906, and the transfer of the dockyard followed. The *de facto* transfer of Halifax dockyard took place on 1 January 1907, although the formalities were not completed till 1910. The departure of these last imperial garrisons necessitated an increase in the Permanent Force, and the Militia Act was amended to raise its authorized establishment from 2000 to 5000, "if necessary". However the actual strength of the Permanent Force at the outbreak of the First World War was only about 3000.

At the Colonial Conference of 1907 Laurier forced the withdrawal of a resolution recognizing the duty of the dominions and colonies to contribute to naval defence and rejected a suggestion that Canada might build dry-docks capable of taking a dreadnought. However, the temper of Canadian public opinion was changing. The departure of the Royal Navy's squadrons from Halifax and Esquimalt in 1905 was a dramatic event which forced Canadians to think about naval defence. Although the discussion was desultory, newspapers and politicians of both parties began to pay more attention to naval matters. Still, there was little sense of urgency until the "naval scare" of March 1909 burst on the Empire. The "scare" arose when the Admiralty (erroneously) announced that by 1912 Germany might have 21 dreadnoughts as opposed to Britain's 18. Something very like panic seized Britain and spread to other parts of the Empire. New Zealand offered a dreadnought; in

The Royal Canadian Navy's first recruiting poster, exhibited in all the principal towns of the Dominion in February 1911.

Australia, public agitation for a similar offer brought down the Government; and on 29 March the Canadian House of Commons passed, without division, a resolution "cordially" approving "the speedy organization of a Canadian naval service in cooperation with and in close relation to the imperial navy". Soon afterwards the Canadian delegates to a special defence conference in London were presented with two alternative plans for a Canadian navy, one calling for seven, the other for 11 ships.

When Parliament re-assembled in November 1909, the political battle lines were already forming. They were ragged lines, with Liberals and Conservatives inextricably mixed — some favouring a Canadian navy, some favouring Canadian contributions to the British fleet, some favouring both, and a few opposed to all naval expenditures. However, the Canadian navy supporters had a parliamentary majority, and the Liberals had little difficulty in passing a Naval Service Act that

received royal assent on 4 May 1910. Promptly on the passing of the Navy Bill, Laurier created a Department of the Naval Service, which included, besides a Naval Branch, the Fisheries Protection, Tidal and Current Survey, Hydrographic Survey and Wireless Telegraph branches formerly under Marine and Fisheries. The Minister of this latter department was also given the Naval Service portfolio; the Naval Branch was put under a Canadian-born retired Royal Navy officer, Rear-Admiral C. E. Kingsmill, who was given the title of Director. Arrangements were made to recruit personnel and to establish a Naval College to train officers. Tenders were called for the construction in Canada of four cruisers and six destroyers, and since this would take time, two cruisers offered by the Admiralty were purchased as training ships. The *Niobe*, a protected cruiser of 11,000 tons mounting a main armament of sixteen 6-inch guns, reached Halifax on 21 October 1910, and the light cruiser *Rainbow* arrived at Esquimalt on 7 November 1910. The cruisers had been brought to Canada by British skeleton crews, but it was intended to man them with Canadians as soon as possible. Obviously it would be some time before the Naval College, which opened at Halifax in mid-January 1911, could provide even junior officers, but ratings were more easily trained. Recruiting started in earnest early in 1911 and was fairly successful, attracting 223 men in the first year.

When Laurier's Liberal Government was defeated in the general election of 21 September 1911, the victorious Conservatives simply ignored Laurier's Canadian navy while they were working out their own naval policy. As the British sailors completed their tours of service, they went home and were not replaced. And what enthusiasm there was in Canada for a life on the ocean wave soon withered before the jeer of "tin-pot navy". It did not help matters when *Niobe* ran aground on a rocky ledge near Cape Sable during one of her early cruises and was put out of service for over a year.

During the fiscal year 1911-12 only 126 men enlisted in the R.C.N. and 149 deserted. In February 1913 the Deputy Minister confessed frankly that the ships were rotting in harbour and that the Department did not know what to do. Robert L. Borden, the new Prime Minister, took some time to decide on a naval policy. A complication was that most of the Quebec wing of his party and the allied Nationalists wanted neither a Canadian navy nor contributions to the Royal Navy. Eventually, Borden decided to defy his Quebec colleagues, and in December 1912 he introduced a Bill to provide $35,000,000 to build three dreadnoughts for the Royal Navy. The Naval Aid Bill precipitated one of the longest and fiercest political fights since Confederation and passed the Commons only after closure had been applied for the first time in Canadian history. In the Senate the Liberals were supreme, and on 29 May 1913 the Bill was rejected there. Borden did not venture to put the question to the electorate, and consequently the R.C.N. remained in a state of suspended

QUEBEC TERCENTENARY 1908: LAST SCENE IN THE FINAL PAGEANT

The Tercentenary was a tremendous military and naval occasion, climaxed by the Historical Pageant. Ships of the British, French and United States navies fire a salute while a great armed throng led by Montcalm and Wolfe, Murray and Levis, crosses the Plains of Abraham. This water-colour was reproduced in *Historical Souvenir and Book of the Pageants*, a brochure prepared by the National Battlefields Commission.

(Courtesy Colonel J. A. Hilliard.)

animation until just before the outbreak of war the following year.

The Last Years of Peace

As European tensions heightened with recurrent crises in the years before 1914, the militia received more attention than ever before. In 1908 the largest militia concentration in Canada's history took place at Quebec City, as nearly 14,000 officers and men assembled to take part in the celebrations marking the tercentenary of the city's founding. But if the militia was more popular than formerly, it was also more business-like. At the 1907 Colonial Conference Britain had recommended the formation of an Imperial General Staff with Dominion branches, and the Dominions had been encouraged to call on the new Committee of Imperial Defence to guide them in matters of higher strategy. Canada had taken no action at the time, but at a special Defence Conference in 1909 Laurier did not oppose standardization on British patterns or the principle of an Imperial General Staff. In 1912 a Canadian officer joined an Australian and a New Zealander in the newly-formed Dominions Section of the Imperial General Staff. More and more Canadian officers were sent to Britain to further their military education, including a number who attended the Staff College at Camberley, and whereas in 1899 only four British officers had been attached to the Canadian Militia, by 1912 there were 34. The number of qualified Canadian staff officers was also growing: in 1909 there had been only three, but by July 1914 there were eight.

It became ever more apparent that the most important role of the militia would be the provision of an expeditionary force for overseas service. The Militia Council had not even mentioned such a possibility in 1905 when considering militia responsibilities; but five years later, when General Sir John French, the British Inspector General, visited Canada to inspect the Canadian Militia, he was specifically asked to comment on its readiness "to succour other parts of the Empire, in the event of the Dominion Government seeing fit to follow on the precedent set by them in the late war in South Africa." He weighed the militia's readiness and found it wanting, and as a consequence, a mobilization scheme was prepared the following year for an overseas contingent of one infantry division and a mounted brigade "for active service in a civilized country in a temperate climate." The plan was kept secret, because "knowledge of its existence might lead to false inferences and cause much mischief", but it was there, ready for use in an emergency.

By 1914 the militia of Queen Victoria's day had been vastly improved. The establishment had increased from about 35,000 in 1901 to 66,000 in 1913, and — what was more important — the 25,000 who underwent training in 1904 had increased to over 55,000 in 1913. Before the South African War, the annual defence budget had averaged some $1,600,000; in 1911, on the accession of Colonel Sam Hughes to the militia portfolio, it stood at about $7 million; and by 1914 it had almost reached the $11 million mark. In 1911 the militia was organized into the formations in which it might have to fight, and a divisional system was adopted everywhere except in the West. Militia training was far from perfect in 1914, but it was much better than formerly. Advantage was never taken of the 30-day training period authorized in the 1904 Act, but the artillery, cavalry, the city infantry corps and some of the supporting services were occasionally given 16 rather than 12 days' annual training. There was less emphasis on parade-square ceremonial and more on musketry and field-craft; officers and N.C.Os. were better qualified, and the adoption of efficiency pay encouraged recruits to continue training. The Department supported

(Courtesy Mr. L. W. Rogers.)

Preparing *Baddeck I* for trials at Camp Petawawa, August 1909.

cadet corps in public and secondary schools, and by 1911 the University of Toronto had a section of engineers and Queen's University was organizing a complete field company. Canadian Officers' Training Corps contingents were established at McGill University in 1912 and at Université Laval in 1913. The new training camp at Petawawa, more and improved rifle ranges and armouries, and better weapons, uniforms and equipment all contributed to a more efficient militia. When General Sir Ian Hamilton inspected the force in 1913, he found some fault with training but conceded that great strides had been made.

Unfortunately, although several militia officers tried to stimulate an interest in military aviation, they were unsuccessful. However, despite a lack of Government support, some Canadian civilians were prominent in aeronautical research. In 1902 W. R. Turnbull set up a laboratory in Rothesay, New Brunswick, where he made substantial contributions to the science of flight. Alexander Graham Bell, F. W. "Casey" Baldwin and J. A. D. McCurdy, together with two United States citizens, organized the Aerial Experiment Association in 1907. In 1908 Baldwin was one of the first British subjects to fly, and on 23 February 1909 McCurdy was the first to fly from Empire territory, when he took the *Silver Dart* off the ice at Baddeck, Nova Scotia. In August that year, Baldwin and McCurdy demonstrated the *Silver Dart* and the *Baddeck I,* the first aeroplane built in Canada, in several flights at Camp Petawawa, but the militia authorities were not sufficiently impressed and the Deputy Minister ruled that aviation was "too expensive a luxury for Canada to indulge in". Consequently, when war broke out, there was no air branch in the Canadian forces.

In the fateful summer of 1914, the Canadian Naval Service was still in a deplorable state. The whole R.C.N. consisted of fewer than 350 officers and men — not even half the war complement of its largest ship — and the Royal Naval Canadian Volunteer Reserve, which had been established only that year, had but 250 officers and men, all in one company at Victoria, B.C. The *Niobe* lay at Halifax in the care of a skeleton crew,

quite unfit for sea duty without weeks of refitting. The *Rainbow* at Esquimalt was in somewhat better case. Early in July 1914 she had been ordered to prepare for a three-month sealing patrol and had actually steamed as far as Vancouver to overawe a group of recalcitrant Hindus who, when they had been refused entry as immigrants, had seized the ship *Komagata Maru* in Vancouver harbour. But although *Rainbow* could put to sea, she was by no means ready for operations.

Meanwhile, across the Atlantic, the skies were darkening, and the time was fast approaching when the Canadian defence forces would have to carry out their responsibilities, whether they were ready or not.

The decades between 1867 and 1914 saw important changes in the Canadian outlook and situation. The Confederation era witnessed the end of the long period when the United States was a potential enemy and the only conceivable task for Canadian forces was defence against it. Now Canada was occasionally looking towards other continents; the colony in the process of becoming a nation was beginning to think of playing a nation's part in the world, and its armed forces were — as they have continued to be to the present day — the chief instrument by which it asserted itself abroad. Canada's part in the South African War was not the mere reversion to colonial status that some people saw it as being at the time. The decision to send men to that war was a national act, stemming in part at least from a new sense of national strength. Sir Wilfrid Laurier spoke after Paardeberg of the pride that battle had aroused, "the pride of the consciousness of our rising strength, the pride of the consciousness that on that day it had been revealed to the world that a new power had arisen in the West". This was exaggerated, but it was at least a true reflection of Canadian feeling. And in 1914 the Canadian fighting man was about to give a new depth of meaning to Laurier's words. Four years later no one could have much doubt that in all truth a new power had arisen in the West.

FLANDERS FIELDS 1914-1918

In the sleepy summer of 1914 the quarrels and crises of Europe seemed remote and unreal to most Canadians. In June the militia held its largest annual camp since Confederation, with 10,339 all ranks and 4553 horses concentrating at Petawawa; but these manoeuvres were typical of Colonel Sam Hughes, the Minister of Militia, who liked to do things on a grandiose scale, and no one connected them with the imminence of war. For several years, of course, there had been talk of a great European conflict, but in Canada at least such talk engendered only the half-pleasant, wholly unreal, thrill of a ghost story told at bedtime. It meant little to Canadians that the Continent was divided into two armed camps, with Germany, Austria-Hungary and Italy in one and France and Russia in the other. Britain had no formal alliance with either, and no one in Canada knew that she did have informal military understandings with France which were to prove almost equally binding.

Sunday, 28 June, was a quiet Sabbath all across the country from Halifax to Vancouver. People did not learn until the next day what had happened in the quaint, far-off town of Sarajevo in Bosnia. There, at about noon, Gavrilo Princip, a member of the Serbian "Black Hand", had assassinated the Archduke Franz Ferdinand, the heir to the Austrian throne. When they read about it in Monday's newspapers, most Canadians were none too sure where Sarajevo or Bosnia actually were.

On 23 July, Austria, supported by Germany, served a harsh ultimatum on Serbia, and on the 28th declared war. Two days later, Russia, the self-proclaimed protector of the Slav nations, mobilized. On 1 August, Germany declared war on Russia and two days later on France. Italy, claiming that she was committed to support Germany and Austria only in a defensive war, remained neutral until May 1915, then entered the war on the Allied side. As Europe rushed to arms, Britain wavered but nevertheless mobilized the fleet. Germany's criminal folly in invading Belgium, whose neutrality was guaranteed by Britain as well as Germany, turned the scale; popular indignation reinforced the effect of the confidential obligations to France, and on 4 August Britain declared war on Germany. Each country, ignorant of what the terrible future was to reveal, confidently expected an early victory.

In 1914 when Britain was at war Canada was at war; there was no distinction. But in Canada too the war was greeted enthusiastically, for with Germany's attack on "little Belgium", Canadians believed that Britain's cause was just. The most frequently expressed fear of young militiamen and volunteers was that the great adventure would be over before they could take part in it.

Despite the energy of Colonel Hughes, the country was indifferently prepared for war. Nevertheless, in the militia — small, ill-equipped and only partially trained — Canada had at least a nucleus on which to build. Hughes promised the early dispatch to Britain of 25,000 men, but then scrapped the orderly procedures of a carefully drawn mobilization plan in favour of a personal appeal — "a call to arms", he termed it — and a concentration at Valcartier where no camp yet existed. Volunteers flocked to join the colours, and by 8 September an impressive total of 32,665 officers and men had assembled to fill the new camp which Hughes was constructing.

At Valcartier four infantry brigades were formed, each comprising four battalions of 1000 men. The new battalions had only numbers and did not perpetuate the time-honoured names of militia units. This naturally caused some hard feelings, the more so since the organization of Hughes' expeditionary force was almost entirely dependent on the drafts of militia officers and

Recruiting meeting outside Toronto City Hall, August 1916.

naval vessel in harbour dressed ship and the townsfolk warmly welcomed the newcomers. Since the Canadians were not yet trained or equipped to go into battle, they exercised for the next four months on Salisbury Plain under conditions of extreme misery. Housed for the first half of their stay under soggy canvas, the troops endured appalling conditions of rain and mud, but being young and healthy, they kept in surprisingly good spirits. On dismal winter evenings, when the long day's work was done and the battalions were swinging homewards again, they would make the grey Wiltshire landscape echo to *Tipperary* or *The Girl I Left Behind Me*. Training was intensive, and by the end of January the contingent, now organized into the Canadian Division under Lieut.-General E. A. H. Alderson, a British officer, had attained cohesion. On 4 February the Canadians were inspected by King George V and Field-Marshal Earl Kitchener, the British Secretary of State for War. By now the men were smart and steady. Five days later when the Division light-heartedly embarked for France, every man was sure that the worst of his troubles were over.

Second Ypres

At St. Nazaire, the port of debarkation, the Canadians were loaded into uncomfortable French box-cars marked *"Hommes 40, Chevaux 8"* and carried northeast into the level Flanders country. From billets in shell-torn hamlets, battalion groups marched forward for a week's indoctrination with British units holding the line in front of Armentières. Here they received a thorough introduction to the intricacies of trench warfare, and on 3 March the Canadian Division took over four miles of line in the Armentières sector.

Meanwhile, the elaborate war plans of Germany, France and Russia, carefully prepared over many years, had been put into operation — and every one had failed. The French Plan XVII, which had called for an immediate, violent offensive into the two provinces of Alsace and Lorraine, lost to Germany in 1871, had merely conformed to the German strategy. The French had confidently assumed that their assault would cause

N.C.Os. who had eagerly travelled to Valcartier. Time was spent in forming battalions, issuing clothing and equipment, examining and inoculating recruits, writing attestation papers and preparing for reviews. Little training could be done. The area swarmed with contractors hastily delivering horses, wagons, boots, tentage and other paraphernalia of war, much of which later proved unserviceable. By the end of the month the First Contingent — the largest force that had ever crossed the Atlantic — began to embark at Quebec, and one by one the loaded ships slipped away to rendezvous in the smooth waters of Gaspé Basin. On Saturday, 3 October, the fleet of 31 ships, escorted by four British light cruisers, sailed with the ebbtide. That evening the men crowding the rails nostalgically watched the sun go down in a blaze of orange light behind the Gaspé hills.

Eleven days later, when the First Contingent reached Plymouth Sound after an uneventful crossing, every

CANADA'S GREAT ARMADA, 1914. From a painting by Frederick S. Challener (1869-1959). Thirty-one ships, escorted by four British light cruisers, carried Canada's First Contingent to Britain. They are seen leaving Gaspé Basin on 3 October 1914.

(Public Archives of Canada photo.)

Canadian troops on Salisbury Plain near Stonehenge, October 1914.

On Salisbury Plain the winter of 1914-15 was the worst in living memory.

(Public Archives of Canada photo.)

(Courtesy The National Gallery of Canada.)

LANDING OF THE 1ST CANADIAN DIVISION AT SAINT NAZAIRE, 1915 by Edgar Bundy (1862-1922).
The pipes of the 13th Battalion, C.E.F. (Royal Highlanders of Canada), now The Black Watch (Royal Highland Regiment) of Canada, led by Pipe-Major David Manson, play troops ashore from the steamship *Novian* — Among the officers in the right centre foreground are Colonel (later Lieut.-General Sir) R. E. W. Turner, V.C.; Lt.-Col. (later Maj.-Gen. Sir) E. O. W. Loomis; and Lt.-Col. (later Maj.-Gen.) G. B. Hughes.

the Germans to abandon the offensive. In the event, it worked the other way; it was the Germans who had numerical and technical superiority and the French who were forced to abandon their ventures. In accordance with the Schlieffen Plan, nearly three-quarters of the German Army had concentrated on the right wing for a gigantic wheel through Belgium, Luxembourg and northern France. At first the plan had worked well, but then the Germans, with gaps opening between their armies, felt obliged to abandon Schlieffen's intention of sweeping beyond Paris to encircle it. Instead, they changed direction and marched across the front of the Paris defences, exposing their own flank. The Allies counter-attacked on the Marne and forced the invaders to withdraw to the Aisne. Although the German forces facing Russia had deliberately been left weak, Russian drives into East Prussia had met disastrous defeats at Tannenberg and the Masurian Lakes.

After a last desperate attempt to break through on the right at the First Battle of Ypres, the Germans dug lines of trenches to protect their gains in Belgium and northern France, and the Allies, for shelter, did the

same. As autumn turned to winter, both sides strengthened the trench line with wire and sand-bagged parapets and covered No Man's Land with fire. A continuous front, offering no flank that could be turned, was thus established from the North Sea to Switzerland. The Allies were in the unenviable position of having relinquished ground under conditions of fluid, mobile warfare and then of having to retake it in the face of strong defences and dominating positions.

Thereafter French strategy was governed by the idea of liberating northern France by means of a breakthrough — a costly task. Some in Britain advocated a different policy for 1915; they were convinced that for a maritime power the true strategy lay not in flinging armies at barbed wire and machine-guns but in turning a flank by sea to bring arms and ammunition to the poorly-equipped but numerically superior Russians. But when this plan was tried at the Dardanelles, it failed through inadequate planning and half-measures. No Canadian troops took part in this unfortunate expedition, but The Newfoundland Regiment fought there with the 29th British Division. In 1915 Germany decided to launch an offensive in the East against Russia, confining her activities in the West to a strict defensive except for local attacks.

One such attack, to screen the dispatch of the Eleventh German Army to the Russian front, was to be directed against the Ypres Salient, a small flat area, eight miles broad by six miles deep, which had remained in British hands after the First Battle of Ypres. During the first week of April the Canadians marched north to take over part of the Salient from a French division. On the Canadian right were two British divisions, and on their left a French division, the 45th Algerian, guarded the northern flank.

On the higher ground around the circumference of the Salient the Germans had built up a superiority in men and artillery; they had also decided to use chlorine gas, although this was contrary to the Hague Conventions of 1899 and 1906. They installed 5730 cylinders of chlorine in their front-line, but were so dubious of success that they neglected to provide adequate reserves to exploit the gap the gas was to create. In the late afternoon of 22 April the Germans struck their blow. Olive-green clouds of deadly gas formed, merged and rolled forward over the Algerian trenches on the Canadian left. Helpless men sprawled on the parapets, froth on their lips, nauseated and powerfully sick; hundreds more, with seared lungs, died of suffocation; dark figures ran blindly in the gas cloud, seeking escape that could be found only towards the rear; and as if by magic, a four-mile gap opened immediately north of the Canadians. Fortunately, although this was not known to our anxious troops, the Germans halted after advancing two miles. Had they driven on to Ypres, only four miles away, and moved south along the Yser Canal — the chord of the Salient — they would have put 50,000 Canadian and British troops in deadly jeopardy.

All through the night of the 22nd the Canadian Division, with the 2nd and 3rd Brigades in line, worked desperately to close the gap. In addition, Brig.-Gen. Richard Turner, V.C., the commander of the 3rd Brigade, ordered his men to drive the enemy out of Kitchener's Wood, an oak plantation near St. Julien. This midnight attack, carried out with great gallantry by troops never before used in the assault, cleared the wood, but before daybreak the Canadians, reduced to only a quarter of their original strength, were forced to pull back again.* In daylight on the 23rd Turner put in

---

*In September 1934, The Canadian Scottish Regiment, which perpetuates the 16th Battalion, and The Calgary Highlanders and The Winnipeg Light Infantry, which perpetuate the 10th Battalion, were at last granted permission to wear a special shoulder badge, shaped like an oak leaf with acorn, in commemoration of the gallant midnight attack on Kitchener's Wood.

two more attacks against the new German positions; little ground was gained and casualties were very heavy.

Nevertheless, during the 23rd the Germans made no attempt to exploit their breakthrough of the day before. The Canadian counter-attacks north of St. Julien — the Battle of Gravenstafel Ridge — probably account for this. Thus the day's operations, so expensive in terms of blood, bought time to close the open flank. By that evening British, French and Canadian troops had barred the way to Ypres.

The first battle was over; a grimmer one — St. Julien — lay ahead. On Saturday, the 24th, the Germans attacked in an attempt to obliterate the Salient once and for all. A violent bombardment and another gas cloud followed the successful pattern of the first attack. This time the target was the Canadians holding the Salient's blunted apex. The gas at its heaviest drifted over the 8th and 5th Battalions of the 2nd Brigade entrenched on the forward slope of Gravenstafel Ridge and over the 15th Battalion of the 3rd Brigade which was holding the northern fringe of the village of St. Julien. Those men of the 8th Battalion who were not suffocated held on throughout the day, coughing, choking, and with streaming eyes, gaining what little protection they could from cotton bandoliers soaked in water. As their Ross rifles jammed repeatedly under the stress of rapid firing, the men worked desperately to pry back the bolts, using their boot heels and entrenching tools. The wounded, lying in the bottom of the trench, loaded spare rifles and passed them up to the men in the firing-line. Every German rush was met with deadly rifle and machine-gun fire. The men of the 15th Battalion, on the left, had worse positions. They were literally blown out of these by German field guns firing at short range, and they suffered 647 casualties that day. With the 15th Battalion forced back, the 3rd Brigade front withdrew 600 yards to a line south of St. Julien. Brig.-Gen. Arthur Currie's 2nd Brigade, although thinly-stretched, stood firm. At last, in the middle of the afternoon, when it seemed as though the enemy must at last break through by sheer weight of numbers, British reinforcements arrived. The 2nd Brigade held its part of Gravenstafel Ridge until taken out of the line on 26 April, by which time all the Canadians had been relieved.

In their first appearance on a European battlefield, the Canadians had held the critical left flank of the Ypres Salient against superior artillery and many times their numbers, even under attack by a horrible weapon for which they were totally unprepared. They had suffered grievous loss — 6035 Canadians had been killed or wounded during the Division's brief tour in

THE SECOND BATTLE OF YPRES by Richard Jack (1866-1952)
The famous stand of the 1st Canadian Division, April 1915.

Canadian Orchard,
Festubert, May 1915.

the Salient — but, miraculously, they had held the line. Had they given way, the consequences would have been disastrous. In his dispatch to the Secretary of State for War, Field-Marshal Sir John French reported that "the bearing and conduct of these splendid troops averted a disaster which might have been attended with the most serious consequences". That week the fame of the Canadians at Ypres echoed around the world.

Festubert and Givenchy

In May, while the French launched a major offensive against Vimy Ridge, the British mounted diversionary attacks against Aubers Ridge and the German positions about Festubert. Unfortunately, few Allied commanders yet realized how greatly trench warfare favoured the defensive. In sensitive areas the trench system had multiplied into mile-wide belts containing forward trenches, support trenches and reserve trenches. Attacking troops were forced to expose themselves as they stumbled in waves over the shell-pocked ground, while machine-guns, firing up to 450 rounds a minute, cut them down. All too often the few survivors who reached the enemy lines could do no more than rage helplessly in front of uncut wire until death stilled them. Artillery was used to cut the wire — a normal allotment was 150 shells for a gap ten yards wide in a 20-yard-thick entanglement — but the long bombardment inevitably forewarned the enemy. If the attack was sustained and enough men were committed, some might get through, but the casualties were out of all proportion to the gain of ground. Under such conditions, all the Allied offensives of 1915 failed.

The British were bloodily repulsed at Aubers Ridge, losing 11,000 men in 12 hours for no gain. Nevertheless, the attack at Festubert went in as planned on the night of 16 May, although there were few areas on the entire Western Front less promising for offensive operations. Under cover of darkness the assaulting troops captured the German frontline trenches, but the enemy merely retired to his support line. Haig, deciding that this retirement meant German resistance was weakening, ordered further attacks, and on the 18th the Canadian Division was thrown into the battle. The 2nd Brigade's objective was two redoubts in the German line and the 3rd Brigade's a strongly defended orchard. Out in No Man's Land lay the festering bodies of those who had been killed that winter, together with the more recent dead. In this perfectly flat, alluvial plain, commanded by German fire, burial parties were suicidal. Not surprisingly, both Canadian attacks failed at the first attempt, but the 3rd Brigade seized the orchard on the evening of the 20th. (It was afterwards known

as "Canadian Orchard" and remained in Allied hands until the great German offensive in the spring of 1918 swept this and other gains away.) The 2nd Brigade succeeded on the 23rd. Two days later the battle was called off. For one small orchard and two muddy ditches the Canadian Division paid with 2468 casualties, mostly inflicted by machine-gun fire.

For the Canadians the next battle was at Givenchy, a few miles south of Festubert. There, when the 1st Brigade attacked on 15-16 June, they were supported by three 18-pounder field guns that had been dragged into the front line to blast a path for the attacking infantry. In addition, a mine had been driven under the German front line and was exploded just before zero hour. Unfortunately, because insufficient backfill had been used in the tunnel, the mine flashed back, causing as much damage to the attackers as to the defenders. The guns silenced three machine-guns and blew great gaps in the wire before they were put out of action, but the gaps, through which the assault was funnelled, became obvious targets for other machine-guns. The battle followed the usual pattern for 1915 — heavy losses in No Man's Land; a brief hold on the enemy front-line trenches; hand-to-hand fighting; the inevitable counter-attack; and the retirement of an exhausted remnant to its own front line. The next day a second assault, which had no field guns in close support nor any mine to be exploded, withered away in No Man's Land under murderous machine-gun fire from an alerted enemy. With this the battle was halted after the attacking troops had lost about one-third of their effectives, and the Canadian Division was moved to a familiar and quiet sector near Armentières to recuperate and hold the line.

The Canadian Corps is Formed

Unchilled by events overseas, Canadian enthusiasm for the war still remained high. Recruits came forward briskly and a Second Contingent was sent to England in the spring of 1915. Because of the heavy casualties in Flanders, the 4th Brigade, which had remained in England, was broken up for reinforcements and more men were sent from Canada. When the 2nd Division was formed from the Second Contingent in May 1915, it continued training in England until it crossed to France in September. A Canadian Corps was then created, with Alderson as Corps Commander. Turner commanded the newly arrived 2nd Division, and Currie replaced Alderson in command of the 1st.

By now autumn was closing in, and as the steady rain of Flanders began to fall, trenches, shell-holes and craters filled with water. The troops crouched under

THE DEFENCE OF SANCTUARY WOOD. By Kenneth Forbes (1892-   ).

glistening ground-sheets and stared moodily at the mud in No Man's Land, the dissolving breastworks and the raindrops dripping from the rusting wire. Although the trenches were deep in water, few high rubber boots were available. Trench feet, colds and influenza set in and uniforms crawled with lice. There was neither warmth nor comfort even in the shattered, leaky billets behind the line. Only the daily rum issue and Christmas Day were briefly cheering. At Christmas a 3rd Canadian Division was formed in France under Major-General M. S. Mercer. Princess Patricia's Canadian Light Infantry, a battalion of ex-soldiers which had been raised in Canada in August 1914 and had served in France with the British 27th Division for a year, now joined the 3rd Division, as did The Royal Canadian Regiment, back from garrison duty in Bermuda.

St. Eloi

With the spring, the 2nd Division received its baptism of fire in the Ypres Salient when General Sir Herbert Plumer, commanding the Second British Army, decided to force the enemy out of a small salient which thrust 100 yards into the Allied lines from a 600-yard base near St. Eloi. The 3rd British Division carried out the first attack on 27 March 1916, after first blowing six mines under the enemy positions. Four craters, numbers 2, 3, 4 and 5, were well forward in German territory; numbers 1 and 6 had been blown in No Man's Land beside an old crater, Number 7. The enemy stubbornly defended these holes in the ground, and it was not until 3 April that the last crater (No. 5) fell. Next day the 2nd Division, wearing the new steel helmets that had just been introduced, took over the defence of the area.

Early on the morning of 6 April, before the Canadians had consolidated the sodden forward line, the Germans counter-attacked in force. The front was overrun and every crater except one lost; but counter-attacking in turn, the Canadians regained two craters in No Man's Land — numbers 6 and 7. In the confusion, however, they believed these to be Craters 4 and 5, a misapprehension under which the divisional staff laboured for ten days and which had disastrous consequences. Reports reaching Army Headquarters that the Canadians still held Craters 4 and 5, well forward in territory that had formerly been German, misled

36

General Plumer into supposing that the enemy counter-attack had failed. He therefore ordered the Canadians to hold on. Constantly reinforced, they stood their ground despite steadily mounting casualties, whereas a true report of the position would have brought orders for withdrawal from an impossible situation. On the afternoon of 19 April, after a three-hour bombardment, the Germans cleared the dazed defenders out of Craters 6 and 7, and so, after almost a month of fighting, the only gain left was Crater 1 on the extreme right. The price in killed, wounded and missing had been 1373 Canadians.

At the end of May, General Alderson left to become Inspector General of the Canadian troops in England. His successor was another British officer and a future Governor General of Canada, Lieut.-General the Hon. Sir Julian H. G. Byng.

Mount Sorrel

The Canadian Corps' first battle under Byng was fought at Mount Sorrel in the Ypres Salient in June 1916. In it the 3rd Division saw action for the first time. On 1 June the Germans intermittently shelled the Canadian positions, but when the bombardment reopened the next morning, the shelling, which continued for four hours, was the heaviest yet experienced by Canadian troops. Survivors spoke of human bodies and even trees hurled into the air by the explosions. The 3rd Division, having been blown out of its positions, could do little to stop the advance of the German infantry. General Mercer was killed by shrapnel that

morning while visiting the front line, and by afternoon the enemy had made a deep penetration, capturing Mount Sorrel and Hills 61 and 62. In this action, a section of Canadian field artillery was overrun and, although the gunners fought to the last man, the two 18-pounder guns were captured.* Only the ruined hamlet of Hooge on the left still held out. However, by evening, reserves had marched firmly towards the holocaust ahead and had sealed off the German thrusts after stubborn fighting.

At dawn the next morning an impromptu counter-attack by the 1st Division failed, and the enemy made the next move. On 6 June he captured Hooge after exploding four mines under the Canadian front line. The support trenches held firm, and since the gain amounted to only a few yards, the enemy was left in possession of the forward trenches.

The high ground that had been lost in the first enemy assault was a different matter. Byng was determined to win it back, and once again he nominated the 1st Division for the task. This time, however, the attack would be deliberately planned in every detail. On 8 June, the division withdrew behind the lines where the battalions rehearsed their carefully co-ordinated roles. Every day reconnaissance parties, as well as scouting planes, reported any change in the enemy's dispositions. The troops were shown exactly where they were to go, what they were to do and what they would encounter. By

----
*This was the only occasion in the war when Canadian guns were lost, and even these were subsequently recovered when the Canadians counter-attacked on 13 June.

(Public Archives of Canada photo.)

One of the Craters at St. Eloi.

the 12th everything was in readiness. The attack would go in at night, following strong artillery preparation.

After a vicious bombardment, three-quarters of an hour long, the Canadian infantry jumped out of their trenches at 1:30 a.m. on 13 June. Although the night was pitch-black and filled with wind and rain, the well-rehearsed troops went straight to their objectives, which were a shambles after being saturated by the shells of 218 guns from Canadian, British, Indian and South African batteries. The heights lost on 2 June were all retaken, and the Canadians consolidated on what had been the old forward line. The 12-day battle had cost the Canadian Corps some 8000 casualties, but Mount Sorrel was a clear-cut victory and proved that the Canadians were as dashing in the attack as they were dogged in the defence.

The Somme

In spite of numerical superiority, the Allies had failed on the Western Front in 1915. In the East, Russia had lost vast areas and suffered devastating casualties, and although Italy had declared war on Austria in May, Serbia had been overrun. Victory seemed as far away as ever, but an inter-Allied conference at the end of 1915 decided that simultaneous offensives would be mounted in 1916 on the Western, Eastern and Italian fronts. In the West the French and British would launch a major assault on the Somme about the middle of the year.

German initiative dislocated the Allied scheme, for General Erich von Falkenhayn, the German supreme commander, struck first. For his battlefield he chose Verdun, the legendary key to the defence of France, for he was confident that the French would throw in every man they had to hold the place and he intended to lure them into the area, then slaughter them with artillery fire. France, he explained to the Kaiser, would "bleed to death". The operation, codenamed *"Gericht"* (a place of execution), began on 21 February. The battle was indeed one of the most sanguinary of the war, but in the event the Germans lost almost as heavily as the French. Seven months of German offensive action were followed by a two-month French counter-offensive that wiped out the German gains. However, by mid-summer the French were so heavily committed at Verdun that the offensive on the Somme had to be undertaken mainly by the British. While preparations were put in hand, local attacks to keep the Germans occupied — of which St. Eloi was one — were launched along the front. The enemy, on the other hand, attacked to upset the British time-table, as at Mount Sorrel.

At the end of June, the British were ready for the

(Public Archives of Canada photo.)

A German trench captured by the Canadians during the Somme fighting.

"Big Push". There could be no surprise, for weeks of administrative build-up and a seven-day bombardment had clearly revealed the imminence of the assault. Nevertheless, General Sir Douglas Haig, who had succeeded Sir John French as British commander-in-chief the previous December, confidently expected a break-through and massed five cavalry divisions for exploitation to the Channel coast.

At precisely 7:30 a.m. on the cloudless summer morning of 1 July the British trenches came suddenly to life. A wave of steel-helmeted khaki figures, stretching as far as the eye could see, surged out of the ground and began to cross No Man's Land with the sun glittering on their bayonets. Weighed down with equipment, they advanced slowly, one wave following another, until in places as many as eight lines of soldiers were moving towards the tense German front. The enemy front-line troops, who had sheltered securely in deep dugouts in the chalk under even the heaviest shelling, clambered up to man their parapets.

The result was slaughter — 57,500 British soldiers killed, wounded or missing in one day, the heaviest day's toll in the history of British arms. Only on the right, where one small village was captured half a mile within the German defences, was there full success. Elsewhere it was a tale of partial sucess or total failure. As part of the 29th British Division, the Newfoundland Regiment, in action for the first time since Gallipoli, attacked on the left near Beaumont Hamel. In spite of the utmost gallantry in pressing the assault, not one Newfoundlander reached the German line. After the action, only 68 unwounded men answered their names; 710 were casualties. In Newfoundland, 1 July is still a day of pride and mourning.

Undeterred by this inauspicious beginning, Haig

CANADIAN ARTILLERY IN ACTION by Kenneth Forbes (1892-   )

A Canadian 6-inch howitzer at Thiepval Ridge on the Somme, 16 July 1916. German artillery registered on the battery which remained in action despite heavy casualties.

persisted in his offensive against the almost impregnable German positions between the Somme River and its tributary, the Ancre. In the middle of July the Canadian Cavalry Brigade, attached to the 2nd Indian Division, took part in the attack on Bazentin Ridge. By the end of August, when the Canadian infantry entrained for the battlefield, almost all the formidable Pozières Ridge was in British hands. The first task given the Canadian Corps was to clear the Germans from the only portion of it still untaken. In an evening attack on 9 September the 1st Division took exactly 23 minutes to do so. Haig now had a line from which he could batter forward in another full-scale offensive, and this time he had at his disposal 49 tanks, a new and secret weapon potentially capable of breaking the trench deadlock.

The Canadian Corps, now part of General Sir Hubert Gough's Reserve Army, had as its objective an outer bastion of the Courcelette and Martinpuich defences known as the Sugar Factory. Byng nominated the 2nd Division for the main assault and allotted it

seven tanks which proved of considerable help to the attacking infantry. The action opened at daybreak on the crisp, clear morning of 15 September. After being fiercely bombarded by Canadian guns, the Sugar Factory was a blazing heap of ruins, but a dashing attack cleared them of the enemy after a brief hand-to-hand struggle in an inferno of grenade and machine-gun fire. Then, in an impromptu effort to exploit success, the Canadians made a bid for Courcelette. A sunken road crowded with machine-guns barred the way, but although the advancing troops suffered heavy casualties, they swept forward with the bayonet and left the position packed with German dead. By evening two units of the 2nd Division had cleared Courcelette, the 22nd Battalion of French Canadians on the right and the 25th Battalion of Nova Scotians on the left. That night the Germans put in counter-attack after counter-attack — seven against the 22nd Battalion and four against the 25th Battalion — but the Canadians repulsed every assault.

Meanwhile the 3rd Division had advanced on the left. On the 15th it secured a portion of the strongly-defended Fabeck Trench and cleared the remainder the next day. Thereafter momentum waned. Gains became microscopic, and on the 22nd, in the face of steadily mounting enemy resistance, Haig called off the battle. The week's fighting had cost the Canadians 7230 casualties, but morale was high, for all objectives had been taken, all counter-attacks thrown back and the Germans defeated in hand-to-hand fighting. A consciousness of superiority permeated the Corps, a knowledge that would sustain it in battles still to come.

The Battle of the Somme dragged on for eight more weeks. During that entire period the Canadian objective was the next German defence line beyond Courcelette, a ditch of evil memory — Regina Trench. Without surprise such as the tanks had achieved on 15 September, spectacular gains were no longer possible. The line was inched forward by brutal close combat that was very costly to both sides. When the older divisions, shadows now through daily attrition, withdrew from the Somme for the Vimy front in the second week of October, Regina Trench was closer but still untaken. The 4th Canadian Division, commanded by Major-General David Watson, reached the battlefield on 10 October.

No words can adequately describe the ordeal through which the raw division passed. The weather had deteriorated, and the chalk, pulverized by the guns and drenched with rain, assumed a mortar-like consistency. It packed and balled on the foot like slushy snow, and there was no telling where this yellowish mud was merely inches deep or where it had filled shell-holes and even trenches in the folds of the stripped and wasted ground. Soldiers wept with frustration as they floundered forward. When they fell — and they fell often — clothing and equipment, plastered with mud, grew incredibly heavy. Moreover, the Germans had explicit orders that any officer who gave up a yard of trench would be court-martialled and that any section of lost trench must be counter-attacked immediately. And never before, except at Verdun, had artillery fire been so violent and so murderous.

Despite the conditions of ground and weather, enemy resistance, and an almost impenetrable curtain of fire, the 4th Division captured Regina Trench on 11 November. The soldiers found this long-sought objective to be "a mere depression in the chalk, in many places blown twenty feet wide, and for long stretches almost filled with debris and dead bodies". The Canadians went on to take Desire Trench a week later, a remarkable feat of courage and sheer endurance.

Weary Canadian troops returning from a tour in the trenches.

Shrapnel bursts over a reserve trench in the Canadian Sector.

(Public Archives of Canada photo.)

(Public Archives of Canada pl

The Battle of The Somme, 1916. Men of the 78th Battalion fix bayonets before going "over the top".

. . . and going over!

There were no further advances that year. The curtain fell on the Somme offensive in atrocious weather, and on 28 November the 4th Division rejoined the Corps opposite Vimy Ridge. The Somme had cost Canada 24,029 casualties, but the enemy's strength had been worn down and Verdun had been relieved. In the East, the Russians had mounted their last successful offensive. Falkenhayn had not achieved his object and had been dismissed at the end of August. Field-Marshal Paul von Hindenburg and his Chief of Staff, General Erich Ludendorff, the real brains of the combination, were brought from the Eastern Front to succeed him. One of their first acts was to begin the construction of a strong defensive position — the Hindenburg Line — behind the Somme. Rather than endure a second battering, they relinquished ground in the spring of 1917 and fell back to the new and shorter line to release 13 divisions for employment elsewhere.

The war was proving nightmarishly expensive, and as yet the end was not in sight. By January 1916 Canada had sent 120,000 soldiers overseas. A year later a further 165,000 had been dispatched. and the aggregate number of enlistments in Canada since the beginning of the war was nearly 400,000. The absence of these men from home was a sore burden and the uncertainty of their fate a constant pain. Canadian newspapers were filled with long casualty lists, and there was scarcely a community, however tiny, that was not affected. An ever-growing number of homes had a well-remembered face to mourn. Yet the nation faced the future with a grim resolve, for after these sacrifices, anything less than victory would have seemed a betrayal of the dead.

Vimy Ridge

The French, like the Germans, got a new commander-in-chief in 1916. He was General Robert Nivelle, who had been responsible for the successful French counter-offensive at Verdun, and he had a grandiose plan for 1917. He intended nothing less than to break clean through the German lines, roll the enemy back and win the war at a single stroke. Since Lloyd George, who had succeeded Asquith as British Prime Minister, was dissatisfied with Haig's conduct of the Battle of the Somme, he made the British general subordinate to Nivelle for the forthcoming attack.

By withdrawing to the Hindenburg Line in March 1917, the Germans disrupted Nivelle's plan and re-

43

stricted the French thrust to a sector immediately south of the new Hindenburg system. Undaunted by this, Nivelle directed Haig to open a preliminary offensive in the Arras sector to draw German reserves away from the Aisne, where the French would strike their main blow. Haig planned a double battle to help Nivelle. The Third British Army would mount an attack on an eight-mile front astride the River Scarpe, and on the adjoining four miles of front the Canadian Corps would assault Vimy Ridge. The Canadian task was formidable. Vimy Ridge reared out of the plain like a whale, humped in the north, then tapering off gradually until it finally disappeared in the Scarpe valley in front of Arras. The highest points, Hills 145 and 135, dominated the surrounding country, and the irregular slopes of the ridge favoured the enemy. The western slope, up which the Canadians would attack, though gentle, was very open and could easily be swept by fire. The reverse slope, on the contrary, was almost precipitous and well wooded, providing excellent shelter for reserves and guns.

During the previous two years these natural advantages had been greatly enhanced by the Germans who had fortified the ridge with successive lines of well-wired trenches, deep dugouts with interconnecting tunnels, and concrete strongpoints. Vimy was a keystone in the enemy's western wall, for not only did it protect a vital mining and industrial district of France, then in full production for Germany, but it also covered the junction of the Hindenburg Line with the defences running south from the Channel. It would be impossible for the British to hold ground in the Arras sector if Vimy Ridge remained in German hands. No greater compliment could have been paid the Canadians than to be entrusted with its capture.

Sir Julian Byng's planning was very thorough. All four Canadian divisions would attack simultaneously in line — from north to south the 4th, 3rd, 2nd and 1st. In each case the final objective was the far side of the ridge. Each division came into line on the front assigned to it so that the men could have a good look at the ground. Then they were withdrawn again to rehearse

THE TAKING OF VIMY RIDGE, EASTER MONDAY, 1917 by Richard Jack (1866-1952)
The artillery barrage on Vimy Ridge is seen from the gun positions.

44

Above — Men of the 29th Battalion crossing German wire in No Man's Land under shell fire.

(Public Archives of Canada photos.)

Below — Vimy Ridge is taken. Victorious Canadian soldiers above the Douai Plain.

the attack over a full-scale model on which German trenches and strongpoints, kept up to date from ground reconnaissance and air observers' reports, were clearly marked. Training was intensive and realistic, and constant repetition made every man familiar with the ground and with the tactics that would be expected of him in the real attack.

Each night now, under cover of darkness, the forward area seethed with activity. Tunnelling companies dug miles of subways through which troops could move to and from the front line in safety. Chambers for brigade and battalion headquarters, dressing stations for the wounded and great caves for stores were carved in the walls of the tunnels; all had piped water and electric light. Roads and light railways were built in the Canadian forward areas to bring up ammunition, engineer stores and rations. The signallers were no less busy. To existing telephone circuits they added 21 miles of cable buried seven feet deep to protect it from shelling and installed more than 60 miles of unburied cable along the tunnels and trenches.

A great array of guns was placed at Byng's disposal — enough to give twice the density of fire provided at the Somme. A new fuse, designed to burst above the ground, would cut the German wire for the attacking infantry. Great emphasis was placed on "counter-battery" — the locating and destroying of the enemy's guns just before the attack. Finally, and most important, there was to be no noticeable change in the artillery activity, even on the day of the assault. The preliminary bombardment, lasting several days, would be maintained right up to zero hour.

Easter Monday, 9 April 1917, was chosen as the day of the attack. The preparatory bombardment began on 20 March, but to conceal the full extent of the massive artillery support available, only half the guns were used during the first two weeks. On 2 April the guns that had been held silent joined the thundering chorus for a period termed by the enemy "the week of suffering". On the night of 8 April the infantry moved forward through gaps in the wire to occupy jumping-off positions in No Man's Land. The moon, just past the full, clouded over to screen the tensely waiting men. In front of them the dark flank of the ridge pulsed with bursting shells. Towards morning the weather turned bitterly cold and frost glazed the torn-up ground.

Zero hour was half-past five. At about four a raw wind blew up, darkening the sky with clouds and covering the Canadians' backs with snow. The attack began dead on time in a gloomy half-light, while slanting sleet blew in the faces of the Germans. Fifteen thousand Canadians surged forward in the first wave, closely following the line of the barrage which rolled towards the ridge by precise lifts of 100 yards. Two other waves of infantry followed.

The first wave found the defences smashed and the wire effectively cut. Only a few sentries were above ground in the battered front-line trenches; they were quickly dealt with and guards were posted at dug-out entrances until the mopping-up wave arrived. The leading troops swept on to the second line where, although many Germans were trapped below ground, there was some hand-to-hand fighting before the attackers again moved forward.

By now the enemy's distress rockets had curved up into the morning gloom, but because of excellent Canadian counter-battery work, the response of his artillery was feeble and fell behind the attacking troops. Gradually, however, the hostile fire increased, thinning the ranks of supporting units. Beyond the second line, the infantry encountered determined opposition from well-concealed snipers and concrete machine-gun posts, and losses mounted. On the lower slopes and across what had been No Man's Land, columns of dejected prisoners marched back under escort, stretcher-bearers carried the wounded, messengers moved through the lines, and supporting troops brought up mortars, machine-guns, picks, shovels, ammunition, water and grenades for the task of consolidation.

The Canadians reached the crest shortly before eight o'clock in the morning, but hard fighting still lay

King George V visits the battlefield. His Majesty tours Vimy Ridge with Gen. Sir Henry Horne of the First British Army (right) and Lieut.-General Sir Arthur Currie in July 1917.

(Public Archives of Canada photo.)

THE VIMY MEMORIAL

ahead. On the steep reverse slope the enemy opened up with machine-guns and field guns at pointblank range, but the elated troops plunged downhill in a raging blizzard, overran the batteries, and seized the sheltering woods. By early afternoon most final objectives had been taken.

The highest point on the ridge — Hill 145 — still held out. Not before the afternoon of the 10th, after two separate attacks, was the summit cleared and the ground carried on the farther side. With that, the four-mile length of the ridge was entirely in Canadian hands. It remained only to bring up artillery to smash any counter-attacks that might develop and to capture two adjacent features, the "Pimple" and the Lorette Spur. On the 12th the Canadians took the Pimple and the British the Lorette Spur.

The Battle of Vimy Ridge had been a striking success, by far the greatest British victory of the war up to that time. The Canadian Corps had wrested from the enemy one of the most formidable defensive positions on the Western Front, and Ludendorff, who celebrated

his 52nd birthday on this famous 9th of April, confessed that he was "deeply depressed". The Canadians captured 4000 prisoners, as well as 54 guns, 104 trench mortars and 124 machine-guns, at a cost of 3598 fatal casualties. Appropriately, Canada's greatest memorial to her fallen sons now stands, on ground ceded in perpetuity by France to Canada, on the top of Hill 145, the highest point of Vimy Ridge.

By now the United States had entered the war on the Allied side, but to counteract this, Russia had been torn by revolution and was out of the conflict for all practical purposes. Nivelle's offensive, launched in wind and rain on 16 April, came to nothing. Forewarned, the enemy had thinned out his forward zone and then, as the French came confidently forward, had brought down his own bombardment and hurled the attackers back with fierce counter-blows. Meanwhile, the British were keeping up a relentless pressure north and south of Arras, struggling painfully forward in a brutal slogging match against tiny but strongly-held villages of no strategic value. Two of these — Arleux and Fresnoy

Lieut.-General Sir Arthur Currie, Brig.-Gen. J. H. MacBrien (12th Brigade) and Major W. S. Woods (38th Battalion) on the Lens Front, July 1917.
(Public Archives of Canada photo.)

— were captured by the Canadians in some of the hardest and most unrewarding fighting of the war. When the French Government replaced Nivelle by General Henri-Philippe Pétain on 15 May 1917, Haig was free to launch an offensive of his own in Flanders.

Hill 70

On 7 June the Second British Army captured Messines Ridge near Ypres, and while Haig was preparing for the main Flanders offensive, he ordered General Sir Henry Horne's First Army, of which the Canadian Corps formed a part, to hold the Germans on its front and prevent them from reinforcing Flanders. On 6 June, when Byng was promoted to command the Third Army, Currie replaced him at the Canadian Corps. Thus for the first time the Corps had a Canadian commander. Early in July, Horne handed Currie his first major assignment as Corps Commander: he was to break through the Méricourt trench south of Lens and then go on to capture the city. On 10 July the Canadians began to relieve the 1st British Corps opposite Lens and Hill 70.

After looking at the ground, Currie pointed out that the Canadians would be pushing forward into a low and exposed area, dominated by two German-held heights, Hill 70 to the north and Sallaumines Hill to the south-east. Without the capture of one of these features, no attack on Lens would be practicable. Currie therefore suggested the substitution of a tangible objective — Hill 70 — for the frontal assault on Lens. Although Haig warned Currie that the Germans "would not let us have Hill 70", he finally sanctioned the attempt.

Although the hill, a bald dome of chalky downland, was not very high, it directly overlooked the straggling ruined houses and collieries of Lens and provided observation over the Douai Plain beyond. Its possession by the Canadians would be intolerable to the enemy. Aware of this, Currie decided to turn German sensitivity to his own advantage. He was confident his troops could take the hill. He would then provide an artillery killing-ground for the German infantry moving forward

HILL 70

49

to counter-attack. Artillery bombardment preceded the assault and 3500 gas drums were sent thudding against the hill and into the enemy reserve positions in the town and its suburbs. At dawn the screaming shells bombarding the enemy lines and strongpoints were augmented by 500 drums of blazing oil projected at selected targets to build up a smoke-screen and demoralize the defenders.

The infantry assaults went in at first light on 15 August. There were two of them — the main thrust against the hill by the 1st and 2nd Divisions and a diversionary blow directly on Lens by the 4th Division. The ten assaulting battalions hugged a rolling barrage provided by more than 200 field guns and within 20 minutes had gained the crest; by six o'clock most of the hill was in Canadian hands. Only the 2nd Brigade was checked in front of a well-defended chalk quarry. Here machine-gun fire cut down the Canadians in swathes, forcing individual rushes from shell-hole to shell-hole. Only after repeated attacks did the 2nd Brigade finally clear its front on the night of the 16th.

As had been expected, the enemy struck back with great strength and determination. By the 18th, when he at last admitted defeat, he had put in 21 counter-attacks, but strongpoints well dug in on the hill, bristling with Vickers machine-guns, provided close support for the newly-captured line. From the hilltop, artillery observers could clearly see the enemy's movements, and any concentration of troops brought down a cascade of shells, breaking up attack after attack. The gunners

never had better targets. Yet, inevitably, despite well-directed artillery concentrations and machine-gun fire, some Germans got through. The resolute enemy, grotesque in masks and bent double under the weight of flame-throwers, swept the Canadian parapets with sheets of fire. Stick-grenades lobbed into the trenches were closely followed by leaping men. Whole sections of trench were entered, but the Canadians, although sometimes forced out temporarily, would not give them up. They leapt back to tackle the Germans in vicious hand-to-hand fighting. The narrow earthern ditches became an inferno of cursing, lunging figures until the enemy was killed or ejected. For four days and three nights such fighting continued, but by the 18th the Germans had had enough. They recoiled for the last time, leaving Hill 70 in Canadian hands.

The fighting around Lens continued until 25 August, as the Canadians cleared the suburbs of the town, but since artillery had been transferred to Flanders, it was hardly feasible to capture Lens itself with what guns remained. After the 25th, the battle lapsed into stalemate. During the period 15-25 August the Canadian Corps had incurred 9198 casualties against an estimated 20,000 for the enemy. Six weeks later, the Corps moved to a grimmer battlefield in Flanders.

The Conscription Issue

On New Year's Day 1916, Sir Robert Borden, without consulting his Cabinet, pledged Canada to provide an army of 500,000 men, but by the end of the year,

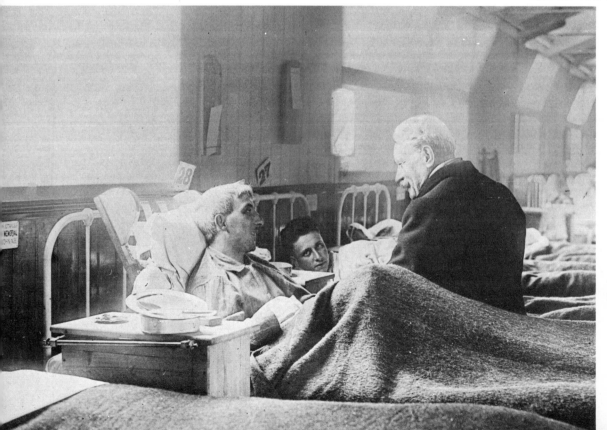

The Prime Minister visits a hos Sir Robert Borden chats wit wounded Canadian soldier dur visit to the Western Front, March

although there had been 384,450 enlistments, the actual strength of the Canadian Army was only 299,937. A National Service Board, set up to "make an appeal for voluntary national service which would render unnecessary any resort to compulsion", failed to achieve the desired results. Early in 1917 the Prime Minister attended meetings of the Imperial War Cabinet in London, and he returned in May convinced that, to obtain the 50,000 to 100,000 recruits needed to maintain the Corps at full strength, "selective" conscription would have to be introduced. After much bitter debate, a Military Service Act was passed by Parliament and became law on 29 August 1917. In October Borden formed a Union Government to administer his policy. In the general election of 17 December, Borden's Government was returned with ease, winning 153 seats out of 235, but 62 of the 82 opposition seats were in Quebec, where the government got only three. Although conscription did eventually produce the reinforcements required, the country was divided as never before, and between 29 March and 1 April 1918, serious rioting occurred in Quebec City.

Passchendaele

Meanwhile, Haig had resumed his northern offensive which had opened so brilliantly at Messines. There could be no surprise, for the Germans had expected an attack and had prepared strong defences. Lightly-manned concrete pillboxes, sited in depth and invulnerable to anything but a direct hit by a heavy shell, could bring down interlocking machine-gun fire all across the front, and the enemy was able to mass his main counter-attack forces well back out of field gun range. The Third Battle of Ypres — better known as Passchendaele — opened on 31 July 1917 with an assault by General Sir Hubert Gough's Fifth Army. A preparatory bombardment of four million shells screamed down to burst on reclaimed bogland, creating in front of the attacking troops a self-inflicted obstacle that doomed the offensive before it started. Pilckem Ridge and the villages of Bixschoote and St. Julien were taken — small gains for 31,850 casualties. Half the available tanks had been squandered on this impossible ground when the battle petered out on 2 August. Gough tried again on 16 August. This time his failure was even more marked, and now there was an ominous aftermath of discontent amongst the previously patient British troops. When Haig entrusted the next attack to Plumer, the complaints died down, but since Plumer called a halt for deliberate planning and the assembly of massive artillery support, he was not ready to resume until late September.

(Public Archives of Canada photo.)
Canadian Pioneers tape a path through the Passchendaele wasteland, November 1917.

A reasonably good phase followed, as infantry attacks were pressed on narrow fronts, following bombardments that were exceptionally heavy even by First World War standards. Three battles, Menin Road Ridge, Polygon Wood and Broodseinde, were all successful. Plumer's Second Army obtained a footing, though at terrible cost, on Passchendaele Ridge. In October the rains set in. However, Haig was determined to have the ridge at Passchendaele for his winter line, and on 5 October, the day following Broodseinde, he decided to employ the whole Canadian Corps in the Salient. After Currie had objected to serving in General Gough's Fifth Army, Haig placed the Canadian Corps in Plumer's Second Army.

Thus the Canadians returned to Ypres in the middle of October, marching forward under drizzling rain into a fantastic desolation of water and mud. On 18 October they reached the line to be taken over from the Australians, which ironically enough was just forward of the line taken over from the French before the gas attack at Second Ypres.

As the Canadians moved forward into the line, they stared in amazed disbelief at the battlefield over which they would be expected to advance. The whole area was covered with water or mud so deep that men had to move at a snail's pace, often being forced to wade up to their waists. And that was on the firmer ground. In some places, even infantry could not cross the half-mile-wide bogs. Guns had been left in badly bunched clusters because it was almost impossible to move them. Not only were they extremely vulnerable to enemy artillery; their rate of fire was very slow. Without firm platforms, a single round would cause the guns to move

51

Canadian wounded and German prisoners make their way back from Passchendaele.

or sink so that they had to be constantly re-aimed. The Germans, on higher and drier ground, overlooked all this terrible morass.

General Currie protested to Haig that no men should be called upon to attack under such conditions, saying that the operation was impossible, except at great cost, and futile. He put the cost of the attempt at 16,000 men and asked if a success would justify the sacrifice. Without giving reasons, Haig overruled him, but Currie determined that the preparations would be very thorough to give the men a fighting chance.

More than 100 field guns "taken over" from the Australians could not be found in the waste of swampland, but at Currie's insistence the deficiency was made good. Firm gun platforms were constructed at various forward sites and connected by roads. The well-tried method of placing a curtain of fire between the enemy and the advancing infantry would be followed, but since to predict the rate of advance over that terrain

Canadian wounded from Passchendaele.

was quite impossible, artillery observers would move with the attacking troops to modify the barrage where necessary and keep it just ahead of the infantry. The front was still a mile from Passchendaele village, and behind the front stretched six miles of shell-ploughed swamp to Ypres. Currie ordered roads, tramways and light railways constructed for bringing up reinforcements, munitions and supplies and for evacuating the wounded; previously, to bring back a wounded man had taken 14 hours of plodding and slipping in the mud. Canadian and British engineers worked night and day, suffering 3000 casualties before their task was finished.

Despite the meticulous preparations, the operation was almost insuperably difficult. Ground conditions were at their very worst. The front had narrowed to a salient, vulnerable from three sides. Only two plank roads, accurately marked and shelled by the enemy, crossed the swamp to the front line. Ahead, the enemy's chequerboard system of pillboxes showed only a few feet above ground.

There was one final change from previous methods. In earlier attacks the troops had been brought up from rest areas just before zero hour, but under the terrible conditions of ground at Passchendaele this meant that the soldiers often arrived more tired than the troops they were relieving. The Canadians came in four days early to recover from the arduous march forward and to study the ground over which they were to attack. The attack was set for 5:40 a.m. on 26 October.

The first phase consisted of a limited assault by the 3rd and 4th Divisions to carry the front forward 1200 yards. The troops shivered through the night in brimming shell-holes. At zero hour they moved slowly forward in a cold, wet mist, having first shed their greatcoats to save as much weight as possible. The barrage, much thinner in these conditions than at Vimy and Hill 70, came down perfectly. Platoons floundered towards the pillboxes which claimed a heavy toll; some men

Canadians of the 16th Machine Gun Company man positions in the mud, November 1917.

(Public Archives of Canada photo.)

(Courtesy The National Gallery of Canada.)

CANADIAN GUNNERS IN THE MUD, PASSCHENDAELE, 1917 by Alfred Bastien (1873-1955)

53

answered the fire with Lewis-guns and rifle-grenades, while others worked round the blind side to toss grenades through the slits.

The mist turned to rain. There could be no impetuous dash forward over this sodden ground where the brown-green mud was liquid, slimy, treacherous and deeper than at the Somme. Almost imperceptibly, the line inched forward as the men tugged and pulled their way towards the higher ground. Some gained the crest, but counter-attacks drove them back. After three days, the limited objectives remained untaken and the men could do no more. Exhausted, they lay in shell-holes under the retaliation of the enemy's guns; fortunately in that soft ground casualties from shellfire were not as severe as they otherwise would have been. Nevertheless, the attack had been costly — almost 2500 casualties had been suffered to win a strip of slightly higher and drier ground.

Currie ordered a pause for the construction of tracks over which mules could bring supplies to each brigade sector. That done, he resumed the assault on 30 November, and it quickly became obvious that the first phase had not been fought in vain. Over firmer ground the Canadians, "matchless attacking troops", swept forward from obstacle to obstacle with the old *élan* of the Vimy days. They gained 1000 yards before nightfall. But the cost in casualties for that one day's fighting was 2321.

It might have been expected that Currie would bid for the remaining quarter-mile the next day, but he would not take chances with tired troops. Instead, he tried Haig's patience to the utmost by insisting on a seven-day pause to reorganize his artillery and bring up and acclimatize the 1st and 2nd Divisions. By 6 November he was ready to proceed, and at dawn that day, behind a tremendously powerful barrage, the fresh troops jumped off from the forward line so rapidly that the German counter-fire fell behind them. Hugging the barrage, they hurled themselves at the last defences, which held out stubbornly until overpowered at close quarters. Three hours later the ridge had fallen. From the pulverized ruins of Passchendaele village, where hardly a brick remained on a brick, the victors looked across the sombre plain towards the distant coast. To obtain this view the Canadian Corps, between 18 October and 14 November, had suffered 15,654 battle casualties, almost exactly the number Currie had estimated the battle would cost.

The German Spring Offensives

During 1917 events in Russia had created an imbalance dangerously in Germany's favour. In November a Bolshevik minority had overthrown the government that had replaced the Tsar, made a truce with Germany in late December and signed a humiliating peace treaty at Brest-Litovsk in March 1918. By the end of 1917, the Germans had transferred several divisions to the Western Front, and by March 1918 they would have 80 reserve divisions as opposed to an Allied reserve of 55 divisions. Although American troops were landing in Europe, the balance would not tip in the Allies' favour until the middle of the year.

In January 1918, to meet the serious shortage of reinforcements, the number of battalions in each British infantry brigade was reduced from four to three. Troops of the surplus battalions were then used to bring the other battalions up to strength. There were thus fewer battalions and weaker brigades; never had the British held so much front with so few men. The Canadian Corps resisted British pressure to do the same. Although reorganization would save a dozen battalions which, with six more available in England, would have enabled two additional divisions to be formed, it would be difficult to keep so large a force up to strength. Conscription had been enacted, but draftees still had to be processed, trained and transported overseas, and American troops were competing for the limited shipping available. Furthermore, the proposed measure would break up an efficient fighting machine. Instead, each of the existing battalions in the Canadian Corps was augmented by 100 men. Without any increase in staff or services, this gave each Canadian division more firepower and 1200 more men in the line. The 5th Canadian Division, then still in England, was broken up for the immediate augmentation of the four divisions in France. Its artillery, however, fought with the Canadian Corps.

On the morning of 21 March the Germans swept forward on a 50-mile front against Gough's Fifth Army and Byng's Third Army farther north. There had been no prior artillery preparation, but the German bombardment paralysed by its very suddenness and mass effect. Storm troops infiltrated through the British lines, ignoring small pockets of resistance. Other troops,

By December 1914 the Western Front had become a continuously defended trench system (thin red line). The first major change occurred in the spring of 1917 as a result of the German withdrawal to the Hindenburg Line.

The enemy offensives of 1918 brought spectacular gains (dotted red line to broken red line), but by September 1918 the Allies had regained most of the ground lost.

Sweeping advances by the Allied armies during the last three months of the war carried them to victory; the Armistice Line (thick red line) shows the position reached by 11 November 1918.

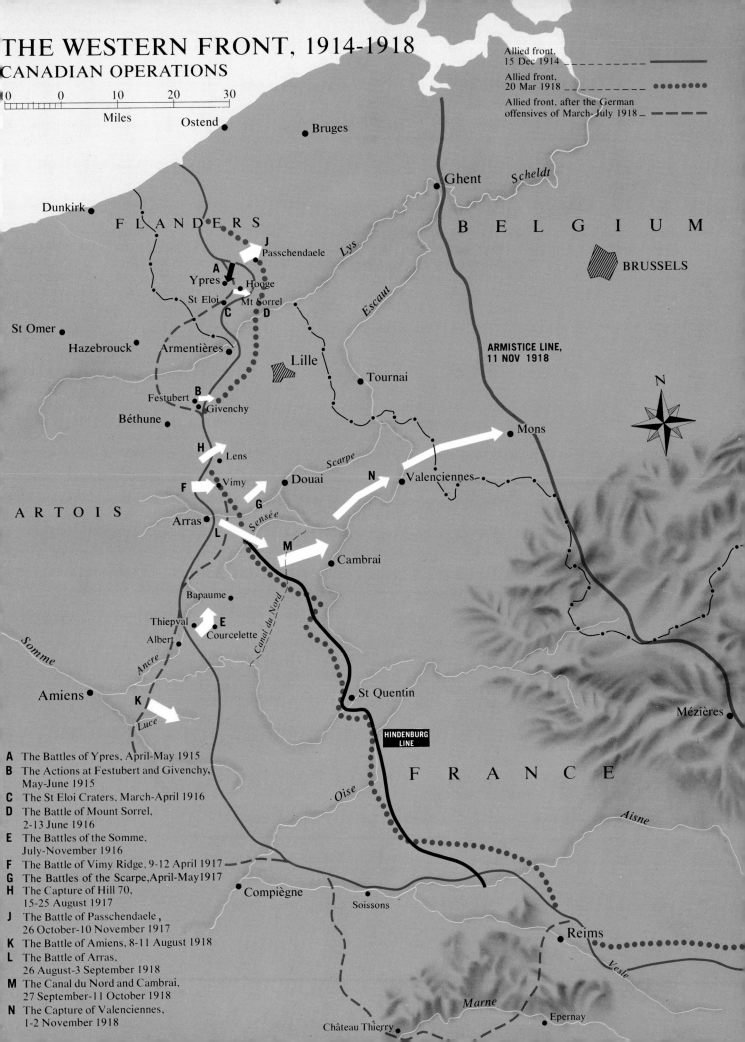

THE WESTERN FRONT, 1914–1918
CANADIAN OPERATIONS

Miles

10	0	10	20	30

Allied front, 15 Dec 1914 ――――――

Allied front, 20 Mar 1918 ●●●●●●●●●

Allied front, after the German offensives of March-July 1918 ― ― ― ―

Ostend

Bruges

Dunkirk

F L A N D E R S

Ghent

Scheldt

B E L G I U M

Passchendaele

Lys

Ypres

Hooge

St Eloi

Mt Sorrel

BRUSSELS

St Omer

Hazebrouck

Armentières

Lille

Escaut

Tournai

ARMISTICE LINE,
11 NOV 1918

Festubert

Givenchy

Mons

Béthune

N

A R T O I S

Lens

Scarpe

Douai

Valenciennes

Vimy

Arras

Sensée

Cambrai

Bapaume

Thiepval

Albert

Courcelette

Canal du Nord

Somme

Ancre

St Quentin

Amiens

Luce

HINDENBURG
LINE

F R A N C E

Oise

Aisne

Mézières

A The Battles of Ypres, April-May 1915
B The Actions at Festubert and Givenchy,
   May-June 1915
C The St Eloi Craters, March-April 1916
D The Battle of Mount Sorrel,
   2-13 June 1916
E The Battles of the Somme,
   July-November 1916
F The Battle of Vimy Ridge, 9-12 April 1917
G The Battles of the Scarpe,April-May1917
H The Capture of Hill 70,
   15-25 August 1917
J The Battle of Passchendaele,
   26 October-10 November 1917
K The Battle of Amiens, 8-11 August 1918
L The Battle of Arras,
   26 August-3 September 1918
M The Canal du Nord and Cambrai,
   27 September-11 October 1918
N The Capture of Valenciennes,
   1-2 November 1918

Compiègne

Soissons

Reims

Vesle

Marne

Château Thierry

Epernay

Canadian wounded and German prisoners meet infantry of the 3rd
Canadian Division and British Mark V tanks moving forward through Hourges, 8 August 1918.

following closely, widened the breaches and thrust still deeper. By nightfall the Germans had broken clean through the Fifth Army and into open country and by 5 April had nearly reached Amiens, where they were finally checked. Rather than tie down his forces in another battle of attrition, Ludendorff called off the attempt to take the city.

Tactically, Ludendorff had scored a huge success, but strategically he had lost the war. The attack had not been decisive. The British and French forces had not been split, and the endurance of German troops, keyed up for what they thought to be the final battle, began to sag as the fighting continued. Badly shaken by these events, the Allies had at last achieved unified command with the appointment, on 26 March, of General Foch to co-ordinate the French and British armies. Three weeks later Foch became Commander-

in-Chief of all the Allied forces.

A second German offensive in April gained ten miles in Flanders before it was stopped just short of Hazebrouck. In May, to attract French reserves from Flanders before turning his attention there again, Ludendorff struck at the French in Champagne. He gained the line of the Marne but could get no further. On 9 June he attempted to widen this southern salient in the direction of Compiègne, gained more ground and was then checked again. It was now the middle of the year and American divisions had redressed the balance of superiority the Germans had enjoyed in March.

In July a further German thrust in the Champagne succeeded in crossing the Marne, but there the German force, badly attenuated, lay wide-open for a counter-stroke by the French. The counter-stroke was duly delivered, and Ludendorff was forced to fight a grim

56

(Public Archives of Canada photo.)

...dian cavalrymen with prisoners, Amiens, August 1918.

defensive battle until 7 August, by which time the Germans had been forced back behind the River Vesle. Since 21 March the enemy had lost a million men, and the lines he had to hold were longer than ever before. Three great newly-won salients offered themselves to Allied attack, and the initiative now lay with Marshal Foch. Ludendorff's final gamble had failed.

During this period the Canadian Corps had been virtually inactive. At the time of the first great German offensive against the British in March, Haig had issued orders to attach the Canadians, division by division, to British formations whenever there was a need to shore up a crumbling front. Currie, left without any of his divisions, protested to the Canadian Overseas Minister in England, pointing out that the efficiency and high morale of the Canadian Corps was due to all its components fighting together under Canadian leadership.

Haig was angry, but he rescinded his orders, apart from those to the 2nd Division, which fought with the British until July. The Canadians held Lens and Vimy Ridge — 16 miles of front — until the crisis had passed. Three Canadian divisions, therefore, were intact and rested when the initiative finally passed to the Allies in August.

Amiens

By mid-July, Haig was already secretly preparing an attack north of the River Luce. It was to be a limited blow to provide a margin of safety around the railway centre of Amiens. Foch approved the plan and placed the First French Army at Haig's disposal to act on the right of Rawlinson's Fourth Army, which would be reinforced by the Canadian Corps.

The forthcoming battle was to be an astonishing

57

departure from the methods of the Somme and Passchendaele, for the British now sought to achieve surprise. There would be no preparatory bombardment to warn the enemy (in fact, the heavy artillery fired without registration); massed tanks would be used instead. Troops slipped stealthily into assembly areas where they lay concealed by day while aeroplanes patrolled the area; the roar of their engines later proved useful to drown the noise of tanks moving to the forward area. To avoid giving the impression that attack was imminent, work on the rear defences continued.

Unsuspected by the Germans, Rawlinson's strength grew by 420 tanks, nine infantry divisions, three cavalry divisions and 2070 guns. It was considered especially important to conceal the presence of the Canadians, for the arrival of these famous troops would be a sure indication that an attack was planned. Therefore preparations for a projected local assault in the Arras sector were continued, and two battalions, medical units and the Corps wireless section were despatched to Flanders to make it appear as though the advance party of the Corps had arrived there. So that the Canadians should not be recognized or captured in enemy

raids, they did not move into the front line until just before the assault. The Australians relieved the French on the right, thinning out the line to make room for the incoming Corps. Even that was a deceptive measure, since the Germans would not expect attack on a front that had the appearance of being spread out defensively. The Germans had only ten under-strength divisions in the line and four in reserve. Moreover, since they had recently been advancing, they had not constructed strong defences. The frontage of the attack was some 14 miles, with the French advancing in the southern half. The Fourth Army was to assault with two corps, the Canadians on the right and Australians on the left, while the British 3rd Corps would act as flank-guard on the Australian left.

An hour before dawn on 8 August, British tanks lumbered forward through a heavy ground mist, their clatter sounding deafening to the expectant soldiers who feared an enemy bombardment that would wreak havoc in the crowded assembly areas. Then, suddenly and reassuringly, British and Dominion guns crashed out all along the front. Surprise was complete. The enemy front dissolved in panic and confusion, as tanks,

Canadian Signallers lay cable, Arras, August 1918.

(Public Archives of Canada photo.)

The "impregnable"
D/Q Line,
October 1918.

escorted by infantry, tore through their positions. The attack swept on impetuously, the main resistance encountered being from pockets of infantry or machine-gun posts which often capitulated when outflanked. For the first time in the war, massed cavalry, accompanied by light "whippet" tanks, came forward to exploit success. Only on the 4th Division's front, where thickly emplaced machine-guns swept the flat fields, were the infantry forced to dig in short of their objective. Elsewhere, the day's objectives had all been reached and a grip obtained on the Amiens Outer Defence Line across the entire Corps front.

It had been a magnificent day. On the Canadian front the German line had been thrown back eight miles, while the Australians had advanced seven miles, the French five and the British two. Fourth Army's casualties had been only about 9000, but the Germans had lost 27,000 men, 400 guns and large numbers of mortars and machine-guns. The Canadian Corps had captured 5033 prisoners and 161 guns, at a cost of under 4000 casualties. Many enemy batteries had been overrun before they had fired more than a few rounds. Greater than the material loss was the moral effect that Amiens had on the German Army — it was, in fact, the decisive engagement of the First World War. "August 8th", Ludendorff later recalled, "was the black day of the German Army. . . ." He confessed that the German

war machine was "no longer efficient" and that he could now see no successful outcome to the four-year-old struggle. When the Kaiser was informed of this, he stated flatly: "The war must be ended."

The Hindenburg Line

Although the Battle of Amiens continued until 11 August, only another three miles were gained. By then the Germans had rushed up 18 divisions; British tank power had dwindled through mechanical failure and enemy action; and more seriously, the attacking troops had come up against the formidable trench lines of the old Somme battleground of 1916. Largely at the instigation of General Currie, Haig broke off the battle in favour of three new thrusts — the Third Army would attack towards Bapaume; the First Army would strike south-east from the Arras sector; and the Fourth Army would exploit any withdrawal from the Somme. The Canadian Corps would fight as part of Horne's First Army.

Horne's task was to force the defences that screened the flank of the Hindenburg Line facing Arras. He was then to break the hinge of the Hindenburg system and, swinging southward, deny those defences to the enemy falling back before the Third Army. The line of Horne's advance would be directly on Cambrai, the hub of the German defence system on the British front. The

Guns captured by the Canadian Corps in the advance on Cambrai, September—October 1918.

Canadian Corps heavy artillery in action.

60

German positions facing the First Army were sited in depth and extremely strong. Immediately in front, in the vicinity of Monchy-le-Preux, were the old British trenches lost in March 1918. Behind this again was the former German front line. Two miles to the east lay another system, the Fresnes-Rouvroy line. A mile farther east the Drocourt-Quéant Switch provided a terribly strong and deep system of trenches with concrete shelters and heavy wire designed to block any advance into the Douai plain. Like the Hindenburg Line, of which it was an extension, the D-Q Line had been under construction for almost two years and was considered absolutely impregnable. Between that and Cambrai, the Canal du Nord formed a major obstacle.

The task of breaking these defences was given to the Canadians, with the 17th British Corps cooperating on their right. It was a tough assignment, calling for successive frontal assaults against a desperately resisting enemy. The battle began on 26 August. By nightfall Monchy and the ground 1000 yards beyond it (including both the old British and German trench lines) was in Canadian hands. The Fresnes-Rouvroy Line, the objective for the 27th, was not reached that day; not before the 30th, after bitter fighting, was the line fully pierced. Currie, appreciating the formidable nature of the D-Q Line, the next objective, obtained Horne's permission to postpone his attack until 2 September when his preparations would be ready. These consisted of powerful artillery support and tanks to roll paths through the belts of wire which were too dense for the preliminary bombardment to cut completely.

At dawn on the 2nd, behind a barrage heartening in its strength, the infantry went forward. Heavy tanks clawed through the wire that remained, snapping the strands like cotton. The infantry's task, although stern enough, proved lighter than had been expected. German morale was cracking, and although some fiercely defiant pockets fought stubbornly to the end, there was little resistance elsewhere along the front. The enemy surrendered in large numbers, and that night the Germans pulled back. Nothing now remained between the captured D-Q Line and the west bank of the Canal du Nord.

In fact, the Germans felt themselves compelled to withdraw behind the Hindenburg defences and, indeed, all along the front as far south as the Aisne and also in Flanders. They relinquished the whole of the gains of the March offensive and also most of those of the April offensive in Flanders. On 3 September Marshal Foch outlined his plans for the Allied campaign on the Western Front. Three British armies, the First, Third and Fourth, were either facing the Canal du Nord or approaching the Hindenburg Line. To prevent the enemy massing all his reserves against them, Foch determined on a general offensive all along the front. Four great blows would be struck — first, by the three British armies against Cambrai and St. Quentin; second, by the French centre beyond the Aisne; third, in the St. Mihiel Salient, by American forces who would later combine with the French in a drive towards Mézières; and finally, by the British and Belgians in the north, who would drive towards Ghent and Bruges. For the Canadian Corps there would be a pause to permit the British farther south to reach the Hindenburg Line.

Meanwhile, Currie studied the ground. He concluded that a frontal attack on the Canal du Nord would be unsound because of the nature of the obstacle — flooded ground, the canal itself, and successive defences from which any advance to the east would be the more dangerously enfiladed the deeper it went. To the south, on the other hand, a 4000-yard stretch of the canal had not been completed; this was dry and the excavated bed ran between higher and firmer ground. He proposed to take advantage of the dry portion of the canal by having the corps boundary extended 2600 yards to the south. Through this one-and-a-half-mile funnel Currie would pass 50,000 men, guns, tanks and transport and, after reaching the farther bank, spread them out fanwise in a 10,000-yard arc to the north and east. It was a daring concept, calling for skilful leadership and strict discipline. If the enemy artillery should become aware of the congestion in the narrow avenue of assault, the resulting slaughter would virtually destroy the Corps. Yet against that risk was the certainty of extremely heavy casualties in a frontal assault, still without assurance of success. With some misgivings, Horne approved Currie's plan.

On 15 September Haig confirmed his intentions. The First and Third Armies would operate jointly towards Cambrai, Horne seizing the great defensive feature of Bourlon Wood, while Byng advanced on the city itself. The Canadian Corps, with the 11th British Division under command, would take the wood and then establish a front along the Sensée Canal, north of Cambrai. The preliminary obstacle, the Canal du Nord, would be crossed on 27 September.

In the dusk of the evening of 26 September the Canadians moved forward. By midnight they were assembled opposite the dry section of the canal, huddled together for warmth, and for the most part in the open. The night wore on, and as yet there was no evidence of enemy counter-preparation. Suddenly, as the eastern sky was brightening, the opening barrage flashed out, shocking the men to action. Before the enemy could

62

retaliate, the initial waves had crossed the canal and were fanning out from the bridgehead. Nevertheless, the follow-up troops suffered casualties as the enemy, alive to his danger, subjected the bed of the canal to a violent bombardment. The results of the first day justified Currie's generalship. His calculated gamble had given him the Canal du Nord at relatively light cost. More than that, Bourlon Wood, the essential objective, had also fallen.

Thereafter, the Germans, sensitive to the threatened loss of Cambrai and the railways converging on it, poured in reinforcements. The enemy strength facing the Corps grew from four divisions on 27 September to ten by 1 October, together with 13 special machine-gun companies which could offer grim resistance under conditions of open warfare. Progress was costly and slow. On the night of 1 October Currie broke off the action because of the exhaustion of his troops. Yet, although it was not immediately apparent, the Canadian thrust, combined with those by the Third and Fourth Armies farther south, had so exhausted German reserves that the enemy was no longer capable of serious resistance.

When the assault was resumed on the night of 8-9 October, it caught the enemy preparing to withdraw. Canadian troops entered Cambrai with ease and by 11 October had pushed on some six miles beyond the city. Since 26 August, the Corps had fought its way forward 23 miles through the main German defensive system which had been manned in turn by 31 identified divisions. The Canadians had suffered nearly 31,000 casualties in the six-week period, but German losses, which were never published, included 18,585 prisoners, as well as 371 guns and nearly 2000 machine-guns.

On 12 September, the First U.S. Army, fighting its first large battle at St. Mihiel, caught the Germans in a withdrawal and straightened out the salient. On 26 September, in conjunction with the French, the Americans opened the Meuse-Argonne battle on the British right. While this did not succeed in drawing off reserves from in front of Haig's three armies until the Hindenburg Line had been broken, it did gain seven miles and eventually caused the Germans to move troops farther south.

The flank protection afforded by the Canadian Corps enabled the Third British Army immediately to the south to breach the Hindenburg Line south-west of Cambrai on 27 September. The Fourth Army, south of the Third, opened a powerful attack two days later; in an impressive display of strength it bored through the Hindenburg defences north of St. Quentin and burst into the open country three miles beyond. The previous day, the Second British Army and the Belgians had ad-

vanced in Flanders, recovered Messines and Passchendaele and gained nine miles before being halted by the condition of the ground.

Behind the German Army, which was still fighting stubborn rearguard actions, the German nation and its allies fell apart. In September, the final British offensive in Palestine tore the Turks to pieces. An offensive in the Salonika theatre succeeded against the Bulgarians, and at the end of September Bulgaria capitulated. On 4 October the German and Austrian governments dispatched notes to President Wilson asking for armistice negotiations.

Pursuit to Mons

On 16 October 1918, with the Hindenburg Line broken and Cambrai lost, Ludendorff ordered his troops back to the Hermann Line. Part of this was based north-east of Cambrai on the Escaut (Scheldt) River in the neighbourhood of Valenciennes. The Canadians crossed the Sensée Canal on the 17th and pushed out cavalry and armoured cars to maintain contact with the retreating enemy. This phase of the war was extremely exhilarating for the Corps. Demolitions could be heard as the Germans systematically cratered roads and destroyed bridges, but there was a strange absence of gunfire. Bands played as battalions marched through liberated towns and villages to the acclaim of French civilians who proffered wine and coffee and bedecked the men with flowers.

On the 20th, however, the enemy began to show his teeth. There was some long-range shelling and road-blocks were now being covered by fire. Resistance stiffened during the next two days. The Canadians were approaching Valenciennes and it became obvious the enemy was about to stand and fight. The Corps paused along the Escaut Canal until the rest of the First Army came into line. As a key point in the Hermann Line, Valenciennes had been well-chosen. The Canal de l'Escaut, covered by trenches and wire, barred approach from the west and north, and the low-lying ground to the west, south-west and north had been extensively flooded. The only dry approaches lay to the east and south, and these were dominated by a heavily defended hill, Mont Houy. Five German divisions held Valenciennes, and three of them were concentrated on or near Mont Houy. On 28 October, a British attack took the hill but could not hold it; the British had to be satisfied with part of the southern slope. Thereafter this objective was entrusted to the Canadian Corps.

The Canadian attack on 1 November was completely successful, due mainly to massive artillery support. Working to a carefully co-ordinated programme, the

— Infantry of the 4th Canadian Division cross the unfinished Canal du Nord, 27 September 1918.

ntre — Cambrai from the forward Canadian positions, 1 October 1918.

ttom — A patrol of the 3rd Canadian Division crossing the square, Cambrai, 8 October 1918.

guns poured a torrent of shells on the enemy positions — in all about 2140 tons were fired, almost as much as had been expended by both sides in the entire South African War. The result was that a single infantry brigade over-ran Mont Houy, taking nearly 1800 prisoners. That night the Germans retreated from Valenciennes and abandoned the Hermann Line. The advance swept on.

The thoroughly defeated Germans were now reeling back from Verdun to the sea before relentless Allied pressure. For a month now armistice negotiations had been in progress, with the Allied terms stiffening as the extent of German demoralization became more and more apparent. On 24 October a final note from President Wilson abandoned the concept of a negotiated armistice for what was virtually unconditional surrender. On 10 November the Canadian Corps reached the outskirts of Mons, the scene of the first engagement between British and German troops in 1914. That night the town changed hands without a struggle.

It was the end of the journey. On 11 November, at eleven o'clock in the morning, hostilities ended and the sound of firing ceased. Wild enthusiasm marked the occasion in every Allied city, but within the Corps there were no elated scenes. It would take time to adjust and grope for thoughts of home. What the future would bring to the men and to Canada was uncertain, but, both for good and ill, the old, pre-war world had disappeared forever.

At Mons the Canadians learned that they were to march to the Rhineland as part of Plumer's Second Army, the British Army of Occupation. Sir Arthur Currie received the news with gratification as an honour his Corps had well earned. Two Canadian divisions formed a sixth of the total occupation force. On the morning of 4 December the leading units reached the German frontier, but the crossing of the Rhine at Cologne and Bonn nine days later was considered more significant. Plumer took the salute at the Cologne crossing, and at Bonn the distinction was accorded to Sir Arthur Currie.

The Russian Venture

On Armistice Day 1918, while their comrades on the Western Front slowly accustomed themselves to the

An armoured car of the 1st Canadian Motor Machine Gun Brigade passes the saluting base in the square at Mons during a Canadian Corps parade celebrating the Armistice.

Lieut.-General Sir Arthur Currie takes the salute on the bridge at Bonn as infantry of the 2nd Canadian Division march into the Rhine bridgehead.

transition from war to peace, Canadian gunners were fighting at a little place named Tulgas, 200 miles south of Archangel in Northern Russia. In all some 5000 Canadians served in Russia. The 16th Brigade, C.F.A., provided the artillery for a British force based on Archangel; 92 officers and N.C.Os. acted as instructors for anti-Bolshevik Russian levies raised at Murmansk in Northern Russia; 41 officers and N.C.Os. served with the British in Mesopotamia and Southern Russia; and a Canadian Expeditionary Force about 4000 strong entered Vladivostok in Eastern Russia.

After the Bolsheviks had taken Russia out of the war, the Allies had intervened in all these places with one purpose in mind: to reconstitute an Eastern Front against the Central Powers. With the Armistice, there was no longer any purpose in an Eastern Front, but anti-Bolshevik governments had grown up under Allied protection and these could not be abandoned to Bol-

shevik reprisals. Thus the intervention, no matter how unwittingly, had become part of the Russian Civil War and was discontinued only when the White Russian cause no longer held any prospect of success. The most hopeful theatre for successful intervention had been Siberia, through the port of Vladivostok where the Japanese had landed 70,000 troops and the Americans 8000, but the private quarrel between these nations over the control of the Trans-Siberian Railway starved the White Russian forces on the Ural front of the munitions and supplies from Vladivostok that they needed to maintain the struggle against the Bolsheviks. Between April and June 1919 the Canadian force, which had taken no part in the fighting, was withdrawn from Vladivostok.

After the White failure in Siberia, the occupation of parts of Northern Russia served no purpose. The Canadians were withdrawn from Archangel in June 1919

Going home.
Men of the 42nd
Battalion embark
at Liverpool.

Canadian gunners
in North Russia.

66

and from Murmansk by September. They had fought against the Bolsheviks through the winter and spring, but fortunately casualties had been light — eight killed and 16 wounded. In the south, a British Mission, known as "Dunsterforce", which included 15 Canadian officers and 26 N.C.Os., had occupied the Caspian port of Baku in August 1918 and denied its oil to the Central Powers at a crucial time. Thereafter, the force was disbanded and its Canadian members returned to England.

In the First World War the Canadian Corps achieved a reputation unsurpassed in the Allied armies. After the Somme, its record had been one of unbroken victory. It emerged successfully from every test, no matter how severe, and its professional ability had proved second to none. Canada had begun the war with little military experience and with practically nothing in the way of a standing army. She ended it with a superb fighting machine, "the greatest national achievement of the Canadian people since the Dominion came into being." A total of 619,636 men and women served in the Canadian Army in the First World War, and of these 59,544 gave their lives and another 172,950 were wounded. That such a war record would carry Canada to full autonomy had been foreseen by Sir Robert Borden, and so it proved. A separate Canadian signature on the Peace Treaty signified that the status of nationhood had been achieved.

THE SEA AND THE SKY 1914-1918

The Royal Canadian Navy in the First World War

On the evening of 4 August 1914, the Canadian cruisers *Niobe* and *Rainbow* were placed "at the disposal of His Majesty for general service in the Royal Navy." When the R.C.N. — much to its surprise — acquired two submarines just after the outbreak of war, these vessels were also placed at the Admiralty's disposal. Thus at the outbreak of the First World War the protection of Canada's coasts and of shipping in Canadian waters was handed over to the Royal Navy.

The acquisition of the two submarines, whose arrival at Esquimalt on 5 August greatly strengthened the naval defences of the West Coast, was entirely fortuitous. They were being built for the Chilean Government in a Seattle yard, but difficulties had arisen between buyer and seller over price and construction details. When this became known in British Columbia, the Premier, Sir Richard McBride, determined to acquire the boats for Canada and wrote out a cheque for them on provincial funds. At 10 o'clock on the night of 4 August 1914, the two submarines cast off their lines and, running on silent electric motors, made for the harbour entrance. Shortly after daybreak the submarines were delivered safely to their new owners just outside Canadian territorial waters; McBride's cheque for $1,150,000 changed hands; and the boats, now under British colours, made for Esquimalt. British Columbia had acquired a navy.

Although it handed over control of all its warships, the R.C.N. did not entirely relinquish responsibility for naval defence. Canadians, both R.C.N. and R.N.C.V.R., made up a substantial part of the ships' companies of the cruisers and submarines, although most of the highly-trained officers and men had to be provided by the Royal Navy. The R.C.N. organized, manned and directed the Examination Service established to check

all vessels entering the principal Canadian ports, and the Naval Control Service directed the movements of shipping. The Radiotelegraph Service of the Department took over control of all wireless stations afloat and ashore and the operation of the coastal stations. The Naval Intelligence Branch, working with the Examination, Naval Control and Radiotelegraph Services, greatly intensified its operations and throughout the war served as a valuable part of the Admiralty's worldwide intelligence system.

Yet another duty assumed by the Naval Service was that of assisting Allied powers to have ships built in Canadian yards. Most vessels constructed in Canada were small, but they were very useful in anti-submarine warfare. A total of sixty 125-foot, steel anti-submarine trawlers and one hundred 72.5-foot, wooden drifters were built for the Admiralty, many of which were turned over to the R.C.N. for service in Canadian waters. Five hundred and fifty anti-submarine motor launches were also assembled for the Royal Navy in Montreal and Quebec from parts manufactured in the United States. Twenty-four steel lighters were built in Canada and shipped to the Near East in sections for use on rivers. Six armed trawlers and 36 coastal patrol motor boats were also built for the French Government. The U.S. Bethlehem Steel Corporation, finding itself prevented by American neutrality legislation from selling submarines to the Admiralty, gained control of the Canadian Vickers plant at Montreal and had American submarine parts shipped there for assembling.

The naval dockyards at Halifax and Esquimalt were another R.C.N. responsibility, for they had been handed over by the Admiralty on condition that they be made available to the Royal Navy when required. The dockyards had not been particularly well main-

H.M.C.S. *Niobe*

Canadian submarines CC-1 and CC-2 at Port San Juan, Vancouver Island, 1

H.M.C.S. *Niobe* coaling alongside Halifax Dockyard, 1916.   (D.N.D. photo.)

tained in the years before the war, but after hostilities began the Naval Service did its utmost to provide repair and refitting facilities and to maintain stocks of provisions and stores for the use of Allied warships. This effort suffered a severe blow when, at the height of the war, Halifax was struck by disaster. The morning of 6 December 1917 dawned fine and clear, and traffic in the port was moving normally when the French-registered S.S. *Mont Blanc* and the Norwegian freighter S.S. *Imo* collided in the Narrows. *Mont Blanc,* carrying a full cargo of explosives, caught fire and was abandoned by her crew. Burning fiercely, she drifted across the harbour towards the piers of Halifax Shipyards Ltd. and there, shortly after 9 a.m., she blew up.

The destruction was terrible. Some 2000 people were killed and another 2000 seriously injured. At least a square mile of the city was destroyed; the port area, with its vital ship repair and refitting facilities, was ravaged, although only three small vessels, besides the *Mont Blanc,* were sunk. Seven sailors aboard H.M.C.S. *Niobe*'s steam pinnace died heroically in an attempt to board and scuttle the blazing *Mont Blanc,* but Canadian naval casualties were lighter than might have been expected: 22 killed and eight wounded. Many years were to elapse before Halifax recovered from the effects of that dreadful December morning, but by supreme efforts the port itself was soon operating at almost normal capacity.

By now the R.C.N. had voluntarily assumed responsibility for recruiting Canadians for the Royal Navy. Some 1700 officers and men joined the Overseas Division of the Royal Naval Canadian Volunteer Reserve, and the Naval Service recruited 264 officers, 635 Royal Naval Air Service pilots, 107 surgeon-probationers and 112 mechanics and chief mechanics for the Admiralty. A considerable number of R.C.N. officers served in Royal Navy ships during the war. The first of the R.C.N.'s more than 150 fatal casualties, and indeed Canada's first war dead, were four young midshipmen who were lost on 1 November 1914 when H.M.S. *Good Hope* went down in the Battle of Coronel. No records exist of how many Canadians enlisted directly into the Royal Navy and its Reserves.

The R.C.N.'s share in naval operations during the First World War was small. Until 25 August 1914, *Rainbow* was the only Allied warship of any size on the West Coast, so on her fell the onus of protecting Canadian ports and shipping from the German cruiser *Leipzig* which was operating in the area. Although for the first fortnight *Rainbow* did not even have any high explosive shells for her two old 6-inch guns, she cruised bravely forth, making forays as far afield as San Francisco to the south and Prince Rupert to the north. Fortunately, she did not meet the *Leipzig,* who with her 23-knot speed and ten modern 4.1-inch guns would have made short work of the Canadian ship. The two new submarines, which were unromantically christened the *CC-1* and the *CC-2,* were a welcome reinforcement for *Rainbow,* for it was believed that their presence would deter enemy raiders from attacking West Coast

A FORWARD GUN ON A PATROL BOAT by Arthur Lismer (1885-   ). This lithograph shows the forward gun on an armed trawler on escort duty off Halifax in rough weather.
(Courtesy The National Gallery of Canada.)

ports. When Japan entered the war on the Allied side, she sent the heavy cruiser *Idzumo* to Esquimalt, and five days later, on 30 August 1914, the British cruiser *Newcastle* also appeared. *Rainbow* could now leave her post in the front line for other tasks more suited to her age and size.

Although the destruction of Germany's Far Eastern Squadron at the Falkland Islands in December 1914 ended any fear of a serious attack on Pacific coast shipping, *Rainbow* still had work to do. Until the spring of 1917 she carried out patrols as far south as Central America to prevent enemy ships in neutral ports from escaping to sea, and during this time she took two prizes. After the United States declared war in April 1917, the *Rainbow* and the two submarines were no longer needed in the Pacific, so the cruiser became the depot ship at Esquimalt and the submarines were transferred to Halifax.

The R.C.N.'s East Coast cruiser, *Niobe,* was not ready for operations until 1 September 1914. After a voyage in the Gulf of St. Lawrence, and a passage to Bermuda and back, escorting the troop transport *Canada, Niobe* served until July 1915 with the British 4th Cruiser Squadron, which was responsible for the blockade patrol off New York City, preventing the entry and exit of enemy warships and merchantmen and searching neutral ships for contraband. After nine months of this, *Niobe* was overdue for refit, but rather than repair her, the Royal Navy handed her back to Canadian control. For the remainder of the war she lay at Halifax, serving as the R.C.N. depot ship for that base.

The Royal Canadian Navy had little to do with the operation of its two cruisers beyond assisting them to prepare for war, helping to man them, and transmitting operational orders to them from the Admiralty. However, the R.C.N. was wholly responsible for the operation of the auxiliary fleet that was built up during the war. The creation of this small-ship force was a slow process, because from the very beginning the Admiralty minimized the need for R.C.N. assistance. An unofficial query from Ottawa in October 1914 brought the Admiralty suggestion that Canada should confine herself to contributions on land because warships could not be built quickly. This advice was reiterated in the late summer of 1915 when Prime Minister Borden was informed that, although a Canadian naval patrol service might not be without value, "exaggerated measures of precaution were to be deprecated." Later the Admiralty was to change its mind.

In 1914 the nucleus of the auxiliary fleet was provided by the ten ships of the Fisheries Protection Service, which, with one exception, were immediately placed at the disposal of the R.C.N. Additional ships came from other government departments, from private citizens and from shipping companies. The Examination and Naval Control Services acquired many of these; others were used for minesweeping in the Halifax

approaches and for patrolling off that port. During the first few months of hostilities, minesweeping at Halifax was carried out by three chartered tugs manned by civilians and by one Fisheries Protection Service vessel.

A two-ship force was created in January 1915 to guard against minelaying operations in the shallow coastal waters off Nova Scotia. This "Bay of Fundy Patrol", as it was called, was carried out by a chartered vessel and a Hydrographic Survey ship, occasionally assisted by a Fisheries Protection ship. It is typical of the R.C.N. at this time that all these ships had civilian crews, although they usually had a naval officer and a few naval ratings aboard.

The St. Lawrence Patrol which was instituted in July 1915 was a more ambitious project, consisting of seven vessels, all of which, including the chartered ones, were commissioned under the White Ensign and manned by uniformed personnel. The Patrol's chief responsibility

H.M.C.S. *GRILSE* ON CONVOY DUTY. Lithograph by Arthur Lismer (1885-). *Grilse*, the former yacht *Winchester*, was secretly purchased in the neutral United States and smuggled to Halifax. Converted into a small destroyer, she spent most of her naval career based on Halifax or Sydney, doing antisubmarine and convey escort work.

was to prevent the use of unfrequented harbours as submarine bases. During the navigational season of 1916 the St. Lawrence Patrol, now known simply as the Patrol Service, acquired a few additional motor boats for local coastal work, and three vessels which the Newfoundland Government had maintained on patrol in 1915 were placed under its operational authority. By now there were ominous signs that Canadian waters would soon be invaded by enemy submarines. Two visits to the United States by the German cargo submarine *Deutschland* in 1916 revealed the enemy's U-boat capabilities, and these were confirmed when the *U-53* sank five ships off the Nantucket Light Vessel in October.

The exploits of *U-53* disturbed the British as much as the Canadian naval authorities, and on 11 November 1916 the Admiralty earnestly recommended the creation of a Canadian patrol force of 36 vessels for use in 1917. Canadian Naval Service Headquarters was surprised at this reversal of the Admiralty's previous policy but at once set to work to assemble the ships. The Royal Navy agreed to supply an experienced officer to organize and command the patrols, a number of trained personnel and the 12-pounder guns that the R.C.N. lacked. Some vessels were obtained from other government departments, some were purchased in the United States and Canada, some were chartered and orders were placed with Canadian shipbuilders for 12 anti-submarine trawlers. Newfoundland promised to provide five armed and manned vessels.

German submarines did not appear in North American waters in 1917, which was just as well, because even by the end of the navigational season in the St. Lawrence the Patrol Service was still far short of its target of 36 ships. The need for a large, efficient Canadian force was becoming ever more apparent, for the adoption of the convoy system during the summer of 1917 had deprived the submarines of much of their prey in European waters, and it seemed likely that they would now venture farther afield. The Western Atlantic was the logical point of attack, and the Admiralty and the R.C.N. agreed that the Patrol Service would have to be expanded greatly before navigation opened in 1918. Fortunately, the means for expansion were at hand in the 60 trawlers and 100 drifters being built for the R.N. Eventually it was decided that the first 20 trawlers and 50 drifters would go overseas and that the remainder would be employed in Canadian waters. In the event, the new ships took longer to build than had been expected, and when they came into service they were allotted as the needs of the moment dictated, some going to Europe, others to the R.C.N. and some

to the United States Navy.

The problem of procuring trained personnel was as serious as that of finding ships. Despite the insatiable demands of the Western Front for manpower, there were always enough volunteers to fill out the crews, but specialists, and particularly gunners, were almost impossible to find. However, earlier in the war the R.C.N. had recruited 1700 men of the Overseas Division of the R.N.C.V.R. for service in the Royal Navy. Many of these sailors now returned to Canada to provide crews for the Patrol Service, and the Royal Navy made up the deficiencies. Plans for 1918 called for a Patrol Service of 112 ships under the command of Captain Walter Hose, a retired R.N. officer who had served in the Royal Canadian Navy since 1911. Yet had it not been for the Royal Navy, which contributed 20 fully-manned drifters, and the United States Navy, which contributed two torpedo boats and six submarine chasers, the R.C.N. would have been hard pressed to meet its commitments on the East Coast in 1918.

Besides handing vessels over to the operational control of the R.C.N., the United States Navy, at the height of U-boat activity in August 1918, dispatched a destroyer and 18 submarine chasers to patrol the area east of Nova Scotia and two revenue cutters to patrol the Grand Banks. It also gave indispensable help to the R.C.N. in the establishment of a Royal Canadian Naval Air Service to provide air cover for shipping in the waters off Halifax and Sydney. The decision to create the R.C.N.A.S. was taken in the spring of 1918, and arrangements were made to recruit and train a force of 500 officers and men while suitable bases were being built at Dartmouth and Sydney. In April the United States agreed to supply aircraft and kite balloons and to lend pilots until Canadians could be trained. Later the offer was extended to include the manning of dirigibles and kite balloons until Canadian crews were available.

Recruiting for the R.C.N.A.S. was slow — only 81 cadets and six airship coxswains were in training at the time of the Armistice — but United States Navy aviators began to arrive at Halifax in early August, and on the 19th Lieutenant-Commander Richard E. Byrd, later famous as a polar explorer, hoisted the Stars and Stripes and took command as Officer-in-Charge, United States Naval Air Forces in Canada. Although the American airmen did not come under the operational control of Canadian authorities, close liaison was maintained to co-ordinate the patrolling activities of United States aircraft and Canadian ships. The first patrol flights over Halifax were made on 25 August by two of the four flying-boats then at the base, and the first

MINESWEEPERS, HALIFAX by Arthur Lismer (1885-   ). Canadian trawler-minesweepers steam in line ahead in the Halifax approaches in 1918. Overhead, Curtiss HS2L flying boats from the Royal Canadian Naval Air Station assist in the daily search for U-boats.

regular convoy-escort flight occurred five days later. The base at North Sydney took longer to complete, and it was 21 September before it reported four machines ready for convoy work. By the end of the war, both stations were employing six flying-boats for convoy protection, coastal surveillance and the investigation of submarine sighting reports. The war ended before any dirigibles were brought to Canada, and by the Armistice only H.M.C.S. *Acadia* was operating a kite balloon.

Fortunately, the submarine attack that had been expected in the spring did not begin in Canadian waters until August and then was only a minor skirmish instead of the dreaded, all-out battle. Only six U-boats operated in the Western Atlantic in 1918, and only three of these, the *U-156,* the *U-117* and the *U-155,* appeared in waters patrolled by Canadian forces. Shipping losses were light. In the area bounded by 43° North and 53°

West, U-boats destroyed only two merchantmen of over 2500 tons and 22 small vessels.

An unusual feature of the attacks in Canadian waters in August 1918 was the use of a disguised "raider", the Canadian steam trawler *Triumph.* This little fishing vessel was peacefully steaming some 60 miles off Canso, Nova Scotia, when, just after midday on 20 August, the *U-156* suddenly appeared out of the water beside her. One warning shot stopped the defenceless trawler, and within half an hour a prize crew had taken over, armed the *Triumph* with two 3-pounder guns, and was ready to begin operations. As a raider, *Triumph* lived up to her name. Since she was known by sight to almost the entire Canadian and United States fishing fleets, she had no difficulty in approaching unsuspecting vessels. Indeed, they frequently ran alongside her to chat about fishing conditions. On the day of her capture,

Triumph sank five fishing boats, while *U-156* dealt with a sixth. The next day the trawler sank another vessel, but that was the last heard of her; presumably she was scuttled by her prize crew. *U-156* continued to prey on the fishing fleets until 26 August and then turned homeward, only to strike a mine and sink in the North Sea.

As far as the Canadian Patrol Service was concerned, one of the more important effects of the U-boat raids in North American waters was the transfer to Quebec of the western terminus of the fast Halifax convoys. At this time the greatest danger to convoys was not the torpedo but the mine, and Halifax was particularly vulnerable to mining. Chiefly because of this, the former Halifax-Channel convoys, which carried large numbers of United States troops, began to run from the port of Quebec early in September 1918. This change upset the R.C.N.'s existing arrangements whereby escort and patrol forces were maintained at both Sydney and Halifax, with a mobile striking force, also based on Sydney, to deal with any special threat. The British admiral commanding the North America and West Indies Station suggested that most of the Halifax force and part of the Sydney force be diverted to protect the new Quebec convoys, but the R.C.N. disagreed — understandably enough in view of the U-boat activity and the outcry over losses in the fishing fleet. The only alternative was to reinforce the Patrol Service, and this was done by diverting to the R.C.N. on temporary loan a number of R.N.-manned drifters destined for overseas service. These vessels, together with those of the St. Lawrence Patrol, provided the necessary protection without disorganizing the regular Halifax and Sydney forces. As it turned out, the convoys were not molested, and the last U-boat left North American waters in October 1918.

The Royal Canadian Navy had made considerable progress in four years. By November 1918 it had grown to a force of some 115 war vessels and about 5500 officers and men. Its future seemed secure and its prospects, if not brilliant, at least promising. In April 1914, the Director of the Canadian Naval Service, Admiral Charles Kingsmill, had expressed the hope that Canada might one day "inaugurate a Naval Service which would be able to carry out its responsibilities." By the end of the war it seemed as though this hope was on the threshold of fulfilment.

The War in the Air, 1914-1918

In 1914 the aeroplane was still a novelty to most Canadians. A few had learned to fly at schools in the United States, Britain or France, and some had built or bought their own aircraft, but most flying in Canada was done by outsiders, principally Americans, who gave exhibition performances and sometimes carried passengers. In August 1914 only a handful of qualified pilots lived in Canada, and in the whole country there was not a single flying field or aeronautical school.

Few could have predicted the technical advances in flying that the next four years were to bring, or the importance of the work that aircraft would be called upon to do. Even fewer could have predicted the part Canada was to play in the air in this new war. When the First World War began, both sides between them could muster only a few hundred first-line machines. Slow, cumbersome and unreliable, they were generally flown only during the daytime, and not even then if the weather was bad. Nevertheless, they soon demonstrated their value and became increasingly important as the war progressed.

The Canadians who flew against the enemy in the First World War did so as members of the Royal Flying Corps, which was a corps of the British Army; the Royal Naval Air Service, which was part of the Royal Navy; or the Royal Air Force, a new third service which was formed in April 1918 by merging the navy and army air services. Accurate figures are difficult to obtain, but between 1914 and 1918 approximately 22,000 Canadians joined the British flying services, two-thirds of them as pilots or observers. By the end of the war, one of every four Royal Air Force officers came from Canada. There was an even larger percentage of Canadians among the thousands of cadets then under training as flyers.

Although the Canadians who fought in the air did so with the British services, no fewer than three separate Canadian air forces were formed during the war or immediately afterwards. The first was the Canadian Aviation Corps, an ill-fated and poorly organized venture of Colonel Sam Hughes, the Minister of Militia and Defence. When the Canadian Aviation Corps sailed with the First Canadian Contingent in October 1914, it consisted of three members and one second-hand aircraft which had been purchased in the United States. The aircraft, damaged in transit, ended in the yard of a Salisbury scrap-metal dealer, and when one of the Canadian pilots was killed while training with the Royal Flying Corps in England early in 1915, the Canadian Aviation Corps quietly faded out of existence.

WAR IN THE AIR by C. R. W. Nevinson (1889-1946).
Action over the lines in France in the First World War.
(Courtesy The National Gallery of Canada.)

Many young Canadians in 1915-1916 received preliminary instruction at the Curtiss Flying School, Toronto, before joining the British flying services. One of three Curtiss flying boats operated by the school in its 1915 season is shown over Toronto harbour.

In the late summer of 1915 the British suggested that distinctive Canadian squadrons be organized, but Canada declined, preferring to limit the Dominion's contribution to providing airmen. Late in the war, when the Canadian Government realized what a large proportion of aircrew in the British flying services was Canadian, it authorized the formation in England of two Canadian squadrons together with a wing headquarters and supporting units, but the wing did not officially come into being as the Canadian Air Force until some days after the Armistice. The Canadian Air Force continued training in England for eight months after the war in the expectation that it would be returned intact to Canada to form the nucleus of a post-war flying service, but in mid-1919 it received orders to disband. During the latter part of 1918 a third Canadian flying force, the Royal Canadian Naval Air Service, was formed to counter the German submarine threat on Canada's East Coast (see page 74 above).

During the first two years of war Canadians often endured months of frustration before they were accepted by the British flying services. A few managed to enlist in 1914, but not until early the following year were procedures established whereby members of the Canadian Expeditionary Force overseas and young men in Canada might join the Royal Flying Corps or the Royal Naval Air Service. Even then few were accepted at first. Those who joined from the Canadian Expeditionary Force were sent to R.F.C. or R.N.A.S. ground and flying schools overseas and were ultimately posted to operational squadrons. A limited recruiting programme was begun in Canada, but until the latter part of 1916 those who joined in the Dominion were first required to gain their pilot certificates at private flying schools and to do this, moreover, at their own expense, although a large part of the cost was refunded to successful applicants. Several private flying schools were established in Canada, but the only successful one was the Curtiss Flying School in Toronto, managed by J. A. D. McCurdy, where students paid $400 for 400 minutes of elementary flying instruction. The school was active during 1915 and 1916, although it closed during the intervening winter. Those accepted by the flying services were given three to six months' operational training after arriving overseas.

Early in 1917 the Royal Flying Corps opened a large-scale recruiting campaign in Canada and established training schools and flying fields in the Toronto area and along the northern shores of Lake Ontario. The largest of the flying fields, Camp Borden, is still in use by the Royal Canadian Air Force. The Cadet Wing and No. 4 School of Military Aeronautics at the University of Toronto and the Armament School in Hamilton gave cadets ground training. Flying training and additional ground instruction were given at Camp Borden, Mohawk, Rathbun and Leaside. Gunnery and combat tactics were taught at the School of Aerial Fighting at Beamsville, and all cadets passed through this course. A School of Special Flying at Armour Heights was attended by those selected to serve as instructors.

The training scheme, which was entirely controlled by the British air services, produced more than 3000 pilots and observers for the Royal Flying Corps and Royal Air Force, and by the end of the war some 280 students were graduating each month. More than 9200 cadets were enlisted for flying training during the nearly two years that the training scheme operated. Most staff personnel and instructors were Canadian, and 7400 mechanics were enlisted in Canada for ground duties.

In addition to its own cadets, the R.F.C. trained pilots and ground crew for ten United States Signal Corps squadrons after the American entry into the war. In return, the Americans provided fields and facilities near Fort Worth, Texas, where the Royal Flying Corps carried out flying training throughout the winter of 1917-1918. The R.F.C. trained 300 American pilots, 144 other flying officers, some 20 administrative and equipment officers and approximately 2000 ground crewmen. Training began in Canada in the summer of 1917 and was completed at Fort Worth. All training equipment in Canada was provided by the Royal Flying Corps. Closely associated with the training programme was an aircraft factory, Canadian Aeroplanes Limited of Toronto, owned by the Imperial Munitions Board (also an agency of the British Government), which produced most of the two-seater biplane training machines used to teach the cadets to fly. The plant was Canada's first large aircraft manufacturing concern, and, including spares, it produced the equivalent of nearly 3000

Cadets under instruction at No. 4 School of Military Aeronautics, Toronto, are shown with a JN-4, the R.F.C.'s standard trainer in Canada in 1917.
(D.N.D. photo.)

JUNIOR OFFICERS' QUARTERS, ARMOUR HEIGHTS by Frank H. Johnston (1888-1949). One of the six R.F.C. training fields in Canada, it was on the then northern outskirts of Toronto.

machines.

While these developments were taking place in Canada, hundreds of young Canadians were daily battling the enemy in the skies overseas. At the beginning of the war, the R.F.C. and R.N.A.S. between them mustered only 113 first-line aircraft and half a dozen small airships. Their combined personnel strength was little more than 2000, fewer than 180 of whom were officers. However, the British flying services, and particularly the Army's R.F.C., grew rapidly. At the end of the war the Royal Air Force had 3300 first-line aircraft and more than 100 airships, and personnel strength had risen to nearly 300,000.

In August 1914 four R.F.C. squadrons flew to France to work with the British Expeditionary Force, their primary duty being reconnaissance. As techniques and equipment were developed to enable guns to range from the air, artillery spotting soon became another

vital role for aircraft. Bombing was at first done only by the R.N.A.S., but the R.F.C. soon added bombing to its duties, and as specialized aircraft and heavier bombs came into service, bombing — both by day and night — became an increasingly important task for both flying services. Pilots and observers occasionally shot at enemy aircraft with pistols or carbines, but there was at first no organized aerial fighting. However, specialized fighting aircraft were soon developed, fitted with machine-guns and charged with defending friendly aircraft employed on reconnaissance, artillery spotting and bombing duties and attacking enemy flyers carrying out similar duties. This often led to the classic "dog fight", in which opposing squadrons of fighter planes engaged in a wild *mêlée* high over the trenches. Both sides strove for air superiority, and a measure of dominance passed back and forth from one side to another as new fighter designs were introduced by the Allies and the Central Powers. When the war ended, the mastery of the air was held by the Allies, although this was rather the result of a heavy numerical superiority than of better aeroplanes.

The air war was fought over the sea as well as over the land, and R.N.A.S. seaplanes and flying-boats operated from bases on the North Sea and both sides of the English Channel, in the Mediterranean and other theatres. From the early days of the war, R.N.A.S. seaplanes operated from naval carriers whose hoists lowered the aircraft to the water and brought it back aboard after its patrol. Later, British fighter aircraft also flew from the decks of sea-going carriers and from small flat-decked lighters which were towed at high speeds behind destroyers.

Nevertheless, most of the flying over the Western Front consisted of daily reconnaissance and artillery spotting flights, and Canada was well represented in the squadrons that performed these routine but always perilous tasks. Although these flyers went almost unnoticed by the public, whose attention was focussed on others whose achievements caught the layman's imagination, reconnaissance and artillery spotting remained the primary *raison d'être* of the R.F.C. in France throughout the war. At first military commanders were hesitant to accept as reliable the reports of reconnaissance aircraft — and perhaps there was some excuse for this scepticism, for there was a lack of trained observers. However, by the late autumn of 1914, aircraft had been recognized as a principal means of obtaining information about the enemy. In the British Expeditionary Force the R.F.C. squadrons were grouped into a wing, whose headquarters provided liaison with army formations. At the beginning of the Battle of the Marne, in September 1914, two squadrons worked directly under the 1st and 2nd Corps for reconnaissance. This was the beginning of a decentralization of the R.F.C. in France. Later certain units were designated as corps squadrons, whose duties included close reconnaissance, photography and artillery spotting on the immediate front of each army corps. Other R.F.C. units, designated as army squadrons, were

LOOKING DUE EAST FROM THE AERODROME by Frank H. Johnston (1888-1949). This reproduction shows the JN-4 in flight at the R.F.C. field, Camp Borden, Ontario, in 1918. Some of the hangars in the background are still standing. *(Courtesy The National Gallery of Canada.*

R.F.C. technician preparing a photograph mosaic of the enemy lines near Arras, 22 February 1918.
(Courtesy Imperial War Museum.)

responsible for air fighting, long-range reconnaissance and bombing. The Royal Flying Corps first used aerial photography on 15 September 1914 during the Battle of the Aisne, and before long, reconnaissance aircraft equipped with cameras were making regular flights. Artillery spotting was also carried out for the first time during this battle, when the airmen signalled the fall of shells on targets by firing different coloured flares. This method of communication was soon replaced by wireless.

The Royal Naval Air Service, as noted above, pioneered aerial bombing in the British forces. The naval flying service went into the war capable of dropping 112-pound bombs. The R.N.A.S. was also the first of the British flying services to attempt strategic bombing. In September, October and November 1914, the navy, flying its aircraft from fields near Antwerp in Belgium and Belfort in north-eastern France, launched several raids against the German airship sheds at Cologne and Düsseldorf and against the Zeppelin factory at Friedrichshafen. Once the war on the Western Front became static, most R.N.A.S. land-based squadrons on the Continent flew from fields in the Dunkirk area. From there they attacked German warships and submarines at Ostend, Zeebrugge and Bruges, railway

centres, and air bases used for raids against Britain.

The first R.N.A.S. unit specifically designed for long-distance strategic bombing, No. 3 (Naval) Wing, holds a particular interest for Canadians, since most of its pilots were from the Dominion. The Wing's first large-scale raid was launched on 12 October 1916, when 20 bombers escorted by seven fighters struck at the Mauser arms works at Oberndorf on the Neckar River. Most of the Wing's bombing was done with Sopwith 1½-Strutters, which carried four 65-pound bombs, and the majority of targets were iron and steel works in the heavily-industrialized Saar basin and northern Lorraine. The Wing operated until mid-April 1917, when the need for additional fighter strength caused its disbandment.

In the R.F.C.'s first bombing operations observers dropped hand-grenades that they had taken aloft with them on reconnaissance flights, but by March 1915 the R.F.C., in its attempts to hamper the movements of enemy reinforcements during the Battle of Neuve Chapelle, was dropping bombs of up to 100 pounds. Thereafter bombing became an important part of the R.F.C.'s work, and improved aircraft, bombs, techniques, tactics and equipment were developed, including the first British bombsight, which came into use in mid-1915. Until early 1916 the Royal Flying Corps bombed only by day, but from then on night attacks were also made. During the Battle of Loos, in September 1915, the R.F.C. dropped only five and a half tons of bombs, but during the Battle of the Somme the following year, it dropped nearly 300 tons.

The R.F.C. did not begin strategic bombing until October 1917, when a special bomber unit, known as the 41st Wing, was formed at the direction of the British War Cabinet. The bomber wing, which was created to retaliate for the German raids against London, consisted of three squadrons, one being an R.N.A.S. unit equipped with the big new Handley-Page night-bombers. Initially the Wing's aircraft operated from Ochey, near Nancy, a field previously used by No. 3 (Naval) Wing. The 41st Wing launched bombing attacks throughout the winter of 1917-1918, striking at the same iron and steel plants that had been hit by the naval bombing wing, and at munitions factories in Mannheim, Kaiserslautern and other points. Redesig-

nated the VII Brigade early in 1918, the bomber wing was provided with two additional squadrons in May.

As a result of a decision to increase the bombing of strategic targets inside Germany, the "Independent Force" was formed on 6 June 1918, under the command of Major-General Sir Hugh Trenchard, who had commanded the R.F.C. in France from mid-1915 until January 1918. The Independent Force initially consisted of the five squadrons of the VIII Brigade, but by the time of the Armistice it had nine squadrons, four of them equipped with twin-engined Handley-Pages. By then the Force's aircraft were operating from five large fields in the Nancy area. During the five months of its existence, the Independent Force dropped 543 tons of bombs, including some 200 tons on German airfields. In addition, during September and October Trenchard was called on to divert part of his force against tactical targets in support of Allied troops. Had the war continued for a few more months, the striking power of

ot and observer of No. 15 Squadron, R.F.C., then near Amiens,
t after a flight behind the enemy's lines, March 1918.

(Courtesy Imperial War Museum.)

Left—NORTH SEA RESCUE, 1917. The cr
a D.H. 4 being rescued by an H. 12 flying-boat flown by
Lieutenant Robert Leckie, who retired as Canada's Chief
Air Staff in 1947. The artist was Charles Dixon, R.I.

Below—Handley Page 0/100 bombers
Dunkirk-area field, April 1918. Many Canadians flew this big,
flying machine, which carried a bomb load of nearly 1800 p
(Courtesy Imperial War M

Sunday morning service in the R.A.F. The pulpit is the forward cockpit of an F.E. 2b night bomber.

Trenchard's force would have been strengthened enormously by the addition of the "Super" Handley-Page V.1500, a big four-engined aircraft which could carry a bomb-load of 7500 pounds.

Although Canadians distinguished themselves in many types of flying, it was generally the fighter "aces" who received the plaudits of the public. Both the R.F.C. and the R.N.A.S. had experimented before the war with airborne armaments, and before the end of 1914 some aircraft had been fitted with light machine-guns. During 1915, both sides introduced machines whose primary role was not to support the ground forces but to attack enemy aircraft.

The Germans made the first significant bid for air superiority in the summer of 1915 by introducing the Fokker monoplane, a single-seater fighter whose combat effectiveness was largely due to its armament. The Fokker mounted a belt-fed machine-gun synchronized with the aircraft's engine so that the bullets passed between the blades of the revolving propeller, and this gave the Germans a degree of dominance in the air that continued until May 1916. The British flying services were able to continue their work, but at heavy cost. In addition, the R.F.C. was forced into defensive measures that necessitated a wasteful misemployment of available aircraft. Orders issued in January 1916 stipulated that a minimum of three fighter aircraft must escort each reconnaissance machine sent across the lines, and formation flying was also adopted as a defensive measure. Fighter operations became a matter of teamwork as the war progressed, and although occasional lone sorties were still flown, pilots normally flew as members of

85

patrols, adhering to stipulated tactical procedures. In addition to aerial combat, the fighter squadrons often carried out "strafing" attacks on enemy positions, a hazardous task that cost the flyers many casualties.

Air superiority swung back to the British and French in the spring of 1916, following the arrival in France of two R.F.C. "pusher" types of aircraft that could outfight the Fokkers. New fighter tactics were also developed during 1916, many of them introduced by No. 24 Squadron, which was the first R.F.C. single-seater fighter squadron to arrive in France and which had several Canadians among its pilots. Prior to and during the Battle of the Somme, the R.F.C. held a marked aerial superiority over its section of the front. By August 1916 all the specialized single-seater fighters of the R.F.C. had been concentrated in squadrons whose primary responsibility was aerial fighting. The Germans

adopted a similar procedure. However, in the autumn of 1916, the first of the new German single-seater fighters appeared. Armed with twin synchronized machine-guns, they were superior to any fighters flown by the British, and, as their numbers grew, British aerial activity continued only at steadily increasing cost. Gradually, as new fighter aircraft arrived in increasing numbers, the Allies began to regain the upper hand.

Canadian fighter pilots established a remarkable record. British authorities have never published an official list of aerial victories, but the many unofficial tabulations that have been compiled are all liberally sprinkled with Canadian names. The highest-scoring fighter pilot of the British services was Lt.-Col. William A. Bishop, V.C., D.S.O. and Bar, M.C., D.F.C., of Owen Sound, Ontario, with 72 victories. Other high-scoring Canadians included Major Raymond Collishaw, D.S.O. and

Many Canadians flew with No. 85 Squadron, shown at St. Omer, France, in mid-1918, with its SE5a fighters.

device of a movable gun platform and target was used to teach aerial
nery at an R.A.F. school in France in 1918.

Bar, D.S.C., D.F.C., of Nanaimo, British Columbia —
60; Major Donald R. MacLaren, D.S.O., M.C. and Bar,
D.F.C., of Vancouver, British Columbia — 54; Major
William G. Barker, V.C., D.S.O. and Bar, M.C. and
two Bars, of Dauphin, Manitoba — 50; Captain Fred
R. G. McCall, D.S.O., M.C. and Bar, D.F.C., of Vernon,
British Columbia—34; and Captain William G. Claxton,
D.S.O., D.F.C. and Bar, of Gladstone, Manitoba — 31.

As the war continued, cooperation between the flying
service and the army grew increasingly close. Prior to
the Battle of Amiens, which opened on 8 August 1918,
British Handley-Page bombers flew in the forward areas
to drown the noise of assembling tanks, and during the
battle itself 147 day bombers, 92 night bombers, 75
fighter reconnaissance aircraft, 376 fighters and 110
corps aeroplanes flew sorties in support of the offensive,
strafing German reserves, laying smoke screens, dropping flares to guide attacking army units and attempt-

ing, although without success, to isolate the battlefield
by destroying the Somme bridges. In its attempt to
interfere with this aerial offensive, the German Air Force
suffered losses from which it never recovered.

Canadian flyers were prominent in the struggle
against the German airships and Gotha bombers that
attacked Britain. The Germans flew 52 bomber raids
over the United Kingdom, killing 857 persons, and
between early 1915 and August 1918 the big Zeppelin
and Schutte-Lanz airships made 51 bombing raids, killing more than 550 persons. Damage to military and
industrial targets was slight, but the public outcry forced
the flying services to divert many aircraft to counter the
night-flying raiders. At first the defending machines were
almost helpless against the attackers, but improved
techniques and weapons wrought a change. Although
a few raids continued into 1918, the threat had been
countered by the end of 1917.

(D.N.D. photo

Above—Captain William A. Bishop of No. 60 Squadron R.F.C., at Le Hameau, France, August 1917, and the Nieuport 17 with which he scored many of his 72 credited victories. *Below*—The brilliant Canadian flyer Major Raymond Collishaw was credited with 60 aerial victories in the First World War. Here, in July 1918, he stands beside a Sopwith Camel of No. 203 Squadron, which he then commanded. In the cockpit is Captain Arthur T. Whealy, another notable Canadian pilot, who was credited with 19 victories.

(Public Archive
Canada ph

Major William G. Barker, whose single-handed combat with a swarm of German fighters shortly before the end of the war won him the Victoria Cross. This photograph was probably taken in the summer of 1918 when Barker commanded No. 139 Squadron, R.A.F., on the Italian Front.

Sopwith Dolphins of No. 1 Squadron, one of the two squadrons formed in England by the short-lived Canadian Air Force shortly after the Armistice. Taken at Upper Heyford, near Oxford, probably in the spring of 1919.

The Royal Naval Air Service's operations against enemy submarines became increasingly successful from 1917 onwards, after large twin-engined flying-boats capable of carrying 230-pound bombs came into service. Canada was particularly well represented at the R.N.A.S. air stations from which these flying-boats operated, and of the seven, possibly eight, submarines sunk by British aircraft, Canadians took part in the destruction of five.

The war in the air was not confined to the Western Front and the waters around Britain, but extended to Italy and the Mediterranean, to Egypt, Palestine and Mesopotamia, and to East Africa and the Indian North-West Frontier. Canadians flew in all these theatres as pilots, observers and balloon officers. After the Armistice some Canadians continued to fly with the British forces fighting the Bolsheviks in North and South Russia.

The development of aviation during the war, and the part played by the Canadians who flew, left the Dominion with more than a new set of national heroes. Five million dollars' worth of aircraft and equipment was presented to Canada by the British Government at the end of the war. In addition to its value to the Canadian Air Force that was formed in 1920, the gift made a considerable contribution to the development of Canadian commercial flying. The Canadian Air Force also benefitted from the R.F.C. Canada training scheme, for the facilities at Camp Borden, including a ready-made airfield complete with hangars, were turned over to Canada.

The deeds of her aviators during the First World War provide Canada with a glowing chapter in her history. Canadian airmen won more than 800 decorations and awards for valour, including three Victoria Crosses. Canadians flew on every major front and in every type of operation, and nearly 1600 Canadian airmen lost their lives.

The names of many Canadian flyers, above all perhaps that of the fighter ace "Billy" Bishop, had become household words at home. Many Canadians who lived near the training fields had come to accept flying as a commonplace occurrence. The thousands of Canadian airmen who returned to their homes brought with them an airmindedness that had not existed before. They, and others, began to think seriously of the future of commercial aviation in Canada. Throughout the 1920s and even later, as commercial flying developed in Canada, most pilots were men who had learned their skills in wartime. The growth of commercial flying in Canada could thus be traced to the exploits of the Canadian aviators overseas. The heritage of the Canadian flyers of the First World War has been passed from generation to generation, making its own contribution in peace and war, and remains today a proud possession and a recognizable national characteristic.

THE TWENTY-ONE YEARS
1918-1939

Canadian Defence Policy Between the Wars

The First World War had everywhere shaken the fabric of society, and in 1919 Canadians shared the prevalent mood of disillusionment and uncertainty. The soldiers in France had sung:

> *When this bloody war is over,*
> *Oh how happy I will be.*
> *When I get my civvy clothes on,*
> *No more soldiering for me.*

And they had meant it. Thus, almost as soon as the war was over, the general revulsion from all things military led the Canadian Government, with the full approval of most citizens, to reduce the armed forces almost to their pre-war level. Whatever else the war changed, it had not changed Canadian military policy.

A period of moderately generous defence appropriations after 1918 was followed after 1921 by sharp reductions; then with growing prosperity the forces regained a little ground. But Canadians had no intention of spending much on defence. In the 1920s defence spending varied from a low of $12,242,930 in 1922-1923 to a high of $21,070,015 in 1929-1930. For the year 1923-1924 Canada's per capita expenditure on defence was $1.46; every other member of the Commonwealth spent far more — Great Britain $23.04; South Africa $4.27; Australia $3.30; and New Zealand $2.33. France spent more than Britain, and the small European countries of Belgium, the Netherlands and Switzerland spent $13.37, $7.87 and $4.04 respectively. The United States per capita expenditure on defence was almost five times as much as Canada's.

In 1922, in order to "promote economy and increase efficiency", Parliament passed a National Defence Act by which the two existing Departments of Militia and Defence and of the Naval Service, and the Air Board which had been formed in 1919 and which adminis-

tered the Canadian Air Force, were replaced by a single Department of National Defence under one Minister. The appointment of Chief of the General Staff, then held by Major-General J. H. MacBrien, was changed to that of Chief of Staff, Department of National Defence. General MacBrien thus became the chief adviser to the Minister on all military matters and the control of all three services was vested in him. The former Militia Council was abolished and a Defence Council created, consisting of the Minister, the Deputy Minister, the Chief of Staff and the Director of the Naval Service. The Adjutant General, the Quartermaster General and the Director, Canadian Air Force, were associate members.

This early attempt at "integration" was hardly a success. The Director of the Naval Service, Captain Walter Hose, felt that he had to resist the subordination of the Navy to the Chief of Staff. Four years of struggle, antagonism and administrative confusion followed, until early in 1927 MacBrien resigned in frustration and the appointment of Chief of Staff, Department of National Defence, was abolished. In March 1928 the position of Director of the Naval Service was renamed "Chief of the Naval Staff", and in November 1938 a similar step was taken with respect to the Royal Canadian Air Force, which until then had reported to the Chief of the General Staff.

Fortunately, the 1920s were peaceful years for Canada. Britain's refusal to renew the Anglo-Japanese Treaty in 1921 and her acceptance in 1922 of naval parity with the United States made it clear that she had no intention of allowing any serious Anglo-American difficulties to develop. Later in 1922, at the time of the Chanak Incident — when Britain suggested the Dominion express a willingness to send a contingent to help hold the line against Mustapha Kemal in the Neutral

Zone of what had been Turkish territory — the aloofness displayed by the Canadian Government let Britain know that she could no longer count on the automatic participation of Canada in imperial wars. From now on the Canadian attitude was clear; Prime Minister Mackenzie King expressed it at the Imperial Conference of 1923 — "to what extent Canada would participate in a war at any time must be considered a matter which her own Parliament will wish to decide."

Late in 1929 the Wall Street stock-market crash ushered in the great Depression. By 1932 almost a quarter of Canada's labour force was unemployed, including an estimated 70,000 single men, who, homeless and hungry, "rode the rods" across the country in search of work or drifted despairingly from town to town and from soup-line to soup-line. A year later wheat was selling for 38 cents a bushel on the Winnipeg Grain Exchange and Canada's national income had been cut almost in half. Defence appropriations were slashed to the bone.

The world's economic difficulties were a major cause of the grave international tensions that began to develop in 1931. That year Japan occupied Manchuria; in February 1932, when the League of Nations condemned this aggression, Japan withdrew from the League, set up a puppet state ("Manchukuo"), and seized a measure of political control in Mongolia. So serious was the situation that the British Government abandoned its "Ten-Year Rule" which stipulated that military planning be based on the assumption that no major war would occur for a decade. In 1934, Japan denounced the Washington Treaty of 1922 governing naval ratios of the Pacific powers. Japan's military expenditure for 1935-36 amounted to almost half the national budget, and Russia's military spending kept pace. Germany, under Hitler, left the League in 1933 and began to re-arm. France grew increasingly concerned about her security and in 1934 moved towards an understanding with Russia. A year later Mussolini defied the League of Nations and added Ethiopia to the Italian colonial empire. In 1936 civil war broke out in Spain.

In the depths of the Depression some military construction had been undertaken under the Unemployment Relief and Public Works Construction Acts, but the forces themselves had been reduced in numbers and efficiency. By 1936, however, the international situation was so menacing that it could no longer be ignored. The next year the Government of Mr. Mackenzie King launched a rearmament programme, in which the Royal Canadian Air Force received the highest priority. But it was on a very modest scale. The Minister of National Defence, Mr. Ian A. Mackenzie,

had found the draft estimates submitted by the services for 1937-38 "staggering", and they were finally reduced from $66,000,000 to $36,194,839. Even this small sum represented an increase of nearly $10,000,000 in three years. For the succeeding year the total was about the same. Then came the "Munich Crisis" of September 1938, which was a severe shock to both the public and the Government. The defence appropriation approved in the final months of peace for the fiscal year 1939-1940 was $64,666,874. Before this sum could be spent, the nation was at war.

The Army Between the Wars

Much had been done to re-establish the members of the Canadian Expeditionary Force after the Armistice. Every soldier who had been overseas for six months or had served in Canada for a full year received a gratuity based on length of service and pay of rank. For example, an unmarried private soldier, who had been overseas, received a payment which varied from $420 (for three years' service or more) to $210 for service of less than a year. Veterans who wanted to establish themselves on the land were assisted with long-term loans. Disabled men received pensions and medical treatment and were given opportunities for vocational training. By the end of 1919 a total of 91,521 pensions had been granted at a cost to the government of some $22,500,000 annually. At that time 8000 ex-servicemen were receiving medical treatment, and more than 23,000 were enrolled for vocational training. In all, 30,000 veterans received loans from the Soldier Settlement Board and were settled on the land. Nevertheless, most returned men deemed these measures inadequate. Their unrest, together with that of labour, which the authorities feared was an echo of the Bolshevik upheaval in Russia, seemed to pose a possible threat to public order.

On 15 May 1919, this unrest flared up in the Winnipeg General Strike, which inspired sympathy strikes in other cities, including Toronto, Vancouver, Edmonton and Calgary. The Winnipeg strike ended in June, not before the militia had been called in; but the Government was apprehensive as to what might happen later in the year when large numbers of returned soldiers would find themselves unemployed throughout a Canadian winter. In June 1919 the Minister of Militia and Defence proposed an amendment to the Militia Act authorizing an increase in the Permanent Force establishment from 5000 to 10,000 men, but he made it clear he had no intention of recruiting to that strength. The Act was amended, but by March 1921 the strength of the Permanent Force was only 4125. Even this total was not exceeded in the next few years.

A step towards the reorganization of the militia had been taken in the spring of 1919 by the appointment of a committee under the chairmanship of Major-General Sir William Otter. On the recommendation of the "Otter Committee", the militia was organized on paper to provide 11 divisions and four cavalry divisions with peace establishments totalling more than 140,000 men. However, the actual strengths of units fell far below establishments; in 1931, for example, the strength of the Non-Permanent Active Militia was only 51,287. These were difficult days for the N.P.A.M., and many units survived only because of the personal sacrifices of officers and men, who frequently gave up their militia pay to regimental funds.

In 1923, in order to help develop the Canadian North, the militia established the first radio-telegraph stations of the Northwest Territories and Yukon Radio System. Men of the Royal Canadian Corps of Signals kept in touch with the outside world from Dawson in the Yukon, along the Mackenzie River basin, in the Great

Slave Lake region and east to Hudson Bay. By means of the radio system, ships in the Arctic were directed from Edmonton; supplies for northern outposts were ordered quickly; communities along the Mackenzie were advised of delivery dates for cargoes on their way down river; and mining syndicates were able to exploit discoveries at once, often gaining a whole summer's work. At some stations a soldier acted as postmaster, airport superintendent and Justice of the Peace, as well as wireless operator. The normal tour of duty was for only three years, but the spell of the North was often stronger than loneliness and primitive conditions, and many signalmen were granted voluntary extensions.

In 1932, when the Depression was at its worst, the Chief of the General Staff, Major-General A. G. L. McNaughton, proposed that the Department of National Defence establish and administer unemployment relief camps where single, homeless, unemployed men might report if they wished to do so. Work useful to Canada would be found for them, and in exchange the men would be clothed, housed and fed until the nation's

A signals station of the Northwest Territories and Yukon Radio System at Ennadal Lake, Northwest Territories.

(D.N.D. photo.)

Unemployment Relief. Highway
construction at Aldridge, British Columbia, April 1934.

economy began to move again and they could be re-established in more regular forms of employment. The plan was authorized in October 1932, and by the following June, 8000 had enrolled and the total was steadily growing. The army supplied the men's rations and administered the camps, and military engineers controlled the works projects, which included building air stations at Trenton and Rockcliffe, repairing the citadels at Halifax and Quebec City and constructing airfields along the proposed trans-Canada air route. There was no militarism whatsoever in the camps, no military discipline, no drill; even the officers and soldiers concerned in the relief projects wore civilian clothes. Nevertheless, the scheme was attacked on the grounds that it served the ulterior purpose of turning single, unemployed men into soldiers and that trades-men in the camps were depriving union members of employment.

The inmates of some camps complained of living conditions, and these complaints were exploited by Communist agitators. Major disturbances, all attributed by the authorities to subversion, occurred at Long Branch in 1933; and in many camps in British Columbia in 1933, 1934 and 1935. The last of these led to the "March on Ottawa" in the summer of 1935, when strikers from Vancouver, swelled by others on the journey East, set out to present their complaints to the Government. The march achieved no change in policy. The Prime Minister, Mr. R. B. Bennett, believing it to be "an organized effort on the part of the various communist organizations throughout Canada to effect the overthrow of constituted authority", remained adamant. A riot in Regina, which resulted in death to a city policeman and injuries to two members of the R.C.M.P. and many marchers, reduced the public sympathy which the plight of the men had aroused. All but a hard core of the marchers dispersed.

In 1936, when the wheels of industry were beginning to turn again, the camps were closed. In all, 170,291 single men had worked in them, and despite complaints and criticism, Unemployment Relief had been successful in preserving the health and morale of a large proportion of the young men of the country and in furthering the development of Canada, especially in its defensive aspects.

As early as 1931 the General Staff, in an appreciation of the state of the Canadian Militia, had decided that Canada's defence requirements could best be served by the provision of a smaller but more efficient force, and had proposed that the 11 infantry divisions and four cavalry divisions be reduced to six infantry divisions and one cavalry division, with a proper proportion of corps and army troops. Canada placed this proposal before the Geneva Disarmament Conference in 1923 and 1933, but the reorganization was not authorized until 1936. It received scant attention in Parliament or the press, for even in 1936 most Canadians were little concerned with defence. The reorganization reduced the militia establishment to dimensions corresponding to its probable role, but, as far as possible, battle honours, traditions and the names of famous regiments were preserved.

Under the reorganization, 135 infantry and machine-gun battalions were reduced to 91, of which six were tank battalions. Thirty-five cavalry regiments were reduced to 20, of which four were armoured car units. By the conversion of surplus cavalry and infantry and the formation of new units, the artillery was greatly expanded, as was the engineer corps. The Royal Canadian Corps of Signals, the Royal Canadian Army Service Corps, the Royal Canadian Army Medical Corps, the Royal Canadian Ordnance Corps, the Royal Canadian Army Veterinary Corps and the Canadian Postal Corps were all reorganized.

No further substantial organizational changes occurred in the militia until the outbreak of war. The years between 1936 and 1939 were taken up with completing the 1936 reorganization and in striving to train, rearm and re-equip the force. Training showed a great improvement from 1937 on, but even so, only 46,521 officers and men were trained in the fiscal year 1938-1939, as contrasted with over 55,000 in 1913. Up to 1936 the arms and equipment of the militia had been seriously inadequate. Annual financial appropriations had been so small that it had been scarcely possible to replace worn-out equipment of 1914-1918 pattern, let alone build up new stocks. The army entirely lacked such items as tanks, anti-tank guns, close-support weapons, armoured cars and armoured machine-gun carriers. Even stocks of such indispensable stores as ammunition were depleted, and by 1935 it was reported that $5,858,645 would be required to bring ammunition stocks up to authorized holdings.

In 1936 some remedial action was taken, but only tiny orders were placed that year. Other orders followed in 1937 and 1938 but again these were by no means large. By the spring of 1939 Canada had received from Britain arms and equipment that included four anti-aircraft guns, five mortars, 82 Vickers machine-guns, ten Bren guns, seven anti-tank rifles, two light tanks, 4000 respirators and one tractor for hauling heavy artillery. Wireless equipment, ammunition to replace the depleted stocks, and fuses had also been obtained.

Carden Loyd Machine Gun Carrier Platoon of The Royal Canadian
Regiment, photographed in 1932 at Wolseley Barracks, London, Ontario.

In addition, 200 field guns had been fitted with pneumatic tires in Canada, some trucks and special vehicles had been obtained from Canadian industry, and 7000 Bren light machine-guns were being produced in Canada. Some items ordered in Britain, including coast-defence, anti-aircraft and anti-tank guns, mortars and light tanks, could not be delivered because of the demands of Britain's own rearmament programme.

In the summer of 1939, therefore, although the militia had been reorganized, its training improved and its re-equipment begun, it was ill-prepared for war. Nevertheless, it did provide a skeleton organization capable of fairly rapid expansion. Far more important was that through the discouraging years of the 1920s and 1930s the militia had kept alive the military spirit which had made the old Canadian Corps so magnificent a fighting-machine and which in the years immediately ahead was to make the First Canadian Army possible.

The Navy Between the Wars

With the end of the First World War, the Royal Canadian Navy soon relapsed into the somnolence that had been its previous peacetime state. At the Armistice, the R.C.N. was a flourishing little service, but within a year, only the drifter *Guelph* and the depot ships *Niobe* and *Rainbow* remained in commission. R.C.N. personnel had been reduced to 500 officers and men, and the Royal Naval Canadian Volunteer Reserve had been completely disbanded.

Nevertheless, the Royal Canadian Navy was very much in the minds of several people. In turn, the British Admiralty, the Canadian Naval Staff, Viscount

Jellicoe of Scapa, Prime Minister Sir Robert Borden and the Canadian Naval Minister all produced plans for its future. As early as May 1918, the Dominion Prime Ministers, gathered in London, had been presented with an Admiralty note suggesting that a single navy was necessary for the security of the whole Empire. The Dominion authorities would superintend dockyards and training establishments, but Whitehall would control everything else. Borden had unhesitatingly rejected this suggestion, since "it did not sufficiently recognize the status of the Dominions" and since it seemed obvious to him that "the acceptance of such a proposal would offend the newly awakened sense of nationhood which pervaded the people of Canada." The Admiralty had then suggested that Admiral Jellicoe, who had just resigned as First Sea Lord, should tour the Dominions to advise on their naval establishments and suggest ways in which unity could be maintained among the various autonomous fleets.

When Jellicoe reached Ottawa in November 1919, he found that the Canadian Naval Staff had fully-matured ideas of its own on what Canada should do about naval defence. The Director of the Naval Service, Admiral Sir Charles Kingsmill, had prepared no less than two dozen occasional papers on naval subjects, in which the most important recommendation concerned permanency of naval policy. He urged that a special Act of Parliament formulate naval policy for a decade or more and recommended a fleet which by 1934 would consist of seven cruisers, 12 destroyers, six submarines, three parent ships, 18 anti-submarine patrol and decoy boats, and 8500 officers and men. The average annual expenditure for such a navy over a 14-year period would be about $13 million.

Jellicoe's *Report,* on the other hand, presented the Canadian Government with a flexible array of alternatives — four different programmes whose annual costs ranged from $4,100,000 to $20,500,000. It also stressed the need for close cooperation between the Canadian and British navies, with similarity of equipment, organization, training, discipline, principles of command, staff work and strategical and tactical doctrine. Jellicoe hoped the Canadian Government might accept his second-cheapest proposal, which called, by 1927, for three light cruisers, eight submarines with a parent vessel, one flotilla leader and four destroyers, four minesweepers, eight patrol boats and a Naval Air Service of 12 aircraft. Most of this equipment would be a gift from the Royal Navy.

However, neither Canadian public opinion nor the Government was prepared to sanction heavy defence expenditures. When the Cabinet discussed Jellicoe's recommendations in December 1920, there was apparently much opposition to even the least expensive of the proposed schemes. Finally, on 20 March 1920, the Naval Minister, Mr. C. C. Ballantyne, was permitted to lay before a Union Government caucus a

modest plan for a navy of eight submarines, four destroyers and some smaller craft.

In caucus the Minister's Cabinet colleagues not only refused to join in urging the agreed scheme, but some even inveighed against it. This so enraged the Minister that he took drastic action. The Minister of Trade and Commerce, Sir George Foster, vividly described the sequel in a letter to the Prime Minister:

> Next day the wires were hot over orders said to have been given by Minister to demobilize the whole force (naval), scrap the old *Rainbow* and *Niobe,* and demobilize the College.
>
> Then the mouse was in the soup sure. The Navy league spent half its revenue on messages, Hfx. and Esq. were up in arms and the rest of the Ministers were asking "who did it?".

A compromise proposal was hurriedly devised and the caucus gave it unanimous approval after less than half an hour's discussion. On 25 March 1920, the Minister announced that, although a permanent naval policy would be deferred, the reorganized R.C.N. would consist of two destroyers and a cruiser donated by Britain to replace the *Rainbow* and *Niobe,* and two submarines, the *CH 14* and *CH 15,* which Britain had given to Canada the preceding January. The Royal Naval College of Canada would be maintained.

Experimental hydrofoil boat, *Hydrodrome-4,* built by Alexander Graham Bell and F. W. "Casey" Baldwin, tested at Baddeck, Nova Scotia, 9 September 1919. It reached a speed of 70.86 miles an hour.

(D.N.D. photo.)

During the summer of 1920, the Admiralty made available the destroyers *Patrician* and *Patriot* and the oil-burning cruiser *Aurora*. The new Director of the Naval Service, Captain Walter Hose, also obtained from the Royal Navy a generous loan of seasoned seamen. Manned mostly by Britons in Canadian uniform, this "small but modern squadron" – the First Canadian Training Squadron – arrived at Halifax on 21 December 1920.

By the spring of 1921, *CH 14* and *CH 15* were in full commission with the Training Squadron. Besides the five ocean-going ships, the navy consisted of the shore establishments *Guelph* and *Naden,* the Halifax submarine depot, the two dockyards and Naval Service Headquarters on one floor of the Hunter Building in Ottawa. There were now 33 officers and 510 men afloat in H.M.C. Ships out of a total personnel of 797 servicemen and 278 civilians. Several officers were on loan to the Royal Navy; 42 cadets were in the Royal Naval College of Canada at Esquimalt; and a new Youths' Training Establishment had been set up in the wrecked college building in Halifax Dockyard to train Canadian ratings. In 1921-1922 the naval organization functioned on a budget of $2,500,000.

But the spectre of financial retrenchment haunted the Navy. All during 1920-22 the Naval Committee* was paring at naval accounts. One young officer serving in H.M.C.S. *Patrician* recalled a typical West Indies cruise:

> Money was so tight we had to shut down [the generator motors] as soon as we entered harbour and rely for the ship's lighting on oil lamps. The heat, the insects and the smell of the oil lamps drove us almost crazy.

Worse was to follow. After the change of government in 1921, the R.C.N. vote was cut by 40 per cent – from $2½ to $1½ million. Now the navy had to decide what it could do with a million and a half. The College could be closed and R.C.N. officers trained in Britain, and the Dockyard could be cut back, but these changes would save only about $200,000. The Naval Committee reported to the Minister:

> If a further reduction in expenditure is considered necessary, the Naval Committee is of opinion that all ships should be paid off and the navy reorganized on an entirely new basis, that is to say, by the formation of a naval reserve force. The ships with a small permanent force would be used for training purposes exclusively. It is estimated that such a naval reserve could be maintained for $1,500,000.

Aurora and the submarines were paid off, and the Royal Naval College of Canada was closed. Since its inception in 1911, the College had been the sole constant element in the R.C.N.'s establishment – a single thread of continuity in a very tattered garment. It had entered

149 boys as cadets and developed a three-year syllabus for turning them into officers. Now the thread was cut. Once more the dismissal notices went out – this time the personnel strength was reduced by 50 per cent to 400. The reduction was accomplished largely by sending back most of the R.N. ratings on loan. Thus passed into limbo the short-lived fleet which had been the R.C.N.'s third false start. Yet although the reorganization of 1922 appeared to result from counsels of despair, it actually contained the seeds of permanent and productive development.

In 1922 *Patrician* and *Patriot* – vessels so tiny that the first reaction of the hands assigned to sail them had been to apply to Ottawa for Hard Lying Money – now became the principal ships of the fleet. *Patrician* was moved to Esquimalt in September 1922, joining the trawlers *Armentières* and *Thiepval*. The trawlers *Ypres* and *Festubert* were stationed at Halifax. The Royal Canadian Naval Volunteer Reserve was established with an approved complement of 1000. Soon, in police stations, warehouses, laundries and armouries all over the land, companies and half-companies of the R.C.N.V.R. were being organized. At first there were 15 units, later 19, each with a permanent R.C.N. instructor. A minimum of 30 evenings' training during the winter was required, and two weeks' training at the Coast in the summer. The Royal Canadian Naval Reserve was authorized to enlist 500 officers and men from those engaged in maritime occupations and provide them with four weeks' naval training each year.

When *Patrician* and *Patriot* wore out in the late 1920s, the R.C.N. built ships of its own to replace them. H.M.C. Ships *Saguenay* and *Skeena* were the first destroyers ever constructed to Canadian specifications. *Patrician* and *Patriot* were sold before the new ships were ready for service, and the Admiralty lent the destroyers *Torbay* and *Toreador* to tide the R.C.N. over the interval. These two vessels, renamed H.M.C. Ships *Champlain* and *Vancouver,* did not have to be returned when *Saguenay* and *Skeena* were commissioned in the spring of 1931. Thus the destroyer portion of the Canadian fleet doubled to four ships. However, natural attrition was occurring among the minesweepers. When *Armentières* was wrecked on a rock off Bamfield, B.C., in 1925, she was refloated and repaired, but in 1930 a similar disaster befell *Thiepval* where no salvage was possible. On the East Coast, *Ypres* in 1932 and *Festubert* three years later were placed in reserve because of boiler defects.

Top— The Canadian submarines *CH 14* and *CH 15* based on Halifax, 1920-1922. *Below—* H.M.C. Ships *Aurora, Patrician* and *Patriot* at Esquimalt, 1921.
(D.N.D. photographs.)

---

*The Naval Committee consisted of the Deputy Minister, the Director and the Assistant Director of the Naval Service.

The trawler-minesweeper
H.M.C.S. *Thiepval* at Petro-
pavlovsk, U.S.S.R., during
her voyage in 1924 across
the Pacific from Vancouver
to Hakodate, Japan.
(D.N.D. photo.)

The Winnipeg Company of
the Royal Canadian Naval
Volunteer Reserve being
reviewed by Governor
General Viscount Willing-
don, 1927.

(D.N.D. photo.)

In 1933 the Government ordered a $3,673,023 reduction in defence expenditure. A new Chief of the General Staff, Major-General A. G. L. McNaughton, recommended that $2 million should be cut from the naval budget of $2,422,000. This would have virtually abolished the R.C.N., but the C.G.S. believed that aircraft could perform many of the navy's tasks in coastal reconnaissance and defence. However, after interviewing Commodore Hose, the Treasury Board decided not to accept McNaughton's advice, and the R.C.N. remained in existence.

By 1936 there were 979 personnel authorized for the R.C.N., about the same number as had been borrowed from the Royal Navy in 1910, but now only four officers and ten men were on loan from the R.N. Besides the permanent force, there were also the Reserves. In March 1927, the strength of the R.C.N.R., which had passed its third birthday, was only 123 officers and men, and ten years later it had grown to only 44 officers and 144 men — 37 per cent of establishment. However, the Volunteer Reserve had been far more successful. The first half-companies, each of about 55 part-time sailors, were formed in Hamilton and Ottawa in March 1923. By 1926 the personnel of the R.C.N.V.R. totalled 848, and ten years later 949.

In 1936 a Joint Staff Committee memorandum presented a five-year programme to bring the R.C.N. to a strength of six destroyers and four minesweepers, enough to guarantee reasonable security on one coast, and recommended that three more destroyers and four more minesweepers be added in the five years following. In the rearmament programme which the Government began in 1937, the scale of priorities did not put the navy last. In 1935-36 the navy's budget had been $2,395,000 — a little below the average level of the previous decade. The next year the vote was doubled and thereafter continued to increase sharply. The ultimate objective, announced in May 1939, was to have 18 destroyers, eight anti-submarine vessels, 16 minesweepers, eight motor torpedo boats and two parent-vessels. This force would cost $13½ million yearly to maintain. By March 1939 the R.C.N. was well advanced on its expansion programme; for the next year, $8,800,000 was allocated — an increase of over 360 per cent in four years.

With the extra money the navy purchased the destroyers *St. Laurent* and *Fraser* from the Admiralty in 1937, and in 1938 the *Restigouche* and *Ottawa*. Four minesweepers, the *Gaspé, Comox, Nootka* and *Fundy,* were built in Canada, and *Armentières* was still in commission, making five vessels of this type. A sail-training schooner, the *Venture,* and the small motor vessel *Skidegate* were also acquired in these years. A Fleet Reserve and a Fishermen's Reserve were established, and the R.C.N.V.R. set up a list of suitable candidates for officers' commissions called the Supplementary Reserve. All these Reserves, rooted as firmly in the prairies as on the coasts, were ready in September 1939 to sail and fight alongside the 191 officers and 1799 men of the permanent service.

A two-seater Bristol Fighter (left foreground), an Avro 504K trainer (centre) and a D.H. 9a (right) of the Canadian Air Force at Rockcliffe, near Ottawa, 1920.

The Air Force Between the Wars

By the Armistice the aeroplane was no longer a novelty. Cheap surplus machines were bought by returning pilots for exhibition flying, passenger-carrying and charter work; and more ambitious projects, such as forestry survey, fire patrols and northern exploration, were in the planning stages. In June 1919 the Government established a seven-man Air Board to control civil and commercial flying and to cooperate with the militia and naval service departments "on all questions relating to the air defence of Canada."

On 18 February 1920 the Government authorized a Canadian Air Force to replace the overseas service that had been disbanded. Under the control of the Air Board, this new C.A.F., with a provisional establishment of 1340 officers and 3905 airmen, would give refresher courses to veterans of the wartime flying services. However, the C.A.F. was to be essentially an air militia; a small number of officers and airmen were to be employed for periods of up to one year, with extensions in special circumstances, but most C.A.F. members were limited to one month of service every two years.

On 23 April 1920 Major-General Sir Willoughby G. Gwatkin, Canada's wartime Chief of the General Staff, was appointed Inspector General of the C.A.F. with

TRANS-CANADA FLIGHT, 1920. The Canadian Air Force's D.H. 9a over the mountains between Calgary and Revelstoke, B.C. From a painting by R. W. Bradford, based on photographs taken during the flight.

(Courtesy National Aviation Museum of Canada.)

the rank of Air Vice-Marshal and became a member of the Air Board. The C.A.F. reported to the Board through him. The C.A.F.'s first Air Officer Commanding was Lt.-Col. A. K. Tylee, who was appointed on 17 May for a nine-month period with the provisional rank of Air Commodore. Other temporary appointments were made to enable an advance party to be sent to Camp Borden, which was to be the C.A.F.'s training centre.

In April the Air Board had been reorganized into three divisions: a Civil Aviation Branch responsible for the control of commercial and civil flying; a Civil Operations Branch charged with all non-military government flying operations; and the Canadian Air Force. Air stations were opened at Dartmouth, N.S.; Roberval, P.Q.; Morley, Alta.; Jericho Beach at Vancouver, and Rockcliffe, outside Ottawa. In addition, a temporary site was established at Haileybury, Ont. The Air Board's pilots and mechanics were employed as civil servants; yet virtually all were also commissioned or enlisted in the C.A.F. and were granted leave for training. Late in 1920 the C.A.F. participated in the first trans-Canada flight between Halifax and Vancouver, but because of bad weather and other difficulties, the aircraft took 10½ days to cover the 3341-mile route.

As part of the reorganization of 1922-1923, when a single Department of National Defence absorbed the Air Board, the air force was provided with a permanent staff; the Operations Branch was consolidated with the C.A.F., and officers and men employed in the Air Board as civil servants were granted temporary commissions or enlisted in the C.A.F., for which a temporary establishment of 69 officers and 238 airmen was authorized. The combined force was placed under a Director, C.A.F., who was responsible to the Chief of Staff. The Air Board's civil flying stations became C.A.F. bases, and the station superintendents became commanding officers.

The next two years were a transitional period in which the air force evolved as a permanent force, but more than a decade was to elapse before it became a wholly military service. Until the early 1930s its major role was civil flying, and its aircraft, bases and training programme were designed to meet this requirement. In March 1923 King George V authorized the C.A.F. to be officially redesignated the Royal Canadian Air Force. The R.C.A.F. adopted the R.A.F.'s slate-blue uniform and its motto, *Per Ardua ad Astra*. A university cadet training scheme began in May 1923, and that summer the R.C.A.F. received its first new aircraft since the war, eight Vickers single-engine amphibians.

The reorganization of the air force was completed on

(D.N.D. photo.)

The formal raising of the Canadian Air Force's new ensign at Camp Borden, 30 November 1921. Overhead are Avro 504K trainers.

1 April 1924, when the new King's Regulations and Orders for the R.C.A.F. became effective. Commissions granted in the C.A.F. lapsed on 31 March and new appointments were promulgated the next day. All airmen were automatically discharged, those who wished to continue in the new permanent force being re-enlisted on 1 April. That date, which marked the end of the transition period and the emergence of the R.C.A.F. in its new status as a permanent component of Canada's defence forces, is regarded as the official birthday of the service.

The new regulations divided the R.C.A.F. into two components, an Active and a Reserve Air Force. The Reserve consisted of officers and airmen liable to be called out for training, but no appointments were made until 1928 and no one was called out until September 1939. The Active Air Force was subdivided into Permanent and Non-Permanent branches, but although numerous commissions were granted in the Non-Perma-

A Short F.3 flying boat of the Operations Branch, Canadian Air Board, at the Victoria Beach, Manitoba, air station, 1921.

nent branch and some airmen were enlisted, no units were formed until more than eight years later. The initial establishment of the Permanent Force provided for 68 officers and 307 men and that of the Non-Permanent Force for 67 officers and 130 other ranks. The R.C.A.F. continued to be administered by a Director who was responsible to the Chief of Staff, and the Officers Commanding Military Districts were charged with the discipline and administration of R.C.A.F. units.

During the 1920s only about half the air force's flying was military, and most of this was logged in elementary and basic training; civil operations accounted for the remainder. The R.C.A.F. provided many services: it photographed vast areas of the country for mapping purposes, flew government officials to isolated regions, undertook mercy flights, and in the Prairie Provinces and British Columbia flew thousands of hours on forestry patrols. Scientists battling forest blights were helped by R.C.A.F. pilots who exposed spore slides coated with grease in the air over the Pacific coast to obtain data on the white pine blister. Similar work was done over the Prairie Provinces on wheat rust research. R.C.A.F. flyers also conducted experimental low-level dusting operations over infested forest and wheat-growing regions and flew patrols over the coastal waters of British Columbia to detect illegal commercial fishing and narcotics smuggling.

In these years the R.C.A.F. blazed new air trails and often operated from remote, temporary bases in regions where aircraft had never ventured before. In 1927-1928, for example, the air force played a prominent part in the Hudson Strait Expedition directed by the Department of Marine and Fisheries to procure information concerning the length of the shipping season through the strait, to test the suitability of aircraft as an aid to marine navigation, and to determine the feasibility of establishing operational air bases in the area. An R.C.A.F. detachment of six officers and 12 airmen carried out the expedition's flying. Bases were established at Port Burwell, Wakeham Bay and Nottingham Island, all on Hudson Strait, and regular patrols were flown between September 1927 and August 1928. Although the severe northern winter tested the fortitude and ingenuity of flyers and ground crew, activities were never interrupted by mechanical failure. There were only three forced landings, all due to weather conditions.

Such northern flying was hazardous and demanded self-reliance from pilots and mechanics, as indeed did much "routine" patrol work, which was often conducted from temporary summertime bases in the wilderness. Landings were often made on uncharted lakes and rivers, where hidden rocks or deadheads lay waiting to rip open pontoon or hull. Lost or broken parts had to be replaced or repaired on the spot with whatever came to hand — a length of piping became an engine-starting

(D.N.D. photo.)

Above—Three of the six Fokker Universals flown by the R.C.A.F. during the Hudson Strait Expedition of 1927-1928 on the ice at Nottingham Island.

Left—The R.C.A.F.'s major flying operation in 1924 was an aerial photographic survey of water routes in northern Manitoba and Saskatchewan. The Vickers Viking flying boat used for the survey is shown at Rabbit River, Manitoba.

(D.N.D. photo.)

(D.N.D. photographs.)

Above—R.C.A.F. civil government operations between the wars involved flying from temporary wilderness bases. This 1931 detachment of Fairchild 71s was at Oskelaneo, Quebec, on a photographic aerial survey.

Below—Two Fairchild F.C. 2s on photographic operations at Churchill, Manitoba, in 1929.

crank, a piece of hardwood from the bush replaced a broken aileron control rod. Navigation was another major problem; the outline of a lake or river below was of little use to the pilot as a navigational aid if his map of the region was blank. The R.C.A.F. flyers who challenged the North were very much on their own, and it was a measure of their worth that the North so seldom triumphed.

In 1927 the Government air services were reorganized into four branches. The R.C.A.F. remained under the Chief of Staff, its role being military air operations; a separate directorate was created to conduct civil air operations; a third branch, under the Controller of Civil Aviation, was established to administer air regulations and perform related duties; and an Aeronautical Engineering Division was formed to serve the other branches of the air services. The R.C.A.F. retained Camp Borden and Vancouver and a stores depot and communications flight, both at Ottawa, but other stations and units were turned over to the new civil branches. The Civil Aviation Branch became essentially civilian in composition, but the Aeronautical Engineering Division and the Directorate of Civil Government Air Operations were staffed largely by service personnel. The separation of civil and military flying was thus more apparent on paper than in fact, for civil flying continued to be per-

A Vickers Vedette, R.C.A.F. workhorse for civil government air operations in the late 1920s and early 1930s, over Orient Bay, Ontario, in 1929 or 1930.

(D.N.D. photo.)

formed by uniformed R.C.A.F. personnel and the flyers themselves were not conscious of any change in status.

After the 1927 reorganization the R.C.A.F.'s military flying was restricted mainly to elementary and basic training at Camp Borden and Vancouver, the latter station being used for seaplane instruction. Although little effort was made to develop the R.C.A.F. as an air defence force, it was able to participate in some joint exercises with the navy and army and to send personnel to artillery cooperation courses.

Air services appropriations had risen steadily since the formation of the R.C.A.F.— from $1,880,850 in 1925-26 to $7,475,700 in 1930-31. The 1927 reorganization, however, resulted in two separate air services' budgets, one for military operations and the other for civil government work. The R.C.A.F. normally received about half as much money as the civil branches. At this time the air force placed orders in Britain for nine fighter aircraft and six army cooperation machines, but no more military aircraft were purchased until 1934. The onset of the Depression did not bring an immediate reduction in the air services' budget, although the R.C.A.F.'s share was reduced. When the appropriations for 1931 dropped by over $2 million, civil operations absorbed most of the reduction, but in 1932 appropriations were slashed to $1,750,000, the sum being lumped in one vote to cover all air operations. This forced the R.C.A.F. to stop its pilot training and reduce its strength by one-fifth. Seventy-eight officers and 100 airmen were released, as well as 110 civilian employees. Most civil government flying operations ceased and some stations were closed.

The need for economy led to a major reorganization. The R.C.A.F. and C.G.A.O. directorates were consolidated on 1 November 1932, and the artificial distinction of the last five years between the military and civil air forces came to an end. Instead of two Directors, one responsible to the Chief of the General Staff and the other to the Deputy Minister, there was now one Senior Air Officer for the reunited service, responsible to the Chief of the General Staff. The separate technical stores and equipment sections of the R.C.A.F. and C.G.A.O. were also consolidated again under the Chief Aeronautical Engineer, who reported to the Senior Air Officer. The stations, substations and detachments previously administered by the C.G.A.O. Directorate were returned to the R.C.A.F. The Civil Aviation Branch was not affected by this reorganization but retained its separate entity under the Deputy Minister.

Although the Depression drastically reduced the

R.C.A.F., it did allow more emphasis to be placed on military training. The R.C.A.F. occupied its new station at Trenton in 1931; an air force signals service was organized; small fighter and army cooperation flights were formed; and in 1932 a flying-boat unit was established at Vancouver. These three small operational units, with only 28 aircraft among them, carried out service training based on that of the R.A.F.

During the Depression, too, the Non-Permanent Active Air Force — later known as the Auxiliary — was transformed. Previously, N.P.A.A.F. personnel had either been seconded to the R.C.A.F. on full-time duty or appointed provisional pilot officers for short-term training, as in the case of the university cadets; there had been no Non-Permanent units and no Non-Permanent training plan. In 1932 an establishment of 128 officers and 624 airmen was approved and three Non-Permanent army cooperation squadrons were formed at Toronto, Vancouver and Winnipeg. These squadrons began ground instruction during the spring of 1933 and commenced flying training the next year. Between 1934 and 1938, nine more Non-Permanent squadrons had made substantial progress in organization and training. Late in 1936 the Civil Aviation Branch was transferred to the new Department of Transport, which also assumed responsibility for most of the civil government air duties previously performed by the R.C.A.F. Apart from its responsibilities for aerial photography and some civil transportation flying, the R.C.A.F. was now free to develop as a purely military force.

The air appropriation for 1933-1934 was slightly lower than the year before, but the appropriation for 1934-1935 rose by $565,000 to $2,262,000. Of this, the R.C.A.F. received $1,930,000, plus $120,000 for civil government operations. As air appropriations continued to increase, a larger share went to the R.C.A.F. The air service's vote for 1935-1936 was $4,302,900 of which the R.C.A.F. received $3,130,000. The trend continued, and of the $6,809,215 voted in 1936-37, the R.C.A.F. received $4,685,028. Five new squadrons were authorized in 1935 and orders were placed for 28 additional aircraft. An additional 24 machines were ordered the following year. For the fiscal year 1937-1938 the air force vote leaped to nearly $11,400,000, and an almost identical amount was provided the next year. The appropriation for 1939-1940, voted in the brief period between the Munich crisis and the German attack on Poland, reached the unprecedented figure of nearly $30 million, almost half the defence estimates.

With more money, the R.C.A.F. began to obtain additional aircraft, and new squadrons whose role was specifically operational were formed. Work was begun

(D.N.D. photo.)

Majesty King George VI inspects an R.C.A.F. Guard of Honour at an Ottawa railroad station during the 1939 Royal Visit.

on new flying bases on both coasts and on an air-firing and bombing range at Trenton. During 1938 Western Air Command was formed and two more commands — Eastern Air Command at Halifax and Air Training Command at Toronto — were authorized. When these commands began to function, the authority over air force units formerly vested in District Officers Commanding was transferred to the senior officers of the air commands.

In April 1939, the Minister of National Defence outlined his programme for the expansion of the R.C.A.F. The objective was an air force of 7259 officers and men: 5025 in the Permanent Force and 2234 in the Auxiliary. It was to have 527 aircraft, 312 of which would be operational machines. Orders already placed would provide 250 aircraft by the spring of 1940 and an additional 107 were to be ordered in 1939. Most of the orders were being placed with Canadian aircraft firms, even though this meant a delay in delivery, "because the development in Canada of a future source of supply for service aircraft is in itself a major contribution to national defence." The R.C.A.F. was to have 23 squadrons, 11 Permanent and 12 Auxiliary. Eight were to be allotted to Western Air Command, nine to Eastern Air Command and the remaining six to a Central Air Command, which was to be established

as an operational reserve.

On the eve of war the air force expansion programme was incomplete, although the R.C.A.F. was greatly changed from the service of five years before. It had a strength of 4061 officers and airmen, of whom three-quarters (298 officers and 2750 airmen) were in the Permanent component and the remainder (112 officers and 901 airmen) in the Auxiliary. There were eight Permanent squadrons: two general purpose, two general reconnaissance, one fighter, one bomber, one torpedo-bomber and one army cooperation. Most of these squadrons were grouped at bases on the two coasts. Three more Permanent squadrons had been authorized but not formed. The Auxiliary Force consisted of three wing headquarters and 12 squadrons: four fighter, four bomber, two army cooperation and two coast artillery cooperation, although five of these were still in the preliminary stages of organization.

However, almost all operational units were under strength in personnel and equipment, and their effectiveness was further limited by their sad lack of modern aircraft. The R.C.A.F. had 270 aircraft of 23 different types, but more than half of these were fit only for training or transport roles. Only 124 aeroplanes were operational types, and many of them were obsolete or obsolescent; only 37 machines were modern first-line service aircraft. Yet, despite these handicaps, the Royal Canadian Air Force was a vigorous, dynamic service, already proud of its past and cheerfully confident of its capabilities as it faced the approaching crisis.

THE ARMY IN THE SECOND WORLD WAR 1939-1945

In 1914 war had broken out with dramatic suddenness towards the end of a peaceful summer. A quarter of a century later the tension in Europe mounted so steadily that by the end of August 1939 war seemed not only probable but inevitable.

Since March, when Hitler had absorbed Czechoslovakia into the German Reich in defiance of solemn agreements made the previous autumn, the powers had moved nearer to what appeared a foredoomed catastrophe. The deteriorating German-Polish situation dominated the European stage, and Britain and France believed that peace could be maintained only if they came to an agreement with Russia. However, preliminary conversations in Moscow foundered during August, and later that month, to the astonishment and consternation of the world, Russia and Germany signed a non-aggression pact. Hitler's fears of a two-front war were now removed, and he was free to settle with the Poles. On 1 September German armies swept into Poland. Three days later Britain and France honoured the pledges they had given Poland in an attempt to preserve the liberties of Europe and declared war on the aggressor.

This time Canada did not automatically enter the war by Britain's act as in 1914. On 7 September the Canadian Parliament assembled in emergency session; and on the 9th it approved the Government's policy of supporting Britain and France. On the 10th the King proclaimed the existence of a state of war between Canada and the German Reich. The years between the wars now seemed nothing more than an uneasy truce. For the second time in a generation Canada was at war with Germany. And throughout the nation there was a clear if reluctant determination to face the ordeal and whatever sacrifices it might bring.

The week before war broke out, Canadian coastal defences had been manned and on 1 September the Government ordered the mobilization of two divisions and ancillary troops from the militia. This time the prepared mobilization plan was followed. The confusion that had marked mobilization in 1914 was thus avoided, as was the creation of new units. Militia regiments mobilized and were brought up to strength by enlistment, and because the unanimity with which the country had entered the war was too precious to be destroyed, and because for the present there was no shortage of manpower, conscription was avoided. Every man attested into the "Canadian Active Service Force" was a volunteer.

Despite the cold realism with which this war was received, men came forward briskly in a determined mood. In September alone, 58,337 men and women joined the army, considerably more than during the comparable month in 1914. Many others were rejected on medical grounds or because of age, and some units were unable to recruit to full strength because of accommodation and clothing shortages.

In December the 1st Division under Major-General A. G. L. McNaughton moved overseas in two main flights. Once again Canadian troops had arrived in Britain in a time of danger. By February 1940, after the third contingent had arrived, there were some 23,000 of them in Britain.

After the opening campaign of the war had ended quickly with the brutal conquest of Poland, Germany built up strength throughout an uneventful winter known at the time as the "phoney war." On 9 April a sudden German attack on Norway broke the uneasy quiet. Aid had to be sent to the small Norwegian forces and, since most of Britain's trained troops were in France, the War Office turned to the Canadians. McNaughton accepted the task, and on 18 April a

(Courtesy Major-General A. B. Matthews, C.B.E., D.S.O., E.D.)

The 9th (Toronto) Field Battery, R.C.A., trains on the parade ground by the University Avenue Armouries, September 1939.

small Canadian force left Aldershot for Dunfermline, the Scottish port of embarkation. However, on the 19th the British plan was changed, and the Canadians never put to sea. Fighting continued in Norway until 8 June when the last French and British soldiers were evacuated.

The Canadians still looked forward to taking their place on the Western Front in France. There the situation remained quiet. French experience in 1914, when a fanatical belief in the offensive had brought enormous casualties, had led to the scrupulous adoption of the defensive. Secure in the Maginot Line, French soldiers stared out from slits in their concrete emplacements, while German soldiers, equally secure in the Siegfried Line, stared back. The British, holding defences constructed during the bitter winter of 1939-40, faced the unfortified Belgian frontier.

The Canadians Go to France

On 10 May the Germans struck — not directly at France, but at the Netherlands, Belgium and Luxembourg. The Netherlands was overrun in a few days of ruthless fighting, and when an Anglo-French army left its prepared positions to assist the Belgians, it was cut off from the main French forces by a German thrust through Luxembourg and the "impassable" country of the Ardennes. German armoured divisions penetrated a gap between the Maginot Line and the British defences along the Belgian border and reached the Channel on 21 May. In the days that followed they worked northwards along the coast, threatening to cut

the communications of the British Expeditionary Force. Farther south, under sudden assaults by aircraft and fast-moving armour, French resistance began to crumble.

In this desperate situation the War Office called upon the 1st Canadian Division (now one of the few trained and equipped formations in England) to restore the communications of the B.E.F. with the Channel ports. General McNaughton was sent by destroyer late on 23 May to study at first hand the situation at Calais and Dunkirk. Meanwhile, his division began to move to Dover for embarkation. At Calais, McNaughton found the British defending a close perimeter; the garrison could not be expected to do more than hold the Germans off. He then left in the same destroyer, reaching Dunkirk before dawn on the 24th, despite attacks by enemy aircraft. The port was weakly held, but two French divisions were moving into position to defend its approaches. That morning the Germans cut the road between Dunkirk and Calais.

Later that day McNaughton returned to London to report what he had seen and heard to a meeting of the defence ministers and Chiefs of Staff over which Mr. Churchill, the new Prime Minister, presided. Obviously, Canadian reinforcements could make little difference to the situation at Dunkirk, which was intended to be the main evacuation port for the B.E.F. The troops, waiting impatiently aboard ship at Dover for the call to action, glumly disembarked and moved back to Aldershot. Two days later their hopes revived when some of them were again sent to Dover; but once more they remained in port. Belgium capitulated on the 28th, but although the Canadians were again warned for movement, none of them ever went to Dunkirk.

The British Isles were now in the gravest danger of invasion. Tanks, artillery and equipment had been left behind in France and little remained at home. The troops ferried back from Dunkirk brought only their small arms. The readiness of the Canadian division therefore assumed a vast importance as it moved with ancillary troops to the Midlands to form a self-contained "Canadian Force" ready to strike at any enemy who might penetrate the flimsy eastern defences. And through "Dunkirk Week" there it remained.

Although the Germans entered Dunkirk on 4 June, they did not attack Britain. To them France was still the primary antagonist, and on 5 June they struck at General Weygand's line on the Somme and Aisne. By the 9th the invaders had reached the Seine. Next day Italy entered the war on the side of Germany. On the 12th Weygand advised his government to seek an armistice. The French army, previously considered the finest in Europe, had been cut to pieces by the German *Blitzkrieg*.

A desperate plan to hold an Anglo-French "redoubt" in the Breton peninsula resulted in the 1st Division's again being ordered to France. One brigade, ancillary units and some artillery disembarked at Brest on 13 and 14 June. However, the military situation in France was beyond repair. On 14 June German troops marched unopposed into Paris, and although the Canadians moved inland, it had already been decided that the

(Courtesy The National Gallery of Canada.)

NORTH ATLANTIC CONVOY
by Will Ogilvie (1901-   )
The convoy carrying the 3rd Canadian Infantry Division to Britain in the summer of 1941.

small forces available could not hold out in Brittany. Late that day the advancing Canadians were abruptly ordered back. So, after only 48 hours in France, the Canadians found themselves again in Aldershot, bitterly disappointed and translating C.A.S.F. as "Canadians Almost Saw France." They had been ordered to destroy their vehicles and guns before re-embarkation, but since the Canadian artillery commander had flatly refused to leave without his guns, these had been stowed aboard and brought back to England where they were more than welcome.

Their Majesties King George VI and Queen Elizabeth visit The Toronto Scottish Regiment (M.G.) at Aldershot in June 1940 when the unit was under orders for France. Lt.-Col. C. C. Thompson, Commanding Officer, is behind the Queen, and Maj.-Gen. A. G. L. McNaughton on the right.

(D.N.D. photo.)

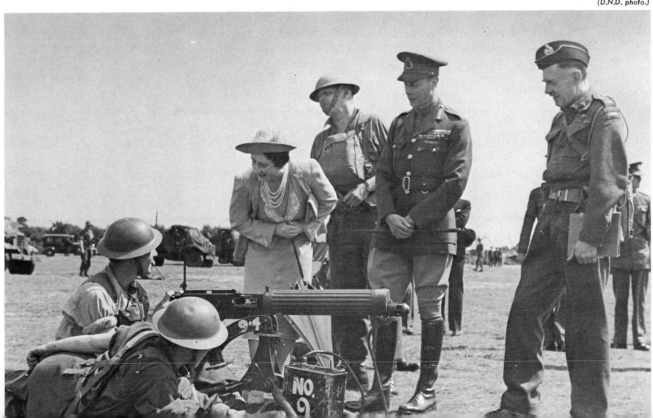

(Courtesy The National Gallery of Canada.)

CANADIAN TANKS MANOEUVRING
by Will Ogilvie (1901-   )

Ram tanks of the 5th Canadian (Armoured) Division's Headquarters Squadron (6th Duke of Connaught's Royal Canadian Hussars) in Ashdown Forest, Sussex, September 1942.

In Defence of Britain

For Britain, midsummer of 1940 was one of the most desperate crises in all her history, comparable (as Churchill said) only to the days when the Spanish Armada was approaching the Channel or when Napoleon's Grand Army waited at Boulogne to invade England. From the North Cape of Norway to the Pyrenees stretched a vast arc of coast-line that had turned hostile almost overnight. From it, submarines, surface ships and aircraft threatened Britain's life-lines — not only from the east as in the First World War, but also from north, south and even west. Every ship bringing cargoes to meet British needs for food and raw materials had to run the gauntlet of enemy attack.

The danger of starvation was serious enough. More immediate was the threat of invasion. Behind the hostile coast the enemy had concentrated 2277 aircraft — fighter planes, medium and dive-bombers and long-range bombers — most of them only a few minutes by air from southern England. The German Air Force outnumbered the R.A.F. by three to one, and under the shelter of this vast umbrella the Germans waited for the signal to invade.

To repel them the British had some 28 divisions, 12 of which were raw training formations. The army had lost almost all its field and heavier guns, anti-aircraft guns, anti-tank weapons, machine-guns, motor vehicles and tanks. Three British divisions were in a better state of training and equipment than the others, but one of them was under strength, another not fully

Left: The Royal Montreal Regiment (M.G.) trains at Larkhill, England, July 1941.

Below: The last men to leave Spitsbergen in 1941 look back on a scene of destruction at Barentsburg.

(D.N.D. photo.)

(D.N.D. photo)

trained or equipped, and the third had left a considerable part of its transport in France.

In these circumstances, the 1st Canadian Division achieved an importance undreamed of two months previously. Although one brigade was still immobile through having had to abandon its vehicles in Brittany, the division was "the strongest element in a very weak fabric" and one of the few that could be counted on for mobile counter-attack. Towards the end of June a reconstituted "Canadian Force" moved to the vicinity of Oxford. By the first week of July the British force available for immediate action had grown to a mobile corps of two divisions north of the Thames and a second corps forming south of the river. The latter corps — the 7th — officially came into being on 21 July under McNaughton. It consisted of the 1st Canadian and 1st Armoured Divisions, some units of the recently arrived 2nd New Zealand Division and certain ancillary troops.

Throughout that ominous summer and fall the 7th Corps laboured to perfect its state of training, but the German invasion did not come. The enemy never achieved the mastery of the skies which was the essential prerequisite to a seaborne thrust. Massive air attacks on England, rightly regarded as the prelude to invasion, switched from shipping and ports to airfields

and aircraft factories. But then, when their object had been almost achieved, the Germans turned to terror tactics and rained bombs on London. The respite thus afforded the British fighter aerodromes turned the scale; and in September the battles fought in the English skies were resolved in Britain's favour. On 20 September the concentrations of German shipping from Oslo to Brest began visibly to disperse. The Führer had decided three days earlier to postpone the invasion indefinitely.

Gradually the Canadians realized that the church-bells announcing the coming of the Nazi invader would not be heard. By now the concentration of the 2nd Canadian Division in Britain was virtually complete,* and on Christmas Day, 1940, the 7th Corps was disbanded. The 2nd Canadian Division came under General McNaughton's command, and the Canadian Corps — a name that stirred the nation's memory and its pride — was formed. In May the heavy air raids, an almost daily feature of the winter and spring, ended for the time being; a month later Germany struck at Russia; and the Canadians, who had been in the front line of Britain's battle, found themselves on the side-lines once again.

In Canada, meanwhile, the Government had begun to call up men for compulsory training under the provisions of the National Resources Mobilization Act which had been passed in June 1940. However, the "N.R.M.A. men" could not be required to serve outside Canada. The expansion of the R.C.N. and the R.C.A.F. led to the appointment of a Minister of National Defence for Naval Services and a Minister of National Defence for Air who administered what were actually, although not technically, separate departments. Newfoundland, not then a part of Canada, agreed that a Canadian battalion should defend Gander airport and the seaplane base at Botwood. Canadian troops remained in the colony until the end of the war. In September 1941 recruiting began for a Canadian Women's Army Corps; all told, during the war, 21,624 women served in the Canadian Army both in Canada and overseas.

Two months after the German invasion of Russia, some 500 Canadian soldiers did find active employment outside Britain. On 19 August 1941, a military expedition, consisting chiefly of Canadians with some British and Norwegian engineers and specialists, and commanded by Brigadier A. E. Potts, a Canadian, sailed for the Arctic archipelago of Spitsbergen to

---

*Two of the 2nd Division's infantry battalions and the 3rd Division's machine-gun battalion had been stationed in Iceland since the summer. The 2nd Division's battalions reached England in November, but the machine-gun battalion spent the winter in Iceland.

destroy or remove the mining gear and the radio and meteorological stations there and to evacuate the local population. These tasks were all performed without opposition, and by 8 September the expedition was back in Britain again.

Hong Kong

That same month, the British Government, which had decided that the Crown Colony of Hong Kong, off the China coast, should be reinforced, proposed that Canada provide "one or two battalions" for the purpose. At the end of September the Canadian Government agreed. The Winnipeg Grenadiers and The Royal Rifles of Canada were selected for the force, as well as a brigade headquarters, a signal section and a few specialists. The Canadians, commanded by Brigadier J. K. Lawson, sailed from Vancouver under Canadian naval escort and reached Hong Kong on 16 November. Three weeks later Japan brought war to the Pacific with almost simultaneous surprise attacks on Pearl Harbor, Northern Malaya, the Philippines, Guam, Wake Island and Hong Kong.

The colony of Hong Kong consisted of Hong Kong Island and the adjacent mainland areas of Kowloon and the "New Territories." All are very mountainous. The defending force consisted of about 14,000 men — British, Indian, Canadian and local — with 29 fixed guns for support. Of the 42 mobile guns and the 18 anti-aircraft guns, only six anti-aircraft guns were not obsolete. Just five military aircraft were based on the colony, and the next nearest R.A.F. station was in Malaya, nearly 1400 miles away. Only a few small naval vessels were stationed at Hong Kong; all larger ships had been withdrawn to European waters or moved south to Singapore.

The Japanese attacked at first light on 8 December, striking on the mainland against the New Territories. At 8 a.m., when the colony's aerodrome was heavily attacked by enemy aircraft, all the British machines were destroyed or damaged. By evening the mainland force had fallen back to the main defence line covering the isthmus between Tide Cove and Gin Drinkers Bay, and the next night the Japanese penetrated the newly-manned line. In the darkness "D" Company of The Winnipeg Grenadiers was hastily dispatched to assist the peninsula force. This company saw some action on the 11th, becoming the first Canadian Army unit to fight in the Second World War.

By the morning of 12 December the defenders had concentrated on Hong Kong Island. Here they were reorganized into two brigades: East, The Royal Rifles and an Indian battalion, under a British officer; West,

HONG KONG
18-25 December 1941

1000 0 1000 2000 3000
Yards

Victoria Harbour

38TH JAPANESE DIVISION
18 DECEMBER

230TH INF REGT
228TH INF REGT
229TH INF REGT

Kowloon Bay

Kowloon

Dockyard

Aldrich Bay *Lye Mun Passage*

5/7 RAJPUT

Sau Ki Wan

Victoria

2/14 PUNJAB

2 R.SCOTS
IN RESERVE

EAST BRIGADE

Mt.
Butler

Mt
Parker

Jardines
Lookout

N

WINNIPEG GRENADIERS

"D" COY
WINNIPEG
GRENADIERS
19-22 DEC

WEST BRIGADE

Aberdeen

Deep
Water
Bay

ROYAL RIFLES OF CANADA

Stanley

JAPANESE ATTACKS
8 DEC

HONG KONG -
MAINLAND
8-13 December 1941

NEW

TERRITORIES

Tai Po

*Tide
Cove*

*Gin Drinkers
Bay*

Kai Tak
Aerodrome

Kowloon

Victoria

HONG KONG

0   5 Miles

Lines of advance are approximate

LAMMA
ISLAND

STANLEY
PENINSULA

Cape d'Aguilar

Japanese advances (black arrows).
British positions, 19 December (broken red lines).
British positions, 25 December (white lines).

a British battalion, an Indian battalion and The Winnipeg Grenadiers, under Brigadier Lawson. There was no hope of relief. Any faint chance of this had been destroyed by the sinking of two British capital ships, the *Prince of Wales* and the *Repulse,* off Malaya on 10 December and by the crippling of the United States fleet at Pearl Harbor. Without aircraft, adequate artillery or naval ships capable of breaking up Japanese concentrations, the defenders awaited the assault in complete isolation.

With darkness on 18 December invasion came. The enemy poured across the strait at its narrowest part, Lye Mun Passage, in assault boats, landing craft and small boats towed by ferry steamers. The Royal Rifles came into action that night, sustaining and inflicting heavy casualties, but the next morning the East Brigade was ordered to withdraw southwards towards Stanley

Peninsula where, it was hoped, a concentration could be made. A new line was established that afternoon, but an enemy thrust to the sea west of Stanley severed all communications with the West Brigade. Attempts to restore them on the 20th failed, and on 21 December contact was re-established only for a day. Stubborn defence and counter-attack marked the next two days, but on the 23rd the entire British eastern force had to be pulled back to Stanley Peninsula. Without artillery support, a counter-attack on Christmas Day, delivered by the tired Royal Rifles to recover lost ground, broke down with heavy casualties.

Meanwhile, The Winnipeg Grenadiers had seen hard fighting with the West Brigade. A portion of the battalion engaged the Japanese during the first night's fighting on the island but, heavily outnumbered, had been cut to pieces. The next day, the 19th, Brigadier Lawson

117

was killed when he went out of his headquarters to "fight it out" with the enemy who were firing into the position at pointblank range. Another company of the Grenadiers held on firmly, and by doing so denied the Japanese the use of the only main north-south road across the island. The Grenadiers' resistance in this area delayed the Japanese advance for three days. The final phase of the fighting on the western part of the island consisted of a brave attempt to maintain a continuous line from Victoria Harbour to the south shore. Christmas morning found the defenders clinging grimly to their positions despite continuous bombardment, air attack and infantry pressure. However, ammunition had run low and most of the island's water supply was in Japanese hands. Since further fighting would bring only useless slaughter, the Governor hoisted the white flag on Christmas afternoon and a messenger was sent to convey the news to the East Brigade.

The fighting, which lasted seventeen and a half days, had imposed delay and some loss on the Japanese. It brought a tragic toll to Canada in dead and wounded:

23 officers and 267 other ranks killed and 28 officers and 465 other ranks wounded. In all, 557 of the 1975 Canadians who sailed from Vancouver in October never returned. The force had been thrust into grim fighting against numerically superior, well-trained troops who were amply supported and finely equipped. The Canadians, on the other hand, had come in the expectation of being garrison troops and had never been allowed time for battle training in their new station. That they had done all that men could do the casualty figures conclusively demonstrate.

The Formation of First Canadian Army

At the end of 1940 the Canadian Corps had been primarily an infantry force, but the emphasis in 1941 was increasingly on armour. In the course of the year, the 1st Canadian Army Tank Brigade, the 3rd Division and the 5th Armoured Division reached Britain. In January 1942 Prime Minister King announced that a Canadian Army of two corps would be created under General McNaughton. The 4th Division in Canada

(Courtesy The National Gallery of Canada.)

DIEPPE RAID
by Charles Comfort (1900-   )
Waterproofed Churchill tanks of the 14th Armoured Regiment (The Calgary Regiment) advance up the beach
to give covering fire to The Royal Hamilton Light Infantry. The large building on the right is the Casino.

118

Off Dieppe, 19 August 1942. At about 11 o'clock, while R.A.F. and naval guns engaged a bomber formation, a Junkers 88 came in low and dropped these bombs, seen bursting among the landing craft.

would be converted into an armoured division and another army tank brigade would be raised. Corps and army troops in large numbers would be provided.

The headquarters of the 2nd Corps was not formed until early in 1943, and by that time the two new armoured formations had arrived from Canada. The new Army was greater in strength than the old Canadian Corps of the First World War. Indeed, this was the *First* Canadian Army. Its future employment was uncertain, but a fighting machine was being perfected to play a distinguished part in winning final victory.

The role of the Canadian force in Britain changed gradually as it grew. By the end of 1941 both Russia and the United States were in the war; Allied strength was increasing; and fears of a German invasion of Britain began to recede. The Canadians came to be regarded less as a safeguard against German invasion than as the spearhead of an eventual Allied offensive against the Continent.

The Raid on Dieppe

In the summer of 1942 the Germans continued to gain ground in Russia. In North Africa the British Eighth Army had been beaten back into Egypt and stood at bay in front of Alexandria; not until October had it recovered sufficiently to spring on Rommel at El Alamein. In Western Europe, powerful German and Allied forces faced each other across the Channel, but the time had not arrived for them to come to grips. In the meantime the British and Americans decided to strike through French North Africa at the enemy in the Mediterranean. This made it desirable to foster German fears of a descent in the West. It was also important to gain experience to assist in planning the great amphibious assault on Western Europe that would come when the time was ripe. Such was the origin of the raid on Dieppe. The venture was a risky one which could be entrusted only to troops of high

quality. Fully realizing its importance, General McNaughton accepted the task, and there is little doubt that his men in Britain, who had waited so long for action, would have violently resented any other decision. The main body of troops taking part, two brigades, came from the 2nd Canadian Division. The 1st Army Tank Brigade provided a tank regiment equipped with Churchill tanks.

When General Montgomery offered the operation to General McNaughton on 30 April 1942, planning for it was already far advanced. Five days earlier, a meeting at the headquarters of the British Chief of Combined Operations, Vice-Admiral Lord Louis Mountbatten, had accepted a basic plan which was essentially that finally carried out. Canadian staff officers agreed that this plan offered a good chance of success. A detailed model of the area to be attacked was constructed and kept up to date by air reconnaissance, and the troops rehearsed the raid on beaches in the Isle of Wight and at Bridport. Major-General J. H. Roberts, the G.O.C. 2nd Canadian Division, was appointed Military Force Commander, with Captain J. Hughes-Hallett, R.N., as Naval Force Commander and Air Vice-Marshal T. L. Leigh-Mallory as Air Force Commander.

The port of Dieppe lies on low ground between high cliffs. The plan of attack called for four preliminary flank landings at dawn, to be followed by a frontal assault on the town itself half an hour later. British Commandos were entrusted with the outer flank attacks on the coastal batteries on the cliffs at either side of the town. Between the eastern Commando landing and Dieppe, The Royal Regiment of Canada would land at Puys and clear a dominant headland overlooking the Dieppe beaches; to the west The South Saskatchewan Regiment would land at Pourville to clear an even higher headland and would be followed by The Queen's Own Cameron Highlanders of Canada, whose objective was an aerodrome farther inland. The main attack on the port itself would be made across the Dieppe beaches by two battalions, The Essex Scottish Regiment and The Royal Hamilton Light Infantry, assisted by the 14th Canadian Army Tank Regiment (The Calgary Regiment); the tanks would push through the town to operate with the Camerons against the aerodrome. General Roberts had as a "floating reserve" Les Fusiliers Mont-Royal and the Royal Marine "A" Commando. Les Fusiliers Mont-Royal were to act as a rearguard to cover the final withdrawal and the Marines were to remove or destroy the barges in Dieppe harbour.

At dusk on 18 August, the raiders' ships crept out into the Channel and for most of the night nosed peacefully towards the distant coast. But about an hour before daybreak, the landing craft on the extreme eastern fringe of the flotilla encountered an enemy convoy of five small vessels with a naval escort. Gunfire flashed out, and there was a sharp little fight. The craft carrying the left Commando were scattered and only seven of 23 craft landed their troops. Furthermore, the noise of the sea fight caused the German coastal defences nearby to be manned within ten minutes of the fight's beginning; from that moment there was little chance of success. One little party of Commando men managed to get within 200 yards of the guns. They could not take them, but accurate sniping neutralized the battery, and for two and a half vital hours its guns fired no shot against our ships. Nevertheless, chances in this sector had been seriously impaired

and most of the Commando had become casualties.

The Royal Regiment of Canada at Puys shared in this ill-fortune. Owing to various mischances, the naval craft arrived late, and when the Royals leapt ashore they met violent machine-gun fire in the growing light. Few men crossed the heavily wired sea-wall at the head of the narrow beach, and of those who did only one came back. The rest remained pinned on the beach by mortar and machine-gun fire until the remnant finally surrendered. The Royals had 209 fatal casualties, the heaviest toll suffered by a Canadian battalion in a single day throughout the war. Failure here left the eastern headland in the Germans' hands. From it they were able to enfilade the beaches in front of the town and nullify the main two-battalion frontal attack.

However, surprise had not been completely lost. The South Saskatchewan Regiment's first wave landed in the western sector without a single opposing shot, and only when the news of this landing was broadcast by the Germans was the general alarm sounded. The Commando attack on the battery on the far right flank was entirely successful; the six German guns were destroyed before the raiders withdrew.

The South Saskatchewan Regiment's assault carried it across the beaches and over the sea-wall, and a good many Germans were killed. Thereafter resistance stiffened and, despite every effort, the high ground east of the little River Scie could not be won. Some Camerons remained to fight with the South Saskatchewans, while the remainder of the battalion pushed along the west bank of the river towards the aerodrome, advancing

This German photograph, probably taken on the afternoon of the Dieppe raid, shows Landing Craft Tank 5, still burning, and stranded tanks of the 14th Army Tank Regiment (The Calgary Regiment (Tank))

HE RAID ON DIEPPE
19 August 1942

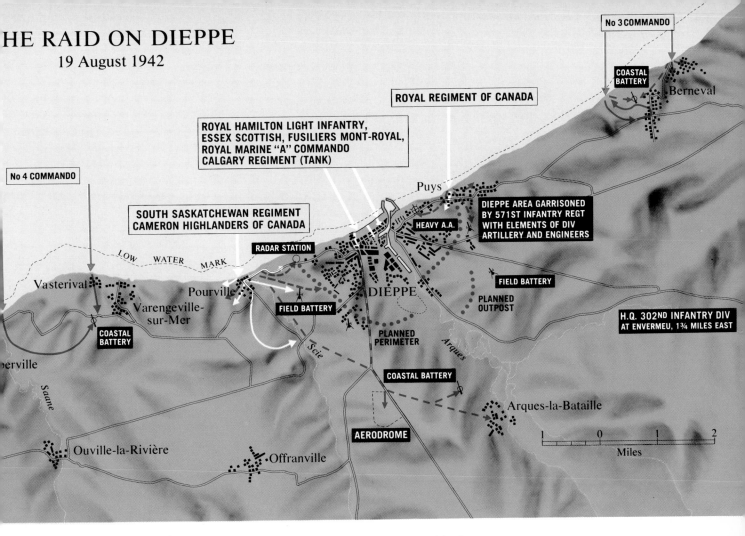

No 3 COMMANDO

COASTAL BATTERY

Berneval

ROYAL REGIMENT OF CANADA

ROYAL HAMILTON LIGHT INFANTRY, ESSEX SCOTTISH, FUSILIERS MONT-ROYAL, ROYAL MARINE "A" COMMANDO CALGARY REGIMENT (TANK)

No 4 COMMANDO

Puys

DIEPPE AREA GARRISONED BY 571ST INFANTRY REGT WITH ELEMENTS OF DIV ARTILLERY AND ENGINEERS

HEAVY A.A.

SOUTH SASKATCHEWAN REGIMENT CAMERON HIGHLANDERS OF CANADA

RADAR STATION

LOW WATER MARK

Vasterival

Pourville

FIELD BATTERY

Varengeville-sur-Mer

COASTAL BATTERY

DIEPPE

FIELD BATTERY

PLANNED OUTPOST

H.Q. 302ND INFANTRY DIV AT ENVERMEU, 1¾ MILES EAST

erville

Scie

PLANNED PERIMETER

Arques

Saane

COASTAL BATTERY

Arques-la-Bataille

Ouville-la-Rivière

Offranville

AERODROME

1   0   1   2
Miles

Landings and movements ashore by Canadian units (solid white arrows), by flanking British units (solid red arrows), movements planned but not completed (broken red arrows).

two miles and destroying parties of Germans along the way. But the upper crossing of the Scie, which had to be passed to reach the aerodrome, was strongly held. Reluctantly the Camerons fell back towards the coast, suffering and inflicting casualties. During the final evacuation both battalions lost heavily from fierce fire from the higher ground, but naval craft came boldly to their rendezvous and took off the greater part of both units. The gallant rearguard had to be abandoned.

In the main assault on Dieppe itself, the Essex Scottish on the open eastern section of the beach could make no progress. Three successive attacks over the sea-wall were beaten back with such grievous loss that the unit could mount no more. Only one small party crossed the promenade, and misleading reports of this success unfortunately led to the commitment of the reserve battalion, Les Fusiliers Mont-Royal. Although the French Canadians stormed gallantly ashore in the face of heavy fire, they too were pinned down on the beach and could accomplish little. To the west The Royal Hamilton Light Infantry landed opposite the Casino on the promenade. Although this building and the pillboxes

near it were strongly held, the Hamiltons cleared them, and groups of infantry and sappers crossed the bullet-swept boulevard behind the Casino and penetrated into the town. Here there was some vicious street-fighting. The last troops to land were part of the Royal Marine "A" Commando, who likewise could accomplish nothing.

Unfortunately, the tanks were late. The craft carrying the first nine Churchills delivered the formidable machines "about 10 to 15 minutes" after the infantry had landed. Guns on the two untaken headlands poured an inferno of fire on the beaches. Yet 27 of 30 Churchills reached shore; some could not get off the beach but engaged the enemy pillboxes with their guns. Others, using rolls of chestnut paling, crossed the shingle and surmounted the low sea-wall, only to discover that road-blocks across the streets leading into the town formed an effective barrier. Not one of these blocks was breached by the engineer demolition parties, although they tried hard. No tank penetrated into the town. Some of them cruised the promenade, silencing enemy positions as they went, but the armoured thrust through Dieppe and on to the aerodrome beyond never took place. About nine o'clock in the morning General Roberts and Captain Hughes-Hallett agreed that orders must be given to withdraw. The tanks covered the evacuation until that operation ended about mid-day.

By two in the afternoon all was over at Dieppe. By then the last craft was almost three miles off the French coast. Enemy air attacks did no serious damage to the ships, but of the 4963 Canadians who had embarked for the operation only 2210 returned to England, and many of these were wounded. There were 3367 casualties, including 1946 prisoners of war; 907 Canadians lost their lives.

"So ended the brave and bitter day", wrote the official army historian in *Six Years of War*. "Under the shaded dockside lights in the English ports, tired and grimy men drank strong tea and told their tales, and the ambulance trains filled and drew slowly out. Back on the Dieppe beaches the Germans were still collecting Canadian wounded, and the Canadian dead in their hundreds lay yet where they had fallen. On both sides of the Channel staff officers were already beginning to scan the record and assess the lessons of the raid; and beyond the Atlantic, in innumerable communities across Canada, people waited in painful anxiety for news of friends in the overseas army — that army which, after three years of war, had just fought its first battle."

Among the awards for Dieppe published in the *Canada Gazette* of 2 October 1942 was that of the Distinguished Service Order to Major-General J. H. Roberts. In April 1943 General Roberts gave up the command of the 2nd Division and was appointed Commander of the Canadian Reinforcement Units in England. It has been asserted in recent years that he was made a "scapegoat" for the failure of the raid and was removed from his command because of it. For this there is no evidence whatever. No adverse official comment on his conduct of the operation is on record; and it would seem that the Emperor Napoleon, had he been in command off Dieppe that day, could not have done much more than General Roberts did. (Napoleon, indeed, might have made an earlier decision to withdraw, and would doubtless have worried less than Roberts about getting as many of his men as possible off the beaches.) Roberts continued to command his division for eight months after Dieppe; and his ultimate relinquishment of command had no connection with the raid.

Events in Canada

In March 1942, when deep concern was being felt in some quarters for the safety of British Columbia, authorization was given for the completion of the 6th and 7th Divisions and for the formation of the brigade groups of an 8th Division. In a plebiscite held in April a large majority of voters endorsed the policy of releasing the Government from its previous pledge not to conscript men for service overseas. Projected Japanese operations against Midway Island and the Aleutians — which Canada heard about in May — led to a redistribution of forces: the 8th Division was given responsibility for the defence of northern British Columbia; the 6th Division took over the defence of Vancouver Island; and the 7th remained as a general reserve for Atlantic Command.

In the summer of 1943, the Active Army had more than 34,000 soldiers in Pacific Command. The anticlimax occurred in August with the "invasion" of Kiska. The 13th Infantry Brigade, under United States command, joined in a carefully planned and lavishly supported operation against this island in the Aleutians, which, it turned out, the Japanese had evacuated more than a fortnight before. Thereafter tension on the Pacific Coast rapidly decreased and a reduction of the force in the area became politically, as well as militarily, feasible.

N.R.M.A. men had gradually been made available for general service in Alaska, Newfoundland, the Caribbean, the United States and the Aleutians, but no conscripted men were sent outside the hemisphere until a critical shortage of infantry reinforcements for overseas formations developed in 1944. The Government then sent N.R.M.A. men overseas. This measure inevitably produced some friction and discontent, but it was clear that the Government had not taken it until forced by circumstances. Thus the singularly deep division which had marked the introduction of conscription in 1917 was avoided. The unity with which the country had gone to war in 1939, though shaken, was not entirely destroyed.

The Invasion of Sicily

By the spring of 1943 the Canadian field army in Britain comprised an army headquarters, two corps headquarters, two armoured divisions, three infantry divisions and two independent army tank brigades. Since January 1943, selected Canadian officers and non-commissioned officers had gained battle experience in North Africa, but no Canadian units took part in the Tunisian campaign. It was urged in Canada that considerations of self-respect, as well as regard for the country's influence in the post-war world, demanded that Canadians fight, and fight soon. It was also argued that large-scale battle experience would be desirable before committing the army as a whole to operations.

(D.N.D. photo.)

The advance in Sicily. This patrol of the 1st Infantry Division near Ipsica commandeered donkey carts to haul heavy weapons and equipment.

In April 1943 agreement was reached with Britain that the 1st Canadian Division (Major-General H. L. N. Salmon) and the 1st Canadian Army Tank Brigade would join the assault on Sicily which would follow the clearing of Tunisia.

The invasion of Sicily would be carried out by two armies, Lieut.-General George S. Patton's Seventh U.S. Army and General Sir Bernard L. Montgomery's Eighth British Army, both under the command of General Sir Harold Alexander. General Dwight D. Eisenhower, the Supreme Allied Commander in the Mediterranean, exercised overall control. On 13 May 1943 General Alexander telegraphed to Mr. Churchill: "It is my duty to report that the Tunisian Campaign is over . . . We are masters of the North African shores."

However, the invasion of Sicily could not begin at once. The various assaulting forces had to embark at widely scattered points – the United States, Algeria, Northern Tunisia, Southern Tunisia, Egypt, Malta and Britain – and they would gather at sea on the eve of attack. The Canadians would be a part of the Eighth British Army. When General Salmon was killed in an

aeroplane crash at the end of April, Major-General G. G. Simonds assumed command of the 1st Division.

On 28 June the bulk of the Canadian troops left the Clyde by fast assault convoy; a slow assault convoy carrying transport and equipment had preceded them. The Tank Brigade sailed in "follow-up" convoys. Fifty-eight Canadians were drowned when three ships of the slow assault convoy were sunk by enemy submarines, and 500 vehicles and a number of guns were lost, but shortly after midnight on 10 July the ships dropped anchor seven miles from the Sicilian beach and quietly rode out the night. The armada of Allied ships presented an enormous target but the enemy made no move. In the early hours of 10 July, while it was still dark, the sea assault (preceded by airborne landings) went in.

The Italians had little stomach for fighting. The Canadians, assisted by British commando units, seized all their objectives, including Pachino Airfield, at small cost. Success was general all along the front. The lessons learned at Dieppe had been put to use: no port was attacked frontally; instead, the attackers assaulted, and were maintained, over open beaches, as was to happen again in Normandy in 1944. But ports soon fell – Syracuse on the first day and Augusta three days later. The Eighth Army now struck northward along the narrow coastal plain to seize Messina at the north-eastern tip of Sicily and cut the defenders' escape route. German forces reacted swiftly to the British thrust, concentrating in front of the great cone of Mount Etna and blocking the coastal road to the port of Catania. Thus in the next phase of the campaign the Americans on the Allied left found themselves confronted in western Sicily only by Italian troops, while the Eighth Army on the right had to deal with stubborn German defenders.

The Canadian axis of advance, through rugged hills far to the left of the main route along the coastal plain, grew increasingly important as the campaign continued. By 20 July it became clear that the Eighth Army's right could make no progress south of Catania and that the main effort would have to be on the left. The Canadians received orders to drive on Adrano, which lies

at the foot of Mount Etna some 20 miles north of Catania. The Seventh U.S. Army, after sweeping through western Sicily, was to come into line and join in a combined offensive to burst through to Messina. Meanwhile the Germans had been reinforced with the best part of two divisions from Italy.

Through the sweltering days of July and August the Canadians pushed forward along dusty mountain roads dominated by towns and villages perched on lofty crags. At first all went well, and by 12 July the troops were 30 miles in a direct line from their point of landing and much farther over mountain roads. They had covered most of the distance on foot in a "continuous cloud of fine white dust". Resistance now stiffened, and from 15 July the Canadians were engaged increasingly with German troops who fought stubborn delaying actions from the towering villages and rocky hills. The first such action was fought at the town of Grammichele. There were many others. The advance along two main axes

Leonforte. This Sicilian hill-town was captured by the 2nd Canadian Infantry Brigade in July 1943.

(D.N.D. photo.)

to Regalbuto in the north and Catenanuova farther south cleared the way to Adrano. Valguarnera, where Panzer Grenadiers of the 15th Division were encountered, was taken only after a two-brigade Canadian attack and much confused and costly fighting. Nor was the capture of Leonforte and Assoro easy. Both towns stood on very high ground and the attackers had to approach them across a river valley dominated by German guns. At Agira, progress could be made only behind a tremendous barrage which moved forward in successive 100-yard lifts. This method, so reminiscent of the First World War, brought speedy results and cleared the enemy off two features that guarded the town. Air attacks and bitter infantry fighting finally gave the Canadians possession of Agira. Catenanuova fell on 30 July, while heavy fighting for Regalbuto still continued. Although The Royal Canadian Regiment penetrated into the town on 31 July, the Germans resisted bitterly. "Throughout 1 August the battalion was in an unenviable situation, holding exposed positions swept by enemy fire from the ridge and scorched by the broiling heat of the Sicilian sun", the regiment's war diary records. But the Germans had had enough. An attack by fresh troops on 2 August found Regalbuto abandoned by the enemy.

The campaign was nearly over. The Germans still held firm along the coast south of Catania but were now confined to the north-eastern corner of Sicily. The Americans had come up on the Canadian left, and both armies would soon press forward towards Messina. The Canadian task was to break through the main enemy position and capture Adrano.

This operation led the Canadians into mountainous and almost roadless country utterly impassable for wheeled transport. Mortars, machine-guns, ammunition and supplies had to be brought forward by mule-trains, but the Canadians, fighting from rock to rock, cleared the Germans from successive positions. On 6 August the Royal 22e Régiment pushed on rapidly to forestall the 78th British Division which was also racing to capture Adrano. To their disappointment, the French Canadians were ordered to hold back, but one of their patrols reached the town before the order was received and found the place deserted. That day the Canadian division moved into reserve and ended its Sicilian operations. Eleven days later American soldiers entered Messina where they met British troops coming from the south. Sicily had been conquered in 38 days.

Throughout the campaign, one regiment of the Army Tank Brigade had fought with the 1st Division and had been of tremendous assistance. The division itself had marched 130 miles, farther than any other formation in the Eighth Army, and during the final two weeks had

(D.N.D. photo.

A tank of the 12th Armoured Regiment (Three Rivers Regiment) advances through the ruined town of Regalbuto, which fell in August 1943.

borne a large share of the fighting on the Army front. Canadian casualties totalled 172 officers and 2138 other ranks, of which 40 and 522 were fatal. Because of their thorough training, the men had been able to acquit themselves like seasoned veterans. They now held themselves in readiness for the next great operation, the invasion of the Italian mainland.

Canadian Operations in Italy — 1943-1945

One result of the Sicilian campaign had been the overthrow of the Italian dictator Mussolini on 25 July. Italy surrendered unconditionally on 3 September, but six days later the Germans occupied Rome. The peninsula would have to be fought for.

Two Allied armies were to carry out the invasion of Italy. The Eighth Army would lead the way across the Strait of Messina and then advance towards Naples; the Fifth U.S. Army would make a seaborne landing in the Gulf of Salerno, south of Naples, cut off the German forces withdrawing before the Eighth Army, seize Naples, and advance on Rome. At the same time the 1st British Airborne Division was to land by sea in the

Taranto area and occupy the heel of the Italian peninsula. For his assault force General Montgomery chose the 13th British Corps, consisting of the 1st Canadian Division, the 5th British Division and the 1st Canadian Army Tank Brigade. The Canadians were directed on the port of Reggio Calabria. The invasion began at 4:30 a.m. on 3 September, and there was even less resistance than at Pachino. The Canadians captured Reggio without difficulty and before nightfall had pushed into the mountainous interior of the Calabrian peninsula. Here tortuous roads and German delaying actions slowed the advance. After some days the Canadians switched to a new axis of advance along the coastal road and made better progress. By 10 September they had reached Catanzaro, 75 miles inland from Reggio.

The previous day the Salerno landings had established a bridgehead, and it was now essential for the Fifth and Eighth Armies to link up. Montgomery ordered Simonds to seize Potenza, a road centre 55 miles east of Salerno. On 20 September the Canadian division did so. Meanwhile the 1st Canadian Infantry Brigade had been operating eastwards; after joining hands with the 1st Airborne Division in the Taranto area, it pushed north. The 5th British Corps seized the Foggia airfields, and on 1 October the Fifth Army entered Naples. The next objective was Rome.

In the centre of the Italian peninsula the 1st Canadian Division advanced towards the towns of Vinchiaturo and Campobasso, while the 1st Canadian Armoured Brigade moved up the Adriatic coast. In this phase the tanks had the harder fighting. A British Special Service brigade captured Termoli on 3 October but the enemy counter-attacked furiously. British infantry and Canadian tanks met these counter-attacks, and in "tank

A Sherman tank of The Calgary Regiment on a ridge overlooking Potenza, Italy, which the Calgaries helped The West Nova Scotia Regiment to take on 20 September 1943.

(D.N.D. photo.)

Soldiers of The Carleton and York Regiment examine a German anti-tank gun, sited to cover the "Bridge of Thirteen Arches" near Gambatesa, which fell to the regiment on 8 October 1943.

(D.N.D. photos.)

Canadian artillery blasts German hill positions before Spinete, Italy, October 1943.

The 10th Battery, 2nd Canadian Field Regiment, R.C.A., puts down a barrage at Torella, 1 November 1943.

ITALY
3 September 1943 –
25 February 1945

GULF OF
GENOA

Genoa

Po

EMILIA

Bologna

Reno

Senio

Ravenna

GOTHIC LINE

Pistoia

Pisa

Arno

Florence

Rimini

Tomba di Pesaro

Pésaro

TUSCANY

Arezzo

Siena

Foglia

Metauro

1ST
CANADIAN
CORPS

Ancona

N

L. Trasimene

MARCHES

CORSICA

Perugia

A D R I A T I C

ELBA

Tiber

UMBRIA

S E A

Viterbo

LATIUM

WINTER LINE

Ortona

ROME

ABRUZZI

Villa Rogatti

SARDINIA

1ST
CANADIAN
CORPS

&

Sangro

Termoli

Biferno

6TH U.S.
CORPS
JAN 1944

Anzio

Liri

Ceprano

MOLISE

Cassino

Campobasso

ADOLF HITLER LINE

Vinchiaturo

GUSTAV LINE

Volturno

Foggia

T Y R R H E N I A N

Naples

CAMPANIA

APULIA

78TH BRIT. DIV.
& 4TH ARM'D. BDE.
22 - 23 SEP 1943

S E A

Salerno

Melfi

Bari

FIFTH
U.S. ARMY
9 SEP 1943

Gulf of
Salerno

Potenza

LUCANIA

Tara

1ST BRITISH
AIRBORNE DIV
9 SEP 1943

GULF OF TARAN

SICILY
10 July – 6 August 1943

Trapani

Palermo

Messina

Reggio

Marsala

Strait of Messina

CALABRIA

Sciacca

Mt
Etna

Catanzaro

Agira

Leonforte

Regalbuto

Valguarnera

Adrano

Piazza Armerina

Catania

Licata

Grammichele

Augusta

1ST CDN
DIV

SEVENTH
U.S. ARMY
10 JULY 1943

Ragusa

Syracuse

Modica

Rosolini

Ispica

EIGHTH
BRITISH ARMY
3 SEP 1943

Messina

Pachino

EIGHTH BRITISH ARMY

Reggio

1ST CANADIAN
DIVISION

0 10 20 30 40 50

Miles

0   20   40   60   80   100

Miles

country" rarely found in Italy, tank fought tank among olive groves in the open plain and the Germans got the worst of it.

In the centre, German resistance stiffened. Now the enemy contested every step, not only with mines and demolitions but also with men. Nevertheless, on 14 October the 1st Infantry Brigade took Campobasso, and the next day Vinchiaturo fell to the 2nd Brigade. The advance continued across the Biferno River, but then the weather broke completely. Rain slashed down from sodden skies, and life under shellfire in the poverty-stricken, filthy little villages beyond the Biferno was uncomfortable and dangerous.

The Canadians were to have returned to Britain when the Sicilian campaign was over, but in October it was decided that they would remain in the Mediterranean theatre and that the 5th Canadian Armoured Division and the Headquarters of the 1st Canadian Corps would join them there. The Canadian Army was to be divided. Soon afterwards, General McNaughton, who favoured keeping First Canadian Army united, retired.

To break the stalemate and assist the Fifth U.S. Army to capture Rome, Montgomery decided to attack along the Adriatic Coast across the broad valley of the River Sangro on which the Germans had established their Winter Line. Only one Canadian brigade, the 3rd, remained in the mountains to drive the enemy across the upper Sangro and, if possible, patrol the opposite bank. At the end of November, Montgomery seized the commanding ridge above the Sangro and burst through the Winter Line, but the Germans clung grimly to the succession of steep valleys beyond. The Canadian division remained on the Campobasso front. In November the headquarters of Lieut.-General H. D. G. Crerar's 1st Canadian Corps reached Sicily; one of its formations, the 5th Canadian Armoured Division, arrived that month and General Simonds left to command it, being replaced in the 1st Division by Major-General C. Vokes. On 2 December Vokes took command of the right flank of Montgomery's Adriatic battle. His immediate task was to force the line of the River Moro and seize the port of Ortona, two miles beyond.

The fighting for Ortona was as bitter as any in the war. The Loyal Edmonton Regiment, The Seaforth Highlanders of Canada, and tanks of The Three Rivers Regiment bore the brunt of the struggle, blasting their way through the walls from one house to the next against determined German paratroopers. On Christmas Day each rifle company was relieved for two hours while the men ate their Christmas dinner, then the soldiers went back to the bloody business of clearing the town.

During the night of 27-28 December the German paratroopers, threatened by a Canadian thrust towards the coast to the north, abandoned Ortona.

Although attempts were made to keep the front in motion during January, the offensive petered out in atrocious weather that turned the ground into a morass. During the lull, Simonds left for England to command the 2nd Corps, and Major-General E. L. M. Burns succeeded him. In March, Burns took over the Corps from Crerar, who returned to command the First Canadian Army in England.

The winter offensive had failed to capture Rome. The Germans stood firm along the Gustav Line and the massive bulk of Monte Cassino blocked the Liri corridor to the Italian capital. During April and May the Eighth Army, including the 1st Canadian Corps, was secretly shifted west of the Apennines to the Liri — Cassino front, where, nine miles behind the Gustav Line, the Germans had constructed the formidable Adolf Hitler Line.

An hour before midnight on 11 May the battle for Rome began. The flashes of over 1000 guns lit up the darkness as the bombardment opened up on the Gustav Line. Tanks of the 1st Canadian Armoured Brigade, festive-looking in their camouflage of green boughs, surged over the first Bailey bridge to span the swirling Gari, but the Corps as such was not yet in action. After four days of hard fighting, the enemy's forward defences were broken from Cassino to the Tyrrhenian Sea. Although Cassino had not yet fallen, the enemy streamed back to the Adolf Hitler Line. The 1st Canadian Division was committed to battle on 16 May. Two days later Polish troops raised their standard over the battered monastery at Cassino and on 20 May General Burns issued the terse order — "The 1st Canadian Corps will break the Hitler Line and exploit towards Ceprano."

Early on the hazy morning of 23 May, for the first time in this war, a Canadian Corps moved into an assault. The men advanced through tall grain behind a barrage put down by over 800 guns. On the centre and the right the Canadians were pinned down by a storm of mortar and machine-gun fire, but within an hour some penetration was made on the left. General Vokes exploited this success with every reserve he could muster. Soon the battlefield was dotted with blazing tanks, and infantry reinforcements moved up through a lurid landscape that glowed weirdly with a hundred fires. That evening a final attack in pouring rain consolidated the hard-won gap and the 5th Canadian Armoured Division poured through. The battle, grimmer even than Ortona, had cost the Corps 879

The 1st Canadian Division landed in Sicily as part of the Eighth British Army in July 1943 and fought its way to the foot of Mount Etna (white arrows).

Landing on the toe of Italy in September 1943, the Canadians had captured the port of Ortona by the end of the year; in May 1944 the 1st Canadian Corps breached the Adolf Hitler Line and advanced along the Liri Valley; two months later the Canadians broke through the eastern end of the Gothic Line and in January 1945 cleared the line of the Senio River, their last operation in Italy.

White arrows show the main axes of Canadian advances; solid black lines show major German defence lines.

"Quadrant"—The Quebec Conference, August 1943. Messrs. Mackenzie King, Roosevelt and Churchill with their service advisers, (left to right) General Henry H. Arnold; Air Chief Marshal Sir Charles Portal; Field-Marshal Sir Alan Brooke; Admiral Ernest J. King; Field-Marshal Sir John Dill; General George C. Marshall; Admiral of the Fleet Sir Dudley Pound; and Admiral William D. Leahy.

casualties.

On the same day, the 6th U.S. Corps, which had landed at Anzio south of Rome, behind the Gustav and Hitler Lines, broke out of the bridgehead where it had been sealed off since January. On 25 May the Americans linked up with the Fifth Army advancing from the south and threatened the German escape routes through the Italian capital. The 1st Canadian Corps, which now had a firm foothold behind the Hitler Line, forced the Melfa River at its confluence with the Liri, and, despite stiff opposition, bridged the stream.

The advance now became pursuit. Since the enemy had no wish to be trapped in the Liri Valley by the American thrust farther west, he pulled back rapidly. The 5th Armoured Division carried the Canadian pursuit on to Ceprano, but north of that town the valley narrowed and razor-back hills lay athwart the path to

Rome. On 30 May the infantry replaced the armour in the chase through the difficult country that lay ahead. But the Canadians were not destined to liberate Rome, and to their intense disappointment they were withdrawn into army reserve. It was American troops that on 4 June entered the famous city, the first European capital to be freed by the Allies. Nevertheless, its liberation had been due in no small part to the breaking of the Hitler Line by Canadian soldiers. The total casualties in the Corps between 15 May and 4 June had been 3368, of which 789 were fatal.

Two days after the fall of Rome, the invasion of Normandy began. It was now more important than ever that the Allies should continue to pin down German troops in Italy. The enemy would certainly stand behind the Gothic Line, a strong system of defences he was building along the Northern Apennines from Pisa to

Rimini. The two Allied armies exploited north of Rome, the Fifth U.S. Army along the west coast to Pisa and Pistoia, the Eighth British Army up the valley of the Tiber to Arezzo and Florence. Tanks of the 1st Canadian Armoured Brigade, supporting the 13th British Corps, were continuously in action through the difficult country west of Lake Trasimene and in the vineyards and maize fields of eastern Tuscany. With mines, demolitions and strong rearguards the Germans won time to strengthen their defences farther north. In mid-August, Ontario Regiment tanks helped the 8th Indian Division clear Florence. Beyond lay the Etruscan Apennines and the Gothic Line. To the west, the Fifth U.S. Army entered Pisa on 2 September. By this time, however, three American and four French divisions had been withdrawn for a landing in the south of France designed to assist the main campaign in Normandy, and accordingly General Alexander modified his plan to assault the central part of the Gothic Line. The Eighth Army would now strike at the eastern end of the line in the Adriatic sector in a narrow thrust that would swing left towards Bologna once the mountain barrier had been passed. The Fifth U.S. Army would advance north-eastwards from Florence in a converging attack intended to trap the German Tenth Army.

After two months' rest and training in the Volturno Valley, the 1st Canadian Corps secretly moved northwards to the Adriatic to play its part in breaching the eastern end of the Gothic Line, which reached the sea 20 miles down the coast from Rimini at Pesaro. No fewer than six rivers lay across the path of the advance to Rimini — the Metauro, the Foglia (which flowed to the sea at Pesaro), the Conca, the Melo, the Marano, and the Ausa. Most formidable was the Foglia, on whose north bank defensive works stretched over the low hills running back to the Apennines' backbone. Here were Panther tank turrets embedded in concrete emplacements, reinforced dugouts and slit trenches, an anti-tank ditch and belts of mines.

On 25 August the Canadians crossed the Metauro, but it took four days to fight through the intervening dozen miles to the Foglia. The Allied air forces had softened up the Gothic defences, and on the afternoon of 30 August two Canadian brigades crossed the Foglia River and fought their way through the Gothic Line. That night General Burns reported: "The Gothic Line is completely broken in the Adriatic Sector and the 1st Canadian Corps is advancing to the River Conca."

Although this thrust had taken the enemy by surprise, he soon recovered, and by thinning out other sectors, reinforced his Adriatic positions. In doing so, although he slowed the advance on Rimini to bitter, step-by-step

(Courtesy The National Gallery of Canada.)

VIA DOLOROSA   by Charles Comfort (1900-   ).
During Christmas-week 1943 Ortona was the scene of bitter street fighting. This debris-filled street leads to the Church of San Tommaso in the old town.

progress, he weakened his central front. Here on 13 September, the Fifth U.S. Army opened its attack north of Florence. Not before 22 September, after fierce fighting, did the 1st Canadian Corps break through the Apennine barrier. The hills fell away, and before the gratified eyes of the Canadians stretched the level northern plains that seemed to beckon their tanks to Bologna and the Po.

But the vision glimpsed from the Apennines of a triumphant sweep to the west was to prove illusory. The hot Italian summer suddenly gave place to the steadily falling rain of autumn. Across the axis of advance, little streams turned overnight into raging torrents; mud replaced the powdery dust; and even drainage ditches, brimming with water, became tank obstacles. All mechanical transport bogged down in the reclaimed swampland, and only by interminable bridging and rafting could the advance creep forward. The Germans still resisted; when bridgeheads were established with difficulty across the many obstacles, they counter-attacked them strongly.

131

THE HITLER LINE
by Charles Comfort (1900-   )
Men of the 1st Canadian Division overrunning a German anti-tank position, 23 May 1944.

Meanwhile, the Fifth U.S. Army struggled across the Apennines until by 22 October it was within ten miles of Bologna. The 1st Canadian Armoured Brigade, still operating with the 13th British Corps in the Fifth Army's sector, crawled through gorges, gullies and canyon-like valleys to support the infantry. Finally on 27 October General Mark Clark, the Fifth Army Commander, reluctantly called off the offensive nine miles from Bologna. On the plain, the Canadian Corps, now commanded by Lieut.-General Charles Foulkes, captured Ravenna on 4 December and by the 21st reached the River Senio. Here, in marked contrast to the previous Christmas at

Ortona, a watchful truce was observed by Canadians and Germans facing each other across the river. Early in January the Corps, in its last operation in Italy, cleared the line of the Senio, which was stabilized thereafter into the Winter Line. In appalling weather, both sides adopted a wary defence from fixed positions. By April the general collapse of Germany had begun; the Allies broke into the Po Valley and raced northward towards the Italian Alps. On 2 May the Germans surrendered. The long Italian campaign was over.

The Canadians had contributed greatly to the final victory, but they were not in Italy to see it. In February

132

Infantry of the 1st Canadian
Division move up through Rimini,
September 1944.

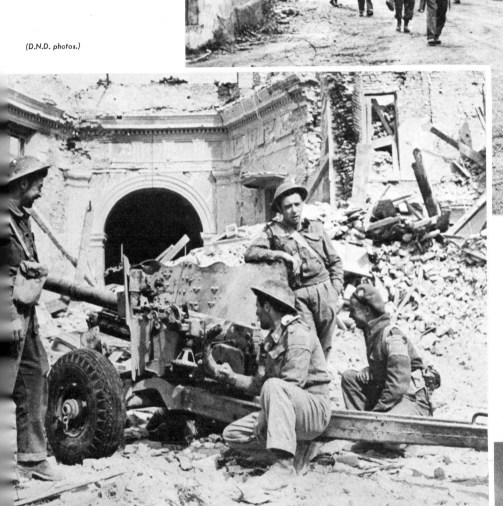

A Canadian 6-pounder anti-tank gun in a
churchyard of the battered town of Rimini.

The Marecchia in flood. During the
breaching of the Rimini Line in September
1944, the Royal Canadian Engineers
bridged the Marecchia under German
fire. Heavy rains brought a flood which
swept the bridge away, and a second
met the same fate. The third Bailey bridge
held, and men and material again moved
forward to the front.

(D.N.D. photo.)

Into the Romagna. Camouflaged Canadian tanks find heavy going as they cross the shallow Uso River.

1945 the Corps had begun to move to North-West Europe to be re-united at last with First Canadian Army.

Across the Channel to Victory

On 6 June 1944 the long-awaited invasion of North-West Europe began with Allied landings on the coast of Normandy. The task was incredibly formidable, and on it depended the outcome of the war. For four years the Germans had strengthened their "Atlantic Wall" with guns, pillboxes, wire, mines and beach obstacles.

Under General Dwight D. Eisenhower as Supreme Allied Commander and General Sir Bernard Montgomery as Commander of 21st Army Group, two armies attacked: the First U.S. Army (Lieut.-General Omar N. Bradley) on the right, and the Second British Army (Lieut.-General M. C. Dempsey) on the left. Five divisions — two American, two British and one Canadian — launched the seaborne assault. The Canadian sector, code-named "Juno", was in the centre of the British front. The 3rd Division (Major-General R. F. L. Keller) and the 2nd Canadian Armoured Brigade assaulted over two beaches. Before the seaborne assault three airborne divisions had been dropped to cover the flanks of the Allied bridgehead; on the left flank with the 6th British Airborne Division was the 1st Canadian

Parachute Battalion.

The first day's objectives on the Anglo-Canadian front were: 3rd British Division — Caen; 50th British Division — Bayeux; 3rd Canadian Division — the line between these towns. The Canadian assaulting brigades, the 7th and 8th, would establish a shallow beachhead and would then push on to intermediate objectives. The reserve brigade, the 9th, would pass through the 8th to seize the left sector of the final objective, the high ground north-west of Caen. Simultaneously the 7th Brigade would seize the right sector of the final line.

D Day had originally been set for 5 June, and elaborate security precautions were taken. By 3 June almost all the 3rd Division and the 2nd Armoured Brigade had been embarked in landing ships and craft about the Isle of Wight, but bad weather caused General Eisenhower to postpone the invasion for 24 hours.

For six hours on the night of 5-6 June R.A.F. and R.C.A.F. bombers saturated the German defences and communications on the coast of Normandy. American bombers took over the task after daylight, their first attacks coinciding with the explosions of naval shells delivered by the escort vessels of the great armada approaching the French coast. Off the Canadian sector, the 3rd Division's four regiments of field artillery on tank landing craft pounded the beaches with high-ex-

(D.N.D. photo.)

Training for Normandy. Firing over their comrades' heads, men of The Regina Rifle Regiment use a 2-inch mortar to lay smoke during an exercise in England, April 1944.

Le Régiment de la Chaudière, the brigade's reserve unit, comes ashore at Bernières-sur-Mer on the morning of D Day. The landing craft were borne in H.M.C.S. *Prince David*, one of the R.C.N.'s invasion craft "mother ships".

(Courtesy Lieutenant R. B. Arless)

D-DAY, NORMANDY: THE RHINO FERRY
by Orville Fisher (1911-   )
Constructed of pontoon units and propelled by outboard motors, these ferries were used to move supplies and vehicles to the beaches from large
landing ships anchored off shore.

plosive shells. By now the assault landing craft, packed with infantry, were butting through the rough sea behind the amphibious tanks which composed the first wave of the attack. For once, too, all three Canadian services were fighting together. Of the 15,000 Canadian troops that hit the Normandy beach on D Day, one-third debouched from R.C.N. landing craft, while R.C.A.F. bombers and fighters flew overhead and Canadian destroyers and minesweepers were at work in the Channel.

On the 7th Brigade's beach The Royal Winnipeg Rifles on the right and The Regina Rifle Regiment on the left encountered fierce opposition. Seven tanks of the 6th Canadian Armoured Regiment (1st Hussars) had failed to reach shore but the remainder went for the German pillboxes, most of which were still intact despite the preliminary bombardment. One company of the Winnipegs, caught in fire from these positions, suffered severe loss while disembarking. A reserve company of the Reginas, coming in later, incurred heavy casualties from mined beach obstacles which had been hidden by the rising tide; only 49 men got ashore. The assault engineers, who were to have destroyed enemy strongpoints and prepared vehicle exits from the beach, had been delayed by the rough weather and were sorely missed. The guns of the 12th Field Regiment R.C.A. had to be brought into action on the beach.

However, by 8:30 a.m. the reserve battalion, The Canadian Scottish Regiment, was coming ashore and the forward battalions pushed inland behind the tanks. After fierce fighting, the Reginas seized Courseulles-sur-Mer, and the Winnipegs, with the Canadian Scottish close behind them, captured the inland villages of Ste. Croix-sur-Mer and Banville. By evening the brigade had penetrated some four miles from the coast and was firmly on its intermediate objective south-east of Creully.

On the 8th Brigade front the assault engineers landed in better time and were able to engage the enemy strong-points. The Queen's Own Rifles of Canada on the right and The North Shore (New Brunswick) Regiment on the left captured the beachhead objective and moved inland to seize Bernières. The tanks of the 10th Armoured Regiment (The Fort Garry Horse) were landed shortly after the leading infantry. By 9:00 a.m. the reserve battalion, Le Régiment de la Chaudière, was ashore, and half an hour later a battery of the 19th Army Field Regiment R.C.A. was in action off the beach. Beyond Bernières the Chaudières' progress was slow. Meanwhile the 9th Brigade had landed. It was ordered to pass through the 8th to its final objective as soon as Beny-sur-Mer, a village on the main road to Caen, was captured. However, the Chaudières did not take Beny until midafternoon. By then the Queen's Own had captured Anguerny and were on high ground beyond it.

The 9th Brigade moved from Bernières shortly after 4 p.m. with The North Nova Scotia Highlanders in the van. The battalion passed through Beny and made good progress as far as Villons-les-Buissons, less than four miles from Caen. Here machine-guns held up the advance and the North Nova Scotias were ordered to consolidate for the night short of Carpiquet airfield, the final divisional objective.

The experience of the British divisions on either flank was similar. The 50th had got within a mile of the Bayeux — Caen road but had not taken Bayeux itself; nor had the 3rd Division taken Caen. The 1st Canadian Parachute Battalion, which dropped with the 6th Airborne Division on the extreme left flank of the bridgehead, had been badly dispersed on landing and consequently had fairly heavy losses. Nevertheless, it performed all its assigned tasks, which included demolishing two bridges over the Dives and the Divette rivers and capturing a strongpoint near Varaville. On

the right flank the Americans had had a grimmer experience in the "Omaha" sector, but even here a beachhead had been won.

By nightfall it was apparent that the great and hazardous venture had succeeded magnificently. A bridgehead had been gained, and although casualties had been high, the cost had been lighter than had been feared. The Canadians lost 1074 killed, wounded and missing, including 113 casualties suffered by the 1st Canadian Parachute Battalion, far less than the price that had been paid for the experience at Dieppe that had helped to make the D Day triumph possible.

Later, the official army historian, in *The Canadian Army 1939-1945,* wrote: "The Canadian soldiers who gave their lives in this great enterprise and in the further bloody fighting to which it was the prelude take their rest today north of Beny-sur-Mer. Their place is high, and from beside the Cross of Sacrifice that guards it one looks down over the pleasant green fields and woods of the Bessin to the sea they traversed and the little seaside towns where they waged what was, for many, their first battle and their last. Courseulles, Bernières and St. Aubin — there they lie, marked by their church-spires rising above the trees. Nothing could be more peaceful now, or more unlike that wild June day when devastation rained from the skies and the Allied armies stormed ashore; and the visitor may think, perhaps, of other peaceful little towns, far away, from which these lads came of their own will to fight and die for the freedom of man on the beaches of Calvados."

The Fighting in Normandy

The Germans could now be expected to mount a powerful armoured counter-offensive against the Allied beach-head. General Montgomery's plan, developed in increasing detail as June advanced, was to attract the maximum German strength to the Anglo-Canadian front while the Americans overran the Cotentin Peninsula, captured the port of Cherbourg, and finally broke out of the enlarged bridgehead, wheeling towards the Seine and driving the Germans against that obstacle. The British army group on the left would wheel on the hinge of the Orne, moving on the Seine in cooperation with the Americans.

On the morning of 7 June General Dempsey's army resumed its advance. The 7th Brigade of the 3rd Canadian Division gained the final D Day objectives against light resistance. The 9th Brigade, in the eastern sector, also made good progress at first. The North Nova Scotias and tanks of The Sherbrooke Fusiliers Regiment entered Authie, two miles from Caen, and shortly afterwards experienced the first real counter-attack, delivered by the crack 12th S.S. Panzer Division, which had just reached the battleground. In a fierce encounter the Canadians had heavy losses and were thrown back to Les Buissons.

The Allies had been held short of Caen. The pattern of the next month was attacks to enlarge our bridgehead and violent counter-attacks by the enemy's best formations to prevent penetration of an area they recognized as vital. The Germans made mistakes. Fearful of another attack in the Pas-de-Calais, they held large numbers of their infantry divisions inactive there. Thus they had to use their armour piecemeal to hold the line in Normandy. Although they eventually placed no fewer than eight of their best armoured divisions on the Anglo-Canadian front, in these circumstances their counter-attacks never had sufficient weight to jeopardize the Allied bridgehead. Behind the bridgehead perimeter Allied forces were steadily built up. On the western flank the Americans rapidly gained ground, taking Cherbourg on 26 June and clearing the upper part of the Cotentin Peninsula by 1 July. Farther south their forces got within striking distance of St. Lô.

On 12 June the Allies had 326,547 men and 54,186 vehicles in the bridgehead; a month after D Day nearly a million Allied soldiers were in Normandy. Some units of the 2nd Canadian Division and the Headquarters of the 2nd Canadian Corps arrived by the end of the first week in July. On 4 July the Canadians were again directed on Carpiquet. The 8th Canadian Infantry Brigade plus The Royal Winnipeg Rifles carried out the attack with heavy tank and artillery support. The village was taken, but fanatical enemy resistance delayed the capture of the airfield until the 9th.

On 8 July Montgomery launched a strong offensive against Caen itself. Powerfully supported from the air and by massed land artillery and naval guns, two British divisions, the 3rd Canadian Division and three armoured brigades, including the 2nd Canadian, swept forward. By afternoon the Canadians were on the western outskirts of Caen, and by the 10th the ruined city was in our hands as far as the Orne. The streets were so choked with debris that it was a major task to bulldoze a passage for the continuing advance.

The 2nd Canadian Division (Major-General Charles

Men of The Queen's Own Rifles of Canada at Carpiquet Airfield, 6 July 1944, after capture of the northern hangars. The south end of the field was still in German hands.

(D.N.D. photo.)

Left: Bulldozers clear a way through the shattered streets of Caen. William the Conqueror's two great abbeys still stood.

Below: The build-up in Normandy. By 20 July, when this photograph was taken, the build-up of troops and equipment in the bridgehead was proceeding rapidly.

(D.N.D. photo.)

Divine Service, Sunday, 18 June 1944. H.M.C.S. Algonquin on passage to Normandy with General Crerar and his staff. In centre foreground left to right are Brigadier A. E. Alford; Brigadier C. C. Mann; Captain F. L. Houghton, R.C.N., Lieut.-General K. Stuart; Lieutenant-Commander D. W. Piers, R.C.N. (commanding the destroyer); General H. D. G. Crerar.

Foulkes) came into the line on the night of 11-12 July. With the 3rd Canadian Division and the 2nd Canadian Armoured Brigade it formed the 2nd Canadian Corps under Lieut.-General G. G. Simonds' command. The first task given the Corps was to break out of Caen across the Orne. The 8th British Corps with three armoured divisions would attack through the airborne troops holding the eastern flank across the Orne and then wheel southwards. Simultaneously the Canadian Corps would thrust directly south across the Orne below Caen itself. This operation was to be supported by the heaviest aerial bombardment yet provided in the war. On 18 July the great attack went in. In the chosen section 7700 tons of bombs pulverized enemy targets, but although ground was gained, a breakthrough was not achieved. A formidable anti-tank screen halted the British armour four miles south-east of Caen; the 2nd Canadian Corps, after capturing Faubourg de Vaucelles, a suburb of Caen, advanced a similar distance before the enemy stabilized the situation. However, the bridgehead was now large enough to permit employment of the additional divisions required for a full-scale breakout. The attack had served another purpose. Not only had it held enemy strength on the Anglo-Canadian front but it had also compelled the Germans to withdraw additional armour from the centre. The American breakout in the west was thus facilitated.

To keep the enemy busy until the very moment of the Americans' main attack General Montgomery ordered General Dempsey to strike the final blow of the holding phase on the 2nd Canadian Corps' front.

On 25 July both divisions of the Canadian Corps attacked on either side of the Caen-Falaise road in the direction of Falaise. The powerful German force in the sector held its ground. Only slight gains were made in return for the heaviest casualties the Canadian Army suffered on any single day of the war except Dieppe. The attack nevertheless served its purpose. That day, at the western end of the Allied line, the First United States Army broke through the enemy positions near St. Lô.

The 4th Canadian Armoured Division (Major-General George Kitching) arrived from England late in July. Almost simultaneously General Crerar, who had been waiting impatiently for his army to become operational, took over the Caen front. The First Canadian Army had under its command the 2nd Canadian Corps and the 1st British Corps. On 3 August General Montgomery ordered Crerar to mount an attack towards Falaise. On the Allied right, the Americans had now penetrated into the Brittany Peninsula and were also swinging east to threaten the rear of the German forces facing the Anglo-Canadian front. When the enemy withdrew four armoured divisions from opposite Caen, Montgomery exploited the opportunity thus presented. The Second British Army had already made some gains in the Caumont area and had established a bridgehead across the Orne north of Thury-Harcourt. It was now the Canadians' turn.

General Crerar used the 2nd Canadian Corps for the thrust to Falaise. In addition to his Canadian formations, General Simonds had under command the 1st Polish Armoured Division and the British 51st (Highland) Division. He placed the latter on the left and the 2nd Canadian Division on the right, reserving the armoured divisions for exploitation. The attack was planned on original lines. The infantry would attack in tight columns, riding in improvised armoured carriers behind a spearhead of tanks (and "flails" to explode the German mines), while more tanks brought up the rear. Half an hour before midnight of 7-8 August, after heavy bombing, the columns surged forward through the darkness. Direction was maintained with the help of wireless and of Bofors guns firing tracer ammunition along the axis of advance. The first phase of the attack was spectacularly successful, but the subsequent armoured thrusts failed to take the high ground overlooking Falaise. Despite early progress by the 4th Canadian Armoured Division, the final objectives were not reached and further attempts were deferred until the 9th. When the attack was resumed that day, the 28th Armoured Regiment (The British Columbia Regiment) lost its way in moving across

Forward to the Laison. Tanks of the 2nd Canadian Armoured Brigade, leading the 3rd Canadian Infantry Division, move to the start line for Operation "Tractable", 14 August 1944.

country and was virtually annihilated. The Corps had advanced nine miles but was still only halfway to its final objectives. By nightfall it was obvious that no further progress could be made without mounting another deliberate attack.

Falaise had to be captured without delay. Hitler had ordered every available armoured unit to the west for a counter-attack aimed at cutting the American lines of communication running through Avranches. There, about Mortain, the First U.S. Army had blocked their progress and pushed them back. Meanwhile the Third U.S. Army had swept eastward to Le Mans, turned north, and was now driving on Argentan, only 15 miles south-east of Falaise. If the Canadians moving through Falaise could unite with the Americans moving up from Argentan, large German forces would be encircled.

Simonds' next major attack went in at noon on 14 August, using much the same tactics as before, though

in daylight. Medium bombers softened the enemy position 20 minutes before the assault, which was launched by the 3rd Division, the 4th Armoured Division and the 2nd Armoured Brigade. Smoke screened the advancing columns. Armoured carriers again proved their worth, carrying the infantry in relative safety to the line of the little River Laison where the main enemy line of resistance had been established. Here the infantry dismounted and began to clear the valley. However, the river delayed the tanks and inaccurate Allied aerial bombing inflicted casualties on our men. By evening, nevertheless, the heights above Falaise, four miles from the town, had been secured.

On the 15th, both the 2nd and 3rd Canadian Divisions moved forward again, and the 1st Polish and 4th Canadian Armoured Divisions thrust south-eastward on Trun to seal the gap through which the enemy was now desperately trying to extricate his battered forces. Not

141

Top: Men of Les Fusiliers Mont-Royal follow a tank of the 27th Armoured Regiment (The Sherbrooke Fusiliers Regiment) while clearing Falaise, 17 August 1944.

Right: An artillery convoy passes through the ruins of Falaise, August 1944.

142

Liverpool · Hull ·
· Birmingham

NORTH
SEA

FRISIAN ISLANDS
Wilhelmshaven · Cuxhaven
Emden · Wismar
Groningen EASTERN FRONT 6 MAY 1945
NETHERLANDS Oldenburg Elbe
Bremen
AMSTERDAM Zwolle Hamburg
Cardiff · ENGLAND Utrecht Apeldoorn Weser
Bristol · Rotterdam Arnhem BERLIN
LONDON Nijmegen Wesel
WALCHEREN Antwerp Duisburg Dortmund
Dover · Scheldt Düsseldorf
I. OF WIGHT Ostend Maas
Calais BRUSSELS
Boulogne BELGIUM
ENGLISH CHANNEL Remagen WESTERN FRONT, 6 MAY 1945
FIRST SECOND Dieppe Rochefort
U.S. ARMY BRIT ARMY FIRST CANADIAN ARMY
6 JUNE 1944 LUX Frankfurt GERMANY
Cherbourg · Le Havre FRONT
Bayeux · Rouen SECOND BRITISH ARMY 1 NOV 1944 Rhine
St-Lô · Caen FIRST U.S. ARMY Reims Karlsruhe
Thury-Harcourt Falaise PARIS Nancy Strasbourg Danube
Mortain Argentan THIRD U.S. ARMY U.S. ARMY FIRST FRENCH ARMY Munich ·
Le Mans Troyes SEVENTH
St-Nazaire · FRONT Orleans Seine Basle ·
25 AUG 1944 Dijon ·

FRANCE Loire

Vichy ·

3RD CANADIAN INFANTRY DIV
H.Q. 2 ARMOURED BRIGADE
9TH INF BDE CANADIAN
ASSAULTS
"D" DAY
5TH BRIT 7 INF BDE 8 INF BDE
INF DIV la German resistance nests
Rivière BEACHES MIKE NAN
Bordeaux · Ste Croix- Courseulles- St Aubin-sur-Mer 3RD BRIT
sur-Mer sur-Mer INF DIV
Banville Bernières-
Seulles sur-Mer Lion-
Creully Beny- Tailleville sur-Mer
sur-Mer
FRONT LINE Anguerny
6 – 7 JUNE

VICTORY
IN EUROPE Villons- Benouville Orne
les-Buissons
6 June 1944 – 8 May 1945 0 1 2 3
Miles
50 100 200
Miles 716TH INFANTRY DIVISION
BAYEUX Authie 21ST PANZER
DIVISION
Carpiquet Caen

...er the initial landings in North-West Europe on 6 June 1944 and the breakout from the bridgehead, which involved the Canadians in the bitter and bloody fighting
...t centred around Caen and Falaise, the First Canadian Army (full white arrows) assumed the task of clearing the coastal belt and opening the ports to supply the
...ied armies sweeping across Europe.
...earing the approaches to Antwerp, which was the greatest port in North-West Europe and essential to the maintenance of the Allied armies, was "a hard and bloody
...siness"; and the Battle of the Scheldt cost the First Canadian Army almost 13,000 in killed, wounded and missing.
...wever, the facilities of this great port enabled the Allies to build up for the grim battles that lay ahead, such as those fought by the Canadians in the Reichswald and
... Hochwald, which culminated in the final defeat of Germany on 8 May 1945.

until the 18th did the infantry finally clear Falaise after savage fighting. On the same day the 4th Division occupied Trun and high ground to the north; the Polish Division moved on Chambois. By the 18th the gap separating First Canadian Army from the First U.S. Army had narrowed to some three miles. As the desperate Germans attempted mass moves in daylight towards the steadily-closing gap, the Allied air forces came in for the kill, diving on the enemy columns time and again until the smoke of hundreds of burning vehicles rose into the sky. Never before had airmen had such targets and never before had an army been so harried from the skies.

Furious German resistance continued about Chambois and Trun, yet on the evening of 19 August the gap was closed, when the Poles entered Chambois and linked up with the Americans. But there was as yet no continuous line, only groups struggling savagely in chaotic fighting. On 20 August the encircled German formations battled desperately to break out at St. Lambert-sur-Dives, and although their losses were extremely heavy, substantial numbers did manage to escape. Many Germans however, collided with units of the 1st Polish Armoured Division who, themselves surrounded and pressed by Germans from both inside and outside the pocket, fought heroically until relieved by Canadian troops the next day. German counter-attacks continued with diminishing violence on the 21st. All about Trun and Chambois lay the wreckage and the dead of the Seventh German Army, which had been virtually de-

Major D. V. Currie of The South Alberta Regiment, his face marked by the strain and grime of the three days' fighting that won him the V.C., stands by, pistol in hand, (left) as German officers and men surrender at St. Lambert-sur-Dives.

(D.N.D. photo.)

144

The 400 Germans captured in the underground passages of the Herquelingue Hill march into Boulogne, 21 September 1944.

stroyed. Remnants of the decimated Fifth Panzer Army were falling back, incapable of fighting more than skilful rearguard actions at certain selected points.

Clearing the Coast

A great victory had been won, but the enemy was still formidable. The Allies could not maintain their advance unless they opened up a major port to supply their armies. Therefore the Germans determined to defend most of the coastal towns. Thus, while other armies swept across upper Normandy, freed Paris, crossed Picardy and Artois and surged on into Belgium and towards the German frontier, First Canadian Army had the task of storming a succession of fortified ports.

The Canadians advanced along the coast at the extreme left of the Allied line, bridging the rivers where they were widest. There was fierce fighting below the Seine with enemy units ensconced in dense woodland, but once the river was crossed the opposition dwindled. Rapid progress was made through Rouen and other towns, where the streets were lined with cheering people. On 30 August General Crerar directed the 2nd Canadian Corps upon Dieppe and on towards the Somme; his other corps (the 1st British) would move against the port of Le Havre. The 2nd Canadian Division, eager to avenge the repulse of 1942, was ordered to take Dieppe, but on 1 September the town was found to be undefended.

Dieppe was a minor port capable of supplying only about a quarter of the needs of 21st Army Group. Le Havre was a different matter, and was strongly held. Not until 12 September, after a deliberate attack, did the 1st British Corps succeed in taking it. On the day the 2nd Division entered Dieppe, the 3rd Division (now commanded by Major-General D. C. Spry) captured Le Tréport, another minor harbour. Farther north, on 4 September, the British, having swept through Brussels, entered Antwerp and found its installations virtually intact. Although Antwerp was a great port capable of supplying all the Allies' needs, the Germans held both banks of the Scheldt River between it and the sea, as

The Leopold Canal. The 7th Canadian Infantry Brigade made its assault crossing here on the morning of 6 October 1944. This photograph, taken in 1946, looks east from the centre of the bridge at Oosthoek.

well as Walcheren Island which commanded the river's mouth. Until these areas were cleared no ship could enter.

On 4 September Hitler issued special orders that certain places, including Boulogne, Calais, Dunkirk and Walcheren Island, were to be held as "fortresses" to the last. On 9 September the 2nd Division, having by-passed Dunkirk, entered Ostend, which had been partly demolished; nevertheless, some supplies flowed in through Ostend from 28 September, pending the opening of Antwerp. The capture of Boulogne and Calais was entrusted to the 3rd Canadian Division; the 2nd Division would clear the coast to the north, and the 4th Division (now under Major-General H. W. Foster) and the 1st Polish Armoured Division would advance on the right.

The plan for Boulogne called for a preliminary bombardment by heavy bombers and artillery, followed by an infantry assault by the 8th and 9th Brigades. The attack was launched on 17 September but Boulogne was encircled by strongly defended hills and its reduction took six days. More than 9500 prisoners were captured at a cost of 634 casualties. The harbour had been extensively damaged and could not be brought into use until 12 October. On 25 September the 7th and 8th Brigades attacked Calais and the adjacent cross-Channel batteries, but in spite of heavy support by the R.A.F. Bomber Command, fighting continued until 1 October; 7500 Germans surrendered. Canadian casualties for the operation were less than 300.

The Second British Army had now entered the Netherlands. Three major waterways – the Maas and the two main branches of the Rhine – separated Dempsey's men from the North German plain. Montgomery's plan was for airborne troops to secure the river crossings and for the Second Army to pass over these and swing south to the Ruhr. The attempt was made on 17 September. A crossing of the Maas was secured at Grave and the great bridge across the Waal was seized at Nijmegen. But the bridgehead established across the Neder Rijn at Arnhem could not be held. After an advance of 50 miles the Second Army could go no farther. The failure at Arnhem made it fairly obvious that the war would not end in 1944 but would continue through the winter and probably into the spring. Thus the opening of the port of Antwerp became absolutely necessary.

The Battle of the Scheldt

This task was given to First Canadian Army. Antwerp was 50 miles from the sea. North of the estuary lay South Beveland, once an island but now joined to the mainland by an isthmus. Beyond it lay the strongly

fortified island of Walcheren. South of the estuary, the flat polder country was below sea-level and protected by dykes. An attack here would have to cross two parallel obstacles, the Leopold Canal and the Canal de Dérivation de la Lys. The prospect was grim.

Broadly, the 2nd Division attacked north of the estuary and the 3rd Division south of it. In both areas the fighting was bitter, as the troops advanced through water and mud in the face of devastating fire. The 2nd Division, advancing north of Antwerp to close the eastern end of the South Beveland isthmus, made good progress until 8 October when the 5th Brigade approached the isthmus itself. Here crack German paratroopers barred the way and casualties were heavy as our men pressed the attack over open, flooded ground. On 16 October, under heavy pressure from General Eisenhower, Field-Marshal Montgomery brought the weight of Second British Army to bear to speed the opening of Antwerp. The British struck westwards to clear the Netherlands south of the Maas, thus sealing off the whole Scheldt region, while General Simonds, now commanding First Canadian Army in place of General Crerar who was sick in England, concentrated on the country immediately north-east of the Beveland isthmus. In this area Simonds employed the 1st British Corps, whose operations permitted the 2nd Division to get forward. On 24 October the isthmus was completely sealed off and the 2nd Division began the advance against South Beveland.

South of the estuary there was equally bitter fighting as the 3rd Division struck towards the little port of Breskens. Entrenched behind the two canals, the Germans resisted tenaciously, and although the Canadians used massed flamethrowers to cover the crossing of the Leopold Canal and later launched an amphibious operation against the rear of the enemy pocket, almost a month elapsed before all resistance ended. However, by 3 November the south shore of the Scheldt was firmly in Allied hands. The 2nd Division's advance into South Beveland, materially assisted by an amphibious landing by the 52nd British Division on the south shore, went well; by 31 October the peninsula had fallen.

Walcheren remained, and it was formidable. The only overland approach was a causeway from South Beveland, over half a mile long and only some 40 yards wide. The flats that the causeway crossed were too soft for infantry, and even at high tide the water was too shallow for assault boats or amphibious vehicles. Simonds planned a three-pronged attack: across the causeway; from the south across the Scheldt; and from the sea. On Simonds' urging, the R.A.F. Bomber Command had breached the dyke surrounding the island so

INFANTRY NEAR NIJMEGEN, HOLLAND
by Alex Colville (1920-   )
An infantry section returns after a tour of duty in the flooded lands between the Waal and the Neder Rijn in the winter of 1944-45.

that the central area was now inundated, and here amphibians could be used. The flooding hampered the enemy's movements, although some of his batteries remained in action on the dykes.

The Canadians attacked the causeway on 31 October. Some indication of the grimness of the struggle may be gathered from the fact that three Canadian battalions, in succession, were needed to establish a very precarious foothold at the far end. The 52nd British Division then passed through to continue the advance in conjunction with the waterborne attacks, also mounted by British formations. On 1 November, in one of the epic landings of the war, the Royal Navy put the 4th Special Service Brigade ashore on the west point of Walcheren. On 6 November the island's chief town fell. Two days later organized resistance on Walcheren ceased. The first Allied convoy entered Antwerp on 28 November.

The Battle of the Scheldt had been costly. Between 1 October and 8 November First Canadian Army suffered 6367 Canadian casualties; but 41,043 Germans had been captured, and — what mattered more — Antwerp had been opened. "The end of Naziism was in clear view", General Eisenhower said later, "when the first ship moved unmolested up the Scheldt."

147

Fighting in the Rhineland

The Canadians now entered a largely static period which lasted exactly three months. In December the Germans, in a last despairing offensive, struck through the snow-clad Ardennes at the First U.S. Army. Although this attack shook the Allies and disrupted their plans, it was speedily contained. The main Canadian force was not called upon to help counter the thrust. The heaviest Canadian fighting in this period was late in January, when units of the 4th Armoured Division had a nasty little battle to clear an enemy bridgehead on our side of the Maas at Kapelsche Veer.

With Antwerp open, Allied strength was built up for a spring offensive which in its first stage would destroy the enemy forces west of the Rhine. It would begin in the north, where Field-Marshal Montgomery had under his command the Ninth U.S. Army as well as his British and Canadian forces. First Canadian Army would thrust from the Nijmegen salient south-eastwards to clear the corridor between the Rhine and the Maas. The Ninth U.S. Army, striking north-eastward from the River Roer, was to link up with the Canadians on the Rhine opposite Wesel. The Second British Army would hold the line of the Maas.

Three main enemy defence lines faced First Canadian Army: first, a strong outpost screen; second, the Siegfried Line running through the Reichswald; and the Hochwald "layback" position covering the Rhine crossings at Wesel. There would be three main phases of attack. In the first, the 30th British Corps would clear the Reichswald. Thereafter the 2nd Canadian Corps would come in on the left and advance abreast of the 30th to the Rhine opposite Emmerich. The final phase called for breaking the Hochwald position and securing the line between the Maas and the Rhine from Geldern to Xanten.

In this battle General Crerar commanded the largest force a Canadian officer has ever directed in action. During February, he controlled in all 13 divisions, including nine from Britain. The 30th Corps struck the first blow with seven divisions under command, including the 2nd and 3rd Canadian.

Crerar's offensive went in as planned on the morning of 8 February "against the yellow light of the rising sun". During the night hundreds of R.A.F. heavy bombers had poured high explosive on towns vital to

Closing with the Siegfried Line. Two Buffalo-borne companies of The North Shore Regiment led the 8th Brigade's attack on 8 February 1945. Here they march to the amphibious vehicles.

(D.N.D. photo.)

Amphibious vehicles swim between the lines of trees marking the Kranenburg road during Operation "Veritable", February 1945.

the enemy's defences. The German forward positions were battered by an artillery bombardment from more than 1000 guns, and tactical aircraft lent close support to waves of tanks which clawed forward as soon as the artillery bombardment died. Behind the tanks came the infantry.

The enemy had not expected attack in this sector and his troops offered rather ineffective resistance. The German infantry division that bore the brunt of the onslaught was shattered. In the first assault, mud and flooded ground hampered the attackers more than armed resistance, but after the Scheldt the Canadians were used to such conditions. Amphibians floated over anti-tank ditches, wire and mines, and at times troops floundered through water three feet deep. By nightfall of the first day the outpost screen was broken. Unfortunately, the Germans had been able to flood the ground in front of the Ninth U.S. Army so effectively that its converging attack could not be mounted on 10 February as planned. Consequently, the enemy was able to reinforce his front in the Reichswald.

For days, violent fighting raged in the vast pine forest, but the Canadians advanced steadily towards the Siegfried Line, whose northern end passed through the Reichswald. On 10 February the 9th Canadian Infantry Brigade broke the tip of the Siegfried defences in the flooded area by the Rhine. The enemy threw in two

parachute and two panzer divisions and Montgomery allotted Crerar another armoured and another infantry division. Not until 13 February was the enemy driven from his defences and the Reichswald finally cleared. With that, the first phase ended; but the offensive continued remorselessly, on a two-corps front now. On 18 February the 30th Corps on the right cleared the last northern sector of the Siegfried Line. On the left the 2nd Canadian Corps, in bitter fighting, overcame a stubborn pocket of enemy resistance centered on Moyland Wood and took the enemy positions along the Goch-Calcar Road.

The last great obstacle before the Rhine was a ridge in front of Xanten, crowned along its crest by two forests, the Hochwald and the Balberger Wald. The 2nd Canadian Corps was ordered to launch a deliberate attack on this formidable position. The floods had at last subsided sufficiently to permit the launching of the Ninth U.S. Army's converging attack on 23 February. This, although it did not initially ease the Canadians' task, eventually made the enemy's defeat a certainty. With powerful artillery and tank support, the 2nd and 3rd Canadian Divisions (the former now commanded by Major-General A. B. Matthews) stormed forward on 26 February against the forward defences of the ridge. The day's objectives were seized after stern fighting. The 4th Division's armoured brigade, thrusting

149

Men of "B" Company, The Algonq[uin]
Regiment, moving forward towa[rd]
the Hochwald Gap, 1 March 194[5]

Churchill with First Canadian Army, 4 March 1945. Others left to right are General
Crerar; Field-Marshal Sir Alan Brooke, Chief of the Imperial General Staff; Lieut.-
General Simonds; and Field-Marshal Montgomery.

forward between the infantry divisions, also reached its objectives.

On the last day of February the 2nd Canadian Corps attacked the main Hochwald position and met fierce resistance, but the American advance to the south now began to affect Crerar's operations. As the Ninth U.S. Army thrust north, the German Command detached forces from the Canadian front, and in the first days of March the Canadians gained ground on the forest ridge. The 2nd Division gradually cleared the Hochwald and the 3rd Division did the same for the Balberger Wald. By the evening of 4 March the Hochwald position had been broken. Thereafter the Germans, still fighting stubbornly in their shrinking bridgehead, were steadily pushed back. Xanten fell on the 8th, and when on 10 March the enemy blew the Rhine bridges at Wesel, resistance ceased west of the Rhine. Thus, after many

perils and vicissitudes, our men stood at last on the banks of the great river which was the historic frontier of the Reich and its last line of defence. Between 8 February and 10 March, First Canadian Army had suffered 15,634 casualties, including 5304 Canadians, but it had captured more than 22,000 prisoners.

The main Allied attack across the Rhine was to be delivered north of the Ruhr by Montgomery's 21st Army Group, which still included the Ninth U.S. Army. A secondary attack would be launched from bridgeheads in the Frankfurt area farther south to encircle the Ruhr. The northern crossings of the Rhine would be made by the Ninth U.S. Army on the right and the Second British Army on the left. Although First Canadian Army as such took no part in the crossings, the 2nd Canadian Corps passed under command of the Second British Army and the 9th Canadian Infantry

Left: "Melville" Bridge. This bridge across the Rhine at Emmerich, completed by the 2nd Canadian Army Troops Engineers on 1 April 1945, is shown under construction.

Below: The bridge in operation, 2 April 1945.

(D.N.D. photo.)

(D.N.D. photo.)

Brigade, fighting under the 51st (Highland) Division, participated in the opening phase of the operation. First Canadian Army, waiting to resume an active role, could now anticipate having the whole Canadian field force under it, for the 1st Canadian Corps had arrived in North-West Europe from Italy.

The Rhine crossings began on the evening of 23 March, the infantry being ferried over in amphibians under the supporting fire of a great concentration of guns. Little opposition was encountered. Next morning 2926 aircraft and gliders, protected by a great force of fighters, launched an airborne attack. The 1st Canadian Parachute Battalion, still with the 6th Airborne Division, dropped successfully with the other paratroopers east of the river.

The enemy had consumed his last reserves in the bitter struggle west of the Rhine. At the beginning of April the Allied armies broke out of the northern Rhine bridgehead and, in step with U.S. forces farther south, began to drive deep into German territory. There was little to stop them now. The situation in the east was equally favourable, for there the Russians were rolling steadily towards Vienna and were on the Oder, ready to advance against Berlin itself.

The End of the War in Europe

The Canadian Army's role in these final days of the war was to open up the supply route to the north through Arnhem, and then to clear the North-Eastern Netherlands, the coastal belt of Germany eastwards to the Elbe, and the Western Netherlands. General Crerar used the 2nd Canadian Corps east of the Rhine to clear the North-Eastern Netherlands and the German coast as far as the mouth of the Weser. The 1st Canadian Corps dealt with the Germans remaining in the Western Netherlands north of the Maas.

(D.N.D. photo.)

Surrender of the Twenty-fifth German Army. At Wageningen, 5 May 1945, Lieut.-General Foulkes (left), G.O.C. 1st Canadian Corps, accepts the surrender of General Johannes Blaskowitz (second from right), commander of German forces in the Netherlands. Left foreground, H.R.H. Prince Bernhard.

152

The 2nd Corps' infantry divisions pushed rapidly forward, clearing Deventer, Zwolle and Groningen. The 4th Armoured Division (now commanded by Major-General C. Vokes) curved east over the flat North German plain to combine with the 1st Polish Armoured Division in thrusts on Emden, Wilhelmshaven and Oldenburg. The 3rd Division (now under Major-General R. H. Keefler) also moved on Emden and the 2nd Division advanced on Oldenburg, which was captured on 3 May.

In the Western Netherlands the 1st Canadian Corps attacked Arnhem on 12 April, clearing the town two days later. The liberation of Apeldoorn followed on 17 April. In a week's fighting, the route north through Arnhem had been opened, and the enemy had been driven back nearly 30 miles from his defences along the Ijssel. The Germans were now behind their defences in the area about and west of Utrecht. The German *Reichskommissar* in the Netherlands stated that, if the Allies would halt, he would refrain from destructive measures, would permit food to be brought in and would surrender his forces if Germany capitulated. On 22 April Montgomery halted the operations in the Western Netherlands, and on the 28th what amounted to a truce came into effect there. American and Russian troops had already met on the Elbe on 25 April, cutting Germany in two. On 30 April, as the Russians fought their way through Berlin, Hitler shot himself, and on 4 May the German forces facing 21st Army Group surrendered unconditionally. For the Canadians, the war in Europe was over. The formal surrender of all the German forces took place three days later at Reims.

After the defeat of Germany, Canada organized a Canadian Army Pacific Force — a division, with ancillary troops — for use against Japan. It was to operate under United States higher command and be organized and equipped on American lines. But on 6 August an atomic bomb was dropped on Hiroshima; and on the 9th a second atomic bomb destroyed Nagasaki. On 10 August Japan sued for peace. Her act of surrender was signed on 2 September, the day after orders had been issued for the disbandment of the Canadian Army Pacific Force.

In all, 730,625 Canadian men and women served in the army during the Second World War; 22,917 were killed and 52,679 were wounded. Men of the Canadian Army had helped defend Britain, they fought the Japanese at Hong Kong; and they paid with their blood for the lessons of Dieppe. Above all they had shared in the stiffest fighting of two great campaigns, in Italy in 1943-1945 and from France into Germany in 1944-1945. Once again, as in the First World War, they had borne the main burden of the nation's losses and had set those who would come after them a high example of courage, service and sacrifice.

THE AIR FORCE AT WAR 1939-1945

The Royal Canadian Air Force, facing the Second World War, was not without sources of spiritual strength. It could find inspiration in the brilliant record of Canadians in the air in 1914-1918 and encouragement in much admirable and original peacetime flying work in Canada in more recent days. The years just ahead were to witness achievements greater in many ways than any in the past. But in September 1939 the R.C.A.F. was materially ill-equipped for the tasks confronting it. No more than eight of the 11 permanent squadrons approved for the Home Defence Force in 1936 had been formed, and of these, only one, No. 5 (General Reconnaissance) Squadron, was fully trained and equipped for its operational role. The 12 auxiliary squadrons authorized in 1936 were in various stages of organization, and the seven that were mobilized absorbed the personnel of the other five.

Nevertheless, during the Second World War the small R.C.A.F. of 1939 expanded into the fourth largest air force of the Allied Powers, exceeded only by those of the United States, the Soviet Union and Britain. Its little group of obsolescent aeroplanes was gradually replaced by thousands of the latest training and operational aircraft; its personnel increased more than fifty-fold, and during the war 232,632 men and 17,030 women served in it. At home it built up a vast training organization, the British Commonwealth Air Training Plan, and put more than 40 operational squadrons into the field for coastal defence, shipping protection and other duties. Overseas the R.C.A.F. was able to provide 48 operational squadrons for duty in the Western European, Mediterranean and Far Eastern theatres. In addition, more Canadian aircrew actually served with R.A.F. than with R.C.A.F. squadrons overseas.

During the war the R.C.A.F. effort was divided into three principal parts. A large force was engaged in the B.C.A.T.P.; another was employed in the theatres of war overseas; and a third, stationed in Canada as the Home War Establishment, conducted operations in the Western Hemisphere.

British Commonwealth Air Training Plan

Even before the beginning of hostilities it was recognized that one of Canada's principal roles would be to provide an air training ground where, as in 1917-1918, instruction could be carried on away from the actual battle area. Representatives of the governments of the United Kingdom, Australia, New Zealand and Canada met in Ottawa, and on 17 December 1939 signed an agreement setting up the B.C.A.T.P., thereby preparing the way for making Canada what President Roosevelt later termed "the aerodrome of democracy".

The original plan provided for three Initial Training Schools, 13 Elementary Flying Training Schools, 16 Service Flying Training Schools, ten Air Observer Schools, ten Bombing and Gunnery Schools, two Air Navigation Schools and four Wireless Schools. Supplementing these were numerous other units for recruiting, training, maintenance and administration, making a total of 74 schools and depots. When fully developed, this establishment was expected to produce every month 520 pilots with elementary training, 544 pilots with service training, 340 air observers and 580 wireless operator-air gunners. (Royal Australian and Royal New Zealand Air Force pupil-pilots received their elementary training before coming to Canada.) The first schools were scheduled to open at the end of April 1940, and all were to be in operation within two years. The responsibility for establishing, administering and operating this great plan was

(D.N.D. photo.)

Briefing student observers before they take off in their Avro Ansons for an air exercise at No. 1 Air Observer School, Malton, Ontario.

placed on the shoulders of the R.C.A.F. and its total complement of scarcely more than 4000 officers and airmen. The number of aircraft required, estimated at 3540, was more than twelvefold the number of military aircraft in all Canada in 1939, and the Plan called for a staff of 33,052 air force personnel and 5951 civilians — a force eight times larger than the entire complement of the R.C.A.F.

It was a gigantic task. Sites for dozens of aerodromes had to be selected, roads and runways built, hangars, barracks and other buildings erected. Incredible quantities of equipment, from thumbtacks to aeroplanes, had to be procured. An army of experts had to be recruited — doctors, dentists, chaplains, technicians, executives, mechanics, bookkeepers, cooks, teachers, flying instructors — to receive, examine, equip, instruct and train the thousands of young men who were clamouring to enlist. Around the nucleus of R.C.A.F. personnel, and the specialist R.A.F. officers who had been sent to assist them, a force of skilled men from all walks of

life rapidly gathered. Among them were many of Canada's leading businessmen and engineers, many of her best-known doctors, bush pilots, scientists and lawyers. From the United States came American commercial pilots, eager to help in what they even then considered the common cause. In the initial stages the Department of Transport gave invaluable assistance in selecting and surveying sites for flying fields, and civilian flying organizations took over the task of running the Elementary and Air Observer Schools.

In the spring of 1940 the first schools opened and training began on schedule. A crisis developed in the late summer when, as a result of the desperate situation overseas after Dunkirk, the delivery of Anson trainer aircraft dropped to about one-half of what was expected. Without hesitation the Canadian Government took the initiative and entrusted the provision of aircraft to a crown company, Federal Aircraft Limited. The Plan was kept moving in high gear, but until the latter part of 1941, when Canadian aeroplanes became

156

available in quantity, many students trained on Harvards obtained from the United States instead of on Ansons. In the fall of 1940 Air Vice-Marshal L. S. Breadner, the Chief of the Air Staff, was able to announce that the success of the B.C.A.T.P. was no longer in doubt.

By the end of September 1941, seven months ahead of schedule, all but three of the B.C.A.T.P. schools were in operation and eight additional elementary schools had been opened. In June 1942, the number of training schools was increased to 67 (including 21 double schools) and ten new specialist schools were added for operational training, training flying instructors and other functions. In addition, the administration of 27 Royal Air Force units which had been transferred to or set up in Canada was also entrusted to the R.C.A.F.

At the close of 1943, when the Plan reached its maximum expansion, 97 B.C.A.T.P. and R.A.F. schools and 184 ancillary units were in operation. Over 3000 students were graduating each month, and the Plan had already produced almost 82,000 trained aircrew. So large was the reserve of aircrew in excess of immediate overseas needs that early in 1944 it was possi-

Students at No. 4 Elementary Flying Training School, Windsor Mills, Quebec, prepare for a flight in their Fleet Finches.

(D.N.D. photo.)

CONTROL TOWER
by Peter Whyte (1905-   )
No. 3 Service Flying Training School, Calgary, Alberta, where many B.C.A.T.P.
aircrew trained on Avro Ansons.

ble to reduce the training programme. The closing of schools was accelerated in October of that year and at the end of March 1945 the B.C.A.T.P. was officially terminated. In 1942 a new cost-sharing arrangement was worked out whereby Australia and New Zealand paid for their air training in Canada by a lump sum or per capita basis instead of accepting a percentage of the total cost as they had in 1939. Britain, however, agreed to accept a large proportion of the overall expense, roughly equal to 50 per cent of the cost of the Plan less the amounts paid by Australia and New Zealand. In 1946 the Canadian Government cancelled

Britain's outstanding indebtedness for the B.C.A.T.P., a sum amounting to $425,000,000.

All this was not accomplished without sacrifices, and more than 2300 air force personnel were killed in Canada during the war, although not all these were B.C.A.T.P. casualties.

In the beginning, only three types of aircrew were trained — pilots, air observers and wireless operator-air gunners — but the expansion of air operations overseas, and in particular the introduction of the four-engined bomber with its larger crew, made it necessary to modify and extend the training programme. Before the war

Left—Embryo aero-engine mechanics learning their trade at No. 1 Technical Training School, St. Thomas, Ontario, which produced over 35,000 technicians during the war.

Below—"Wings parade" at No. 2 Service Flying Training School, Uplands, Ontario, at which pilot graduates were presented with the coveted flying badge. The aircraft are Harvard trainers.

(D.N.D. photo.)

(D.N.D. photo)

ended, the Plan was producing eight different aircrew categories — pilot, navigator, navigator B (bombing training in addition to navigation), navigator W (additional wireless training), air bomber, wireless operator-air gunner, air gunner and flight engineer.

The ultimate total output of the British Commonwealth Air Training Plan was 131,553 aircrew, including almost 50,000 pilots, 18,500 wireless operator-air gunners and 15,900 navigators. More than 55 per cent of the graduates were members of the R.C.A.F. The R.A.F. contributed 32 per cent of the trainees, the Royal Australian Air Force slightly more than seven per cent, and the Royal New Zealand Air Force about five per cent. In addition, 2629 pilots and 704 air gunners were trained for the Royal Navy's Fleet Air Arm.

In Defence of Canada

A year before the war began, Eastern Air Command and Western Air Command had been organized to cooperate with the navy and army in the defence of Canada's coasts. Their squadrons were mobilized in August 1939 and had undertaken patrols even before the British declaration of hostilities. Eastern Air Command suffered the first R.C.A.F. casualties of the war. These two formations continued to conduct operations over the Atlantic and Pacific until the final surrender of Germany and Japan. The number of bases increased until each coast had a network, curving from Labrador

A Hudson patrol bomber of No. 11 (Bomber Reconnaissance) Squadron, R.C.A.F., based at Dartmouth, N.S. circles an R.C.N. "Bassett" Class minesweeper near Halifax in the spring of 1940.

(D.N.D. photo.)

A Liberator of No. 10 (Bomber Reconnaissance) Squadron, R.C.A.F., helps escort the surrendered German submarine U–190 to St. John's, Newfoundland, on 3 June 1945.

through Newfoundland to the Maritimes and from Alaska to the southern part of Vancouver Island. On both coasts, flying conditions were uncertain because of sudden fogs, and many of the bases and posts were virtually inaccessible except by air. Isolation, boredom and the weather were the chief enemies in these lonely places.

As soon as possible, the pre-war Stranraers, Wapitis, Deltas and Sharks with which the home-based squadrons were originally equipped were replaced by more modern Hudsons and Digbys. With the advent of the Catalina and Canso and later the Very Long Range Liberator, it was possible to extend convoy escort and anti-submarine sweeps hundreds of miles out over the

Atlantic — and sometimes right across it. As a protection against the remote possibility of air attack by enemy long-range bombers or shipborne aircraft, fighter squadrons of Hurricanes, Kittyhawks and, later, Mosquitoes, were formed to reinforce the bomber-reconnaissance squadrons on both coasts. The bulk of the work naturally fell to Eastern Air Command, and even after Pearl Harbor the major responsibility continued to be E.A.C.'s, whose Air Officer Commanding, in cooperation with the Royal Canadian Navy, ultimately directed all the work of air protection in the North-West Atlantic.

The first 18 months of the war were relatively quiet, because U-boats had not yet made their way westward,

161

but from the spring of 1941 onwards, the resources of E.A.C. were taxed to their utmost in the grim battle of the Atlantic. Even before the United States entered the war enemy U-boats were sighted and attacked in Canadian coastal waters; later they even penetrated into the St. Lawrence. The most critical period came in 1942 and the first five months of 1943, when submarine activity in the North Atlantic reached its peak. Long-range aircraft played an important part in beating back the attack and turning the tide. Although the introduction of the acoustic torpedo and later of the "Schnorkel" breathing-tube presented serious new problems, the sea and air forces of Britain, the United States and Canada retained the upper hand until the last U-boats surrendered in May 1945.

Aircraft of Eastern Air Command sank six submarines and damaged at least three more so heavily that they were forced to return to port. However, this figure is no full measure of the Command's contribution, nor would the total number of sightings and attacks express it. A better indication is to be found in the thousands upon thousands of hours flown by the aircrew, through weather that was often appalling, carefully searching the grey expanse of water, forcing the enemy to crash-dive or remain submerged, driving him away from our convoys and permitting the ships to continue on their way unmolested. It was weary and unglamorous work, but its importance cannot be over-emphasized, for the battle lines of Western Europe were fed by the long Atlantic sea lanes.

There was much less activity on the Pacific coast, but the Japanese threat led to a general strengthening of Western Air Command in 1941-1942. Many of the elderly Stranraers, which had been replaced by Catalinas in E.A.C. in 1941, were in turn replaced in W.A.C. by Cansos in 1942. In the late spring of 1942 Western Air Command sent one bomber-reconnaissance and two fighter squadrons to Alaska and the Aleutians to help American forces drive the Japanese from Kiska and Attu. For months they carried out reconnaissance patrols and strafing missions in that isolated theatre of war. On one of these missions, a Canadian Kittyhawk pilot shot down a Japanese Zero, the only enemy aircraft destroyed by Home War Establishment squadrons during the war. The Canadians remained in the Aleutians, flying side-by-side with the Americans in "the worst flying weather in the world", until the Japanese withdrew from Kiska in July 1943. Later, another potential threat developed when the Japanese began sending paper balloons carrying incendiaries and small bombs across the Pacific. Although the balloons kept the West Coast fighter squadrons on the alert for many months, they caused no casualties and no appreciable damage in Canada.

To move aircraft and supplies from the United States to Alaska and the Aleutians, a Northwest Staging Route, the air counterpart of the Alaska Highway, was developed within Western Air Command. Along this aerial highway, too, flowed great quantities of aircraft and material for the Soviet Union. The volume and importance of the traffic finally led to the formation, in June 1944, of a new command, North-West Air Command, with headquarters at Edmonton, to administer the chain of airfields and aircraft control facilities.

Before the war the R.C.A.F. had a variety of transport aircraft but no transport organization higher than a flight. Military operations on the home front soon brought an increase in air transport work and resulted in the formation of a few transport and ferry squadrons. The first squadron assigned to air transport work was No. 12 Communication Squadron which was formed in August 1940. Two heavy transport squadrons, Nos. 164 and 165, came into existence in 1943. In December 1943 No. 168 Squadron began flying service mail overseas, using Flying Fortresses, Dakotas and Liberators. This was the first time that the R.C.A.F. maintained a regular trans-oceanic transport operation. It continued for more than two years, during which time 636 Atlantic crossings were completed. In February 1945, No. 9 (Transport) Group was organized with three squadrons and its headquarters at Rockcliffe, Ontario.

On both coasts the Aircraft Detection Corps contributed outstanding service. This was an organization of volunteer civilian ground observers — farmers, woodsmen, schoolboys, housewives, fishermen — who reported movements of aircraft and kept watch for submarines or suspicious surface vessels. As fortune had it, there was little enemy activity to report but on many occasions the network of observer posts helped to rescue aircraft in distress. Although the Corps was officially disbanded on 15 November 1944, observers remained on watch in certain key areas until the end of hostilities.

The R.C.A.F. Overseas

The heavy commitments of the R.C.A.F. in the development and administration of the B.C.A.T.P., in addition to its responsibility for Canadian air defence, made it necessary to retain the greater part of the Force of 1939 at home and, in the early months of the war, only three squadrons could be spared for overseas service. The first of these was No. 110 Army Co-operation Squadron, which was strengthened by personnel from No. 112 and No. 2 Squadrons. It arrived in Britain in February 1940 and began training with the intention of accompanying the 1st Canadian Division to France. The previous month the Overseas Headquarters R.C.A.F. had been formed in London, absorbing the staff and functions of the former Air Liaison Office there. In June, when the general military situation was extremely critical, No. 112 Army Co-operation Squadron and No. 1 Fighter Squadron also went overseas, the latter reinforced by personnel from No. 115 Squadron. The fall of France and the cessation of land operations in Western Europe condemned the two army cooperation squadrons to a long period of waiting, but No. 1 Fighter Squadron saw action in the Battle of

Britain. (below, page 166).

In October 1940 the Chief of the Air Staff advised the Minister that arrangements for the formation of Canadian squadrons under Article 15 of the B.C.A.T.P. agreement, left unsettled a year earlier, should now be completed without delay. In December and January the Minister of National Defence, Colonel J. L. Ralston, discussed the matter with the United Kingdom Secretary of State for Air, Sir Archibald Sinclair, and the "Sinclair-Ralston Agreement", signed on 7 January 1941, provided that the R.A.F. would endeavour to form 25 R.C.A.F. "Article 15" squadrons overseas by May 1942.

By the close of 1940 the first trickle of B.C.A.T.P. graduates began to flow overseas, most being posted to

COASTAL COMMAND HARBOUR, OBAN
by Eric Aldwinckle (1909-   )
Nos. 422 and 423 Squadrons, R.C.A.F., operated their Sunderlands for a time from
this base in Argyllshire, Scotland, on anti-submarine and convoy protection patrols.

(Courtesy The National Gallery of Canada.)

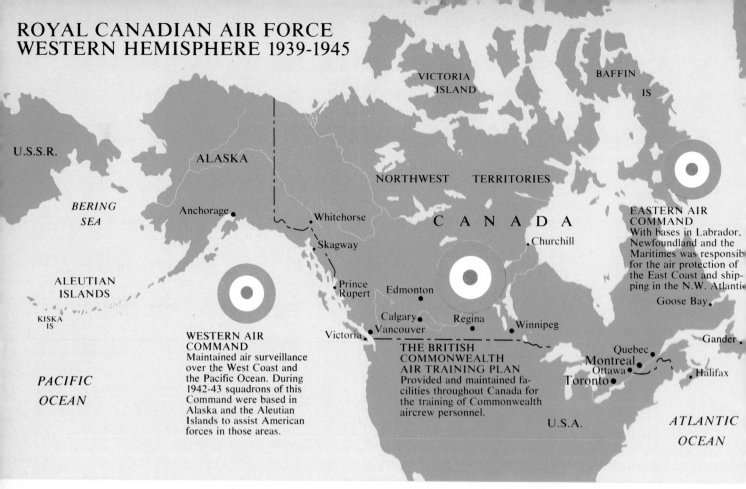

ROYAL CANADIAN AIR FORCE
WESTERN HEMISPHERE 1939-1945

VICTORIA ISLAND

BAFFIN IS

U.S.S.R.

ALASKA

NORTHWEST TERRITORIES

BERING SEA

Anchorage

Whitehorse

C A N A D A

.Churchill

EASTERN AIR COMMAND
With bases in Labrador, Newfoundland and the Maritimes was responsib for the air protection of the East Coast and ship- ping in the N.W. Atlanti

Skagway

ALEUTIAN ISLANDS

Prince Rupert

Edmonton

Goose Bay.

KISKA IS

WESTERN AIR COMMAND
Maintained air surveillance over the West Coast and the Pacific Ocean. During 1942-43 squadrons of this Command were based in Alaska and the Aleutian Islands to assist American forces in those areas.

Calgary. Regina

Victoria Vancouver

Winnipeg

Gander.

Quebec

PACIFIC OCEAN

THE BRITISH COMMONWEALTH AIR TRAINING PLAN
Provided and maintained fa- cilities throughout Canada for the training of Commonwealth aircrew personnel.

Montreal.
Ottawa.
Toronto.

.Halifax

U.S.A.

ATLANTIC OCEAN

In addition to the air defence of Canada, the Royal Canadian Air Force built up the vast training organization for the British Commonwealth Air Training Plan.

R.A.F. units. In the initial stages of the Plan many air-crew graduates had to be retained in Canada as in-structors for the further expansion of the Air Training Plan. As the number of personnel available for service abroad increased, it became more practicable to organ-ize the new Royal Canadian Air Force squadrons in Britain. In the beginning, many of these new units were R.C.A.F. in name rather than fact, until the policy of "Canadianization" eventually changed the situation. When this expansion of the R.C.A.F. overseas began in the spring of 1941, a new system of squadron num-bering was adopted to avoid confusion with R.A.F. units. The 400-449 block was allotted to the R.C.A.F. and the three original squadrons were given new num-bers: No. 110 Squadron became No. 400, No. 1 became 401, and No. 112 (which had been re-organized as No. 2 Fighter Squadron in December 1940) became No. 402 Squadron.

The first R.C.A.F. unit formed overseas was No. 403 Fighter Squadron, which came into being on 1 March 1941; 17 more squadrons were formed that year. By the end of 1941, however, the Air Minister and the Chief of the Air Staff were deeply perturbed to learn that of the 8595 Canadian graduates of the B.C.T.A.P. who had been sent overseas only about 500 were to be

found in the 18 R.C.A.F. squadrons, whereas in the light of the Sinclair-Ralston Agreement about half of them might have been expected to be serving there. It was no secret that many British officers were lukewarm to the idea of national squadrons, preferring instead one air force for the Commonwealth. Months of dis-cussion and argument ensued, and the problem of "Canadianization" was never quite fully resolved. How-ever, after the spring of 1943, when the Canadian Government finally accepted full financial responsibility for R.C.A.F. units overseas,* the situation markedly improved. In February 1944, when the "Balfour-Power Agreement", the last of the Anglo-Canadian agreements governing the B.C.A.T.P., was drawn up by Captain the Rt. Hon. H. H. Balfour, the British Parliamentary Under-Secretary of State for Air, and the Canadian Air Minister, it was specified that for the war against Japan the R.C.A.F. would be as completely under Canadian control as the Canadian Army had been in the German war; but peace came before this new system could be inaugurated.

*Until this time, Canada had paid only the difference between R.A.F. and R.C.A.F. rates of pay for R.C.A.F. men serving in these squadrons, and their equipment was paid for by the R.A.F.

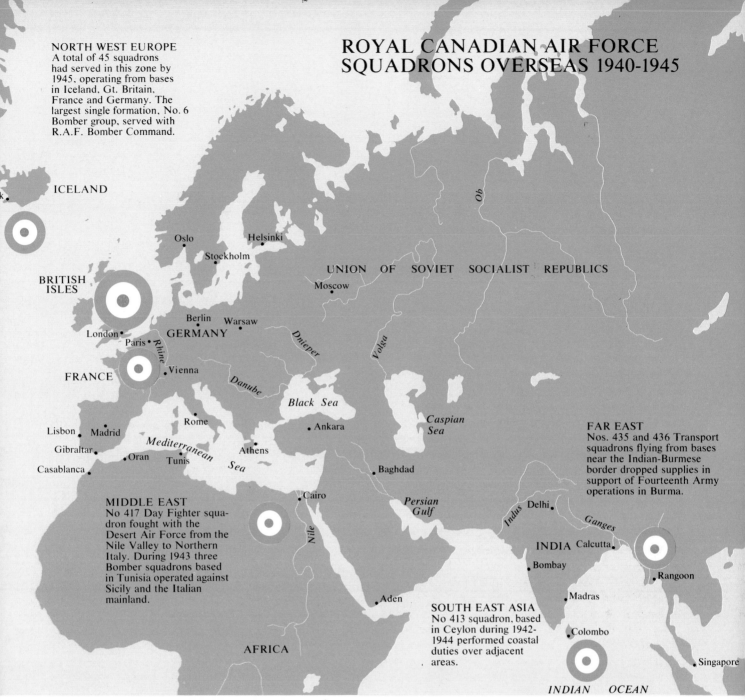

ROYAL CANADIAN AIR FORCE SQUADRONS OVERSEAS 1940-1945

NORTH WEST EUROPE
A total of 45 squadrons had served in this zone by 1945, operating from bases in Iceland, Gt. Britain, France and Germany. The largest single formation, No. 6 Bomber group, served with R.A.F. Bomber Command.

ICELAND

BRITISH ISLES

London

Oslo   Helsinki
Stockholm

UNION   OF   SOVIET   SOCIALIST   REPUBLICS

Moscow

Berlin   Warsaw
GERMANY
Paris   Rhine
FRANCE   Vienna
Danube

Dnieper

Volga

Lisbon   Madrid   Rome
Mediterranean
Gibraltar   Oran   Athens
Casablanca   Tunis   Sea

Black Sea

Ankara

Caspian
Sea

FAR EAST
Nos. 435 and 436 Transport squadrons flying from bases near the Indian-Burmese border dropped supplies in support of Fourteenth Army operations in Burma.

Baghdad

Persian
Gulf

Indus   Delhi

Ganges

INDIA   Calcutta

Bombay

MIDDLE EAST
No 417 Day Fighter squadron fought with the Desert Air Force from the Nile Valley to Northern Italy. During 1943 three Bomber squadrons based in Tunisia operated against Sicily and the Italian mainland.

Cairo

Nile

Aden

SOUTH EAST ASIA
No 413 squadron, based in Ceylon during 1942-1944 performed coastal duties over adjacent areas.

Madras

Colombo

Rangoon

Singapore

AFRICA

INDIAN   OCEAN

The Royal Canadian Air Force provided 48 operational squadrons for service overseas, 1940-1945. This map shows the areas over which the squadrons operated.

Ten more Canadian squadrons were formed in 1942, four in 1943 and nine in 1944, so that by the end of the war the number of squadrons in the overseas 400-series had grown to 44. Included in this number were six squadrons which, after periods of service in Eastern or Western Air Commands, were transferred to Britain in late 1943 and early 1944 to carry out a tour of operations with the Second Tactical Air Force. Moreover, one squadron was detached from Eastern Air Command to operate from Iceland and Northern Scotland. In addition to these 45 units, there were also three Air Observation Post squadrons (Nos. 664, 665 and 666) flown by officers of the Royal Canadian Artillery and maintained by R.C.A.F. personnel. Of the 48 R.C.A.F. squadrons overseas, 15 were bomber, 14 day-fighter, three fighter-reconnaissance, four night-fighter and intruder, six coastal, three transport and three A.O.P.

The R.C.A.F. squadrons overseas, although definitely Canadian, did not function in Canadian commands but came under the operational control of the Royal Air Force. Thus all but one of the Canadian fighter squadrons operated under the R.A.F. Fighter Command or the Second Tactical Air Force, while those squadrons engaged in anti-submarine and anti-shipping duties came under the R.A.F. Coastal Command. The largest R.C.A.F. formation overseas, No. 6 Bomber Group, operated under the R.A.F. Bomber Command, and those squadrons that flew in Asia and the Mediterranean were components of R.A.F. commands there.

R.C.A.F. Fighter Operations

No. 1 Fighter Squadron arrived in Britain in the critical period of May and June 1940, when France was crumbling and the cause of freedom was in peril. After a few weeks' training, the squadron began operations on 19 August 1940, at a time when the *Luftwaffe's* attacks on southern England were increasing in intensity. The first few days resulted only in fruitless "scrambles"; then, on 26 August, the Canadian Hurricane pilots finally encountered a formation of Dornier 215 bombers and shot down three of them. Eight weeks later, when the squadron flew to Scotland for a well-earned rest, its score stood at 31 enemy aircraft destroyed and 43 more probably destroyed or damaged. Sixteen of the squadron's Hurricanes had been lost in action; three pilots had been killed and ten wounded or injured – the first R.C.A.F. combat casualties. In the Battle of Britain the R.C.A.F. had received its baptism of fire and had acquitted itself with distinction.

It was the summer of 1941 before Canadian fighter units, whose number had now increased to five, were again heavily engaged in action. In the interval, the character of the air war had changed. The *Luftwaffe's* daylight offensive against Britain had been repulsed with heavy loss, and Fighter Command, released from its defensive role, lost no time in going over to the offensive. Late in December 1940, aircraft of Fighter Command began daylight operations over northern France, starting an air offensive which grew steadily in magnitude until the day of final victory. In time, many types of offensive operations were developed in addition to the routine work of patrolling over convoys moving along the coast, but broadly speaking the activities of the fighters fell into two categories – "rhubarbs" and "circuses". The purpose of a "rhubarb" was to hit the enemy on the ground where it would damage him most. Hurricanes and Spitfires in pairs or larger formations struck into Nazi-occupied France and Belgium to attack enemy movement by rail and road, munition factories and airfields, and gun positions. The "circus" was a large formation of bombers and fighters which roared high across the Channel to strike at a railway junction, an airfield or a munition plant. It had a twofold object — to destroy the enemy's communications and industries, and to draw the *Luftwaffe* into the air where the fighter escort could engage it. Similar operations were directed against enemy naval and merchant vessels that ventured to move in daylight along the coast of Hitler's *Festung Europa*. These operations forced the Germans to maintain large anti-aircraft defences in the threatened areas and at the same time steadily whittled down the *Luftwaffe's* fighter strength.

In all this work, squadrons of R.C.A.F. Hurricanes and Spitfires played their part. At first the Canadian squadrons flew in formations with R.A.F. units, but presently an all-Canadian wing of three squadrons was formed, and by the time the Normandy D Day arrived there were three of these R.C.A.F. Spitfire wings as well as a wing flying dive-bombing Typhoons and a reconnaissance wing of Spitfires and Mustangs.

On 19 August 1942, when a large raiding force principally composed of Canadian soldiers struck at the German-held port of Dieppe (above, pages 119-122), eight of the 74 Allied squadrons that gave aerial support belonged to the R.C.A.F. The Allied air forces fulfilled their function of protecting our armada of shipping off Dieppe, but the cost was high. The *Luftwaffe* reacted strongly and shot down two Allied aeroplanes for every one it lost itself. The Royal Air Force lost more aircraft over Dieppe than on any other day of the war. R.C.A.F. losses amounted to 13 aircraft.

After some sharp encounters in the air in the summer and autumn of 1943, the German fighter squadrons almost disappeared from the coastal area for the six months preceding the invasion of Normandy. Many had been withdrawn to the Reich in a vain attempt to stem the devastating daylight blows of the U.S.A.A.F. Fortresses and Liberators. However, the squadrons and wings of Second Tactical Air Force had no lack of work as the aerial preparation for D Day gained momentum.

In the spring of 1944 the Spitfires became fighter-bombers, carrying under each wing a 500-lb. bomb to blast bridges, railway junctions, radar posts and coastal defences. Again and again they dive-bombed the carefully camouflaged launching sites the enemy was constructing in the Somme and Pas de Calais areas in preparation for the V-1 "buzz-bomb" offensive against England. An R.C.A.F. wing of Typhoon fighter-bombers, formed early in 1944, also took an active part in all these operations.

The problem of providing the invading armies with immediate air support had received intensive study long before the Allies were ready to return to the continent. Since 1940, when the Germans had demonstrated how effectively formations of dive-bombers could be employed in support of troops, the R.A.F. had been revising its concept of close support. In the pre-war years, obsessed with the idea of dealing a knockout blow against an enemy homeland from the air, the R.A.F. had given little thought to the use of ground-attack aircraft — an oversight which led to a long argument with the British Army. In time the basic weakness in air support organization was overcome and the Desert Air Force had great success with its fighters, fighter-bombers and reconnaissance squadrons which kept in constant touch with the front-line troops and helped them develop their ground attack. For the invasion of Europe two complete groups were formed on these lines.

Neither General A. G. L. McNaughton, the Commander of First Canadian Army, nor Air Marshal H. Edwards, the senior R.C.A.F. officer overseas, was directly involved in determining air support policy but they watched it develop with growing interest and concern. Ever since No. 400 Army Co-operation Squadron had arrived in England in 1940, it had been assumed that the R.C.A.F. would support the Canadian ground forces when the time came to go into battle. Over the years the R.C.A.F. overseas came to have three reconnaissance squadrons, Nos. 400, 414 and 430, which operated as No. 39 Reconnaissance Wing from R.C.A.F. Station Dunsfold (built by the Royal Canadian Engineers). The squadrons were equipped with North American Mustangs, suitable for ground attack as well as for taking reconnaissance photographs, and when not working with the army on training schemes, they frequently skimmed across the Channel on photo-reconnaissance or ground attack sorties. Nos. 400 and 414 Squadrons had taken part in the Dieppe attack, one of the first big experiments in tactical air support.

In March 1943, No. 39 Reconnaissance Wing was part of an experimental composite group which supported the Canadian Army in Exercise "Spartan", when it rehearsed its planned role of breaking out from a beachhead established by another force. Shortly after "Spartan", the British Chiefs of Staff announced that the Second Tactical Air Force, whose main components were the two composite groups, would begin to form in June. The Canadian Government had always assumed that, when the time came, Royal Canadian Air Force squadrons would support the First Canadian Army in battle. After representations by McNaughton and Edwards, Air Chief Marshal Sir Trafford Leigh-Mallory, the C.-in-C. Allied Expeditionary Air Force, agreed in June 1943 to assign No. 83 Group, to which the R.C.A.F. reconnaissance and fighter squadrons were to be transferred, to the First Canadian Army. Out of the discussions with Leigh-Mallory came another suggestion — that some home-defence squadrons from Canada be added to No. 83 Group. With the Japanese

threat from the Aleutians removed, the Canadian Government agreed to sending six home-defence squadrons and about 5000 administrative and technical personnel to the United Kingdom (above, page 165).

Second Tactical Air Force came into embryo existence on 1 June 1943 as planned. In July, six of the seven R.C.A.F. fighter units in Fighter Command were moved to No. 83 Group where they were formed into two tactical wings. Army Co-operation Command also disappeared and No. 39 Reconnaissance Wing, formerly part of that command, joined No. 83 Group in July. Late in the year the six squadrons arrived from Canada and in February were added to No. 83 Group as two tactical wings, one equipped with Spitfires and the other with dive-bombing Typhoons. Although No. 83 Group was not to be an all-Canadian formation, as at one time Edwards had rather optimistically hoped it might be, 15 of its 29 squadrons and half its ground establishment of approximately 10,000 were Canadians.*

The reorganization did not bring an immediate change in the day-to-day activities of the individual pilots. During the summer of 1943 the operations of the two tactical fighter wings continued to be planned and directed by Fighter Command. Their main task was to escort American day bombers to and from attacks on enemy airfields and communication centres in France. All the R.C.A.F. squadrons in No. 83 Group had a dual capacity. The Spitfires could dive-bomb as well as fight, and the Typhoons, primarily dive-bombers, could hold their own against German fighters. So too could the Mustangs whose main work was reconnaissance and low-level attack. For the invasion these activities had to be harnessed in aid of the ground forces, and in the winter the R.C.A.F. wings spent much time in perfecting their air-to-ground communications with army formations. In the spring of 1944 they began to live under canvas and, in anticipation of their mobile existence on the Continent, remained always ready to break camp and move to another airfield.

Although it had been understood that No. 83 Group would work in conjunction with First Canadian Army and No. 84 Group, which contained no R.C.A.F. squadrons, with the Second British Army, the exact opposite occurred. On 26 January 1944, Leigh-Mallory announced that No. 83 Group would support Second British Army and not First Canadian Army, as in the original plan. This announcement came just after it had been confirmed that in the invasion plan First Canadian Army would be used as a follow-up army

*The headquarters staff, however, remained entirely British, although after the group moved to the Continent two R.C.A.F. officers became members of it.

NORMANDY DUST BOWL
by R. S. Hyndman (1911-   )
R.C.A.F. Spitfires of No. 126 Wing taking off from Beny-sur-Mer in the beachhead, June 1944. Note the
distinctive black and white "invasion stripes", designed to protect the aircraft from Allied gunners.

and that the Second British Army would command the one Canadian and two British seaborne assaulting divisions. Consequently, military logic perhaps dictated that No. 83 Group, the more experienced of the two composite groups, should support the assaulting force. No. 84 group, which had begun to form only in the autumn of 1943, would be ready in time to accompany First Canadian Army into action. Thus the expectation that Canadian land and air forces would go into battle together came to an abrupt and disappointing end. The decision was defensible on purely military grounds, but it is interesting to note that it was taken shortly after both McNaughton and Edwards, the prime movers behind the policy of keeping the Canadian fighting forces together, had been posted back to Canada and

at a time when First Canadian Army had only an acting commander.

From Normandy to the Baltic

Just after midnight on 6 June 1944 a force of 190 Halifax and Lancaster bombers of No. 6 Group dropped 870 tons of bombs on gun positions on the coast of Normandy. At dawn the Canadian fighter wings were over the beaches, standing guard while the Allied forces launched the invasion of North-West Europe. The R.C.A.F. Typhoon Wing dive-bombed enemy strongpoints overlooking the beaches just before the Canadian infantry waded ashore. Then, when the beachheads were firmly established, the R.C.A.F. gave air support to the Canadian and British forces during the long and

Above—A Spitfire IX of No. 416 Squadron, R.C.A.F., waits for the next sortie near Bazenville in mid-June 1944.

Left—Pierced steel plate matting enabled tactical aircraft to fly from forward fields which would otherwise have been unusable.

bitter fighting around Caen. By the end of June all five R.C.A.F. wings were based in Normandy in close support of Second British Army. The *Luftwaffe* did not often appear over the battle area, and on the few occasions when it did come out in strength, it lost heavily. On 28 June R.C.A.F. Spitfires had their record day, shooting down 26 enemy aircraft and crippling a dozen others. Four days later they destroyed 20 more and damaged 11.

Ground strafing, which steadily reduced the *Wehrmacht's* armoured fighting vehicles and motor transport, reached a climax in the four days between 17 and 20 August when the German Seventh Army, caught in a pocket between Falaise and Argentan, was seeking to escape eastward. From dawn to dark Spitfires and Typhoons raked the long columns of enemy vehicles with cannon and machine-gun fire and left the roads strewn with blazing, shattered wrecks. The R.C.A.F. wings alone estimated that they had destroyed or damaged more than 2600 vehicles.

Then began the long pursuit across northern France

169

and Belgium into the Netherlands and finally through the West Wall, over the Rhine and across the plains of north-western Germany. The fighter wings covered the advance of the armies, drove the German Air Force out of the sky, blasted bridges and strongpoints and paralysed enemy movement by road and rail. Outstanding exploits were performed by R.C.A.F. pilots during this period. The first enemy jet fighter to be destroyed in aerial battle by Commonwealth forces was shot down by five Spitfires of No. 401 Squadron. On New Year's Day 1945, when German aircraft attempted to surprise the Allies on their airfields in a New Year raid, R.C.A.F. Spitfires and Typhoons destroyed at least 36 enemy machines.

When hostilities ended, No. 126 R.C.A.F. Spitfire Wing had flown 22,372 sorties since D Day and was credited with destroying 361 enemy aircraft, probably destroying 17 and damaging 170. The record of No. 127, the second Canadian Spitfire wing, was equally impressive. During the same period No. 143 Typhoon Wing made 11,928 dive-bombing sorties and dropped 6442 tons of bombs on German defences, lines of communication and other objectives. The Typhoon wing calculated that it had blown up 16 bridges and two lock gates, cut rail lines in 1210 places and destroyed or damaged over 3600 locomotives, freight cars, tanks, vehicles and barges. The pilots had repeatedly been commended for the support given troops on the ground.

Throughout this long period, No. 39 Reconnaissance Wing also performed invaluable services, carrying out photographic and tactical reconnaissances to gather information for the staff planning for "Overlord" and

(D.N.D. photo.)

From a newly-harvested field in Normandy these R.C.A.F Typhoon pilots pare for a rocket-firing against a German tank centration.

then, moving to the continent, continuing this work for the Second British Army as it fought its way from the beaches of Normandy to the banks of the Elbe and beyond. The wing was the first major R.C.A.F. formation to move its base across the Rhine, and it ended the war deeper in Germany than any other Royal Canadian Air Force unit.

With the Desert Air Force

In addition to the squadrons that served in Western Europe with Fighter Command and Second Tactical Air Force, another R.C.A.F. day-fighter squadron, No. 417, flew with the famous Desert Air Force on operations from the Nile valley in Egypt to the plains of northern Italy. Its Spitfires provided protection for the port of Alexandria, participated in the closing stages of the Tunisian campaign, covered the Allied invasions of Sicily and Calabria, guarded the beachhead at Anzio, and then, becoming fighter-bombers, supported the Eighth Army, including the 1st Canadian Corps, as it slogged its way up the peninsula.

Night-Fighting

When the war began, night-fighting was in the experimental stage, the Bristol Blenheim being the first aircraft to use the highly secret interception radar. By the time the R.C.A.F. night-fighter squadrons (Nos. 406, 409 and 410) became operational in the autumn of 1941, Beaufighters equipped with A.I. (airborne interception radar) were in use, and the *Luftwaffe's* large-scale night attacks on England had been checked. Sporadic enemy raids continued, however, and in the winter

of 1943-1944 the Germans made a number of attacks as reprisals for Allied bombing. In the course of these the Canadian night-fighter teams destroyed 55 enemy aircraft, probably destroyed another 100 and damaged 27. The invasion of Normandy opened a new chapter in their history, as the squadrons, now flying Mosquitoes, patrolled over the beach-heads and enemy rear areas to intercept German night raiders. In the last 11 months of the war, the three squadrons shot down or destroyed on the ground more than 150 enemy aircraft and counted 60 more as probably destroyed or damaged.

When the V-1 flying-bombs began buzzing across the Channel in June 1944, two R.C.A.F. Mosquito squadrons were detailed to patrol the night skies as part of the first line of defence. During the comparatively short time it was engaged on this work, No. 409 Squadron destroyed ten flying-bombs. The other squadron, No. 418, shot down 77 over the Channel and five more over the English coast.

Before it entered the V-1 campaign, No. 418 had won an outstanding reputation as an intruder squadron. Flying first Bostons and then Mosquitoes, the crews had been engaged on a counter-offensive against the enemy's night operations, patrolling over enemy airfields to attack bombers as they returned from raids or enemy night-fighters that sought to intercept our own bombers. When no targets were to be found in the air, the intruder crews dropped bombs on runways, bridges or rail junctions. Many victories were scored on these night sorties, but the squadron achieved its greatest success with daylight intrusions deep into enemy-held territory when the crews sometimes penetrated as far as the

405 Squadron was the
r R.C.A.F. Bomber unit
ned overseas and the
t to fly on operations.
e its twin-engined Wel-
tons are shown being
pared for a night raid
the Pocklington, York-
e, base in the summer
1941.

.D. photo.)

Baltic Coast.

In the three years between November 1941 and November 1944, when No. 418 was employed as an intruder unit, it destroyed 105 enemy aircraft in the air and 73 on the ground and damaged 103 in combat or strafes. Then, in the last five months of the war, the squadron was converted to close support work for the armies in Western Europe, making night bombing attacks on enemy concentrations and communications.

The R.C.A.F. in Bomber Command

When the war began, R.A.F. Bomber Command's aircraft consisted of single-engined Battles and twin-engined Blenheims, Whitleys, Hampdens and Wellingtons. Five years later these sturdy warplanes of the early days had been replaced by fast twin-engined Mosquitoes and great four-engined heavy bombers, the Halifax and Lancaster. Mosquitoes were regularly carrying 4000-pound "block-busters" as far as Berlin, and the normal bomb load for the heavy bombers was four to five tons of high explosive and incendiary bombs. The Command increased in size until, at the end of May 1942, with some assistance from the bombers of its Operational Training Units, it could muster

1000 aircraft for a single operation. In addition, it had its own force of intruders which contributed to the offensive by harassing the enemy's fighter defences.

Bombs, too, grew from the 500-pounders used in the first raids of September 1939 to the giant earth-shaking "Ten-Ton Tessie" of 1944 and 1945. Moreover, the whole technique of bombing had been transformed by the use of radar, which guided the aircraft to the target, identified the objective even when cloud completely covered the ground, and told the bomb-aimer precisely when to let his missiles drop. Pathfinders led the way for the main bomber force, pinpointing and marking the target with flares, while Master Bombers directed the ensuing attack. Instead of using small forces to scatter bombs individually over several targets, Bomber Command now concentrated its great strength on one objective at a time to saturate it with devastating effect, as was done at Cologne, Bremen, Hamburg and Berlin.

The remarkable expansion of R.A.F. Bomber Command was reflected in the development of the Canadian bomber squadrons. On the night of 12-13 June 1941, the first Canadian bomber operation was carried out by three Wellingtons of No. 405 Squadron. A year later,

Many R.C.A.F. flyers took part in a daylight raid by 94 Lancaster bombers on the Schneider Armaments Arsenal at Le Creusot, France, on 17 October 1942. Here the bomber "swarm" is seen in loose formation near Montrichard, 150 miles west of the target.

(British Ministry of Defence photo.)

The famous Lancaster aircraft was flown by 12 British-based R.C.A.F. squadrons.

in May 1942, when the first 1000-bomber raid was staged, 68 R.C.A.F. aircraft participated, and by the time the war ended Canadian squadrons were sending out more than 200 heavy bombers in single raids with 900 tons of bombs in their bomb-bays.

The first Canadian bomber squadrons, No. 405 (Wellingtons) and No. 408 (Hampdens), were formed in April and June 1941. In December, No. 419 and No. 420 squadrons were organized and began operations a month later with the same two types of aircraft. For more than a year these four squadrons represented the R.C.A.F. in Bomber Command, participating in almost every major raid. When the first three 1000-bomber raids were carried out in May and June of 1942, a number of four-engined Halifaxes joined the veteran Wellingtons and Hampdens in the Canadian bombing force.

By October 1942 the number of Canadian bomber units had grown to five, with the addition of No. 425 ("Alouette") Squadron, and six more Wellington units were organized before the year ended. The most significant development in the Canadianization of the R.C.A.F. came at the beginning of 1943 when the 11

Canadian bomber squadrons were brought together to form an all-Canadian Bomber Group, No. 6, under the command of Air Vice-Marshal G. E. Brookes, who was succeeded a year later by Air Vice-Marshal C. M. McEwen.

While No. 6 Group continued operations from its bases in Yorkshire, three R.C.A.F. bomber squadrons were detached to the Mediterranean theatre to take part in the invasion of Sicily and Italy. In May and June 1943, Nos. 420, 424 and 425 Squadrons, comprising an all-Canadian wing, moved by sea and air from Yorkshire to Tunisia. For over three months their Wellingtons went out almost every night to bomb airfields, harbours, freight yards and rail junctions in preparation for the landings by British, American and Canadian troops. When Italy deserted the Axis, the wing returned to Britain and rejoined No. 6 Group.

The Group had by now been strengthened by three more squadrons, making a total of 13 (not including No. 405, which was in the Pathfinder Group). Its striking power had also grown, as more and more units converted to heavier four-engined bombers, the Lancasters and Halifaxes. In the first great raid on Essen, delivered

MARSHALLING OF THE "HALLIES"
by Paul Goranson (1911-   )
Halifax bombers of No. 419 (Moose) Squadron preparing for a raid at their base in County Durham, England, in the spring of 1943.

on 4 March 1943 by 442 aircraft, No. 6 Group was represented by 78 aeroplanes. For the next four months Canadians participated nightly in the attacks on the Ruhr, known with grim irony as "Happy Valley". Losses were alarmingly high, as the Germans concentrated their defences to meet this threat. During the Battle of the Ruhr, between March and July 1943, No. 6 Group lost 638 aircrew and 118 aircraft. In mid-July the Allied bombers were switched to other targets, but during 1943, its first year of operations, No. 6 Group flew more than 7300 sorties and dropped 13,630 tons of bombs. It lost 340 aircraft, almost five per cent of the number dispatched. In 1944 the scale of operations increased sharply as the Group undertook tactical operations in addition to its long-range strategical offensive against the Reich. It poured high explosive on scores of targets on the "rocket coast", assisted in the

preparations for D Day, took part in the actual assault, and then gave valuable support to the army in the Battle of Normandy. All the R.C.A.F. squadrons were now equipped with Lancasters or Halifaxes, and a new unit, No. 415, which had originally been in Coastal Command, had been added to the Group, giving it a total of 14 heavy bomber squadrons. Operations reached their peak in August, when the Group made 3704 sorties, dropping 13,280 tons of bombs.

The winter months of 1944-1945, with their long periods of fog and rain, brought a decrease in the Group's operations, but in the early spring of 1945 the tempo again quickened in the final all-out offensive. However, targets were rapidly becoming scarcer, as the Allied armies drove into Germany from east and west. The enemy's fighter defences were overwhelmed, and daylight attacks with escorts of long-range Mustangs

fax bombers of Nos. 431 and 434 Squadrons, R.C.A.F., at their base near Croft, Durham, England, in the
ng of 1944, wait for darkness before thundering off to strike at enemy territory.

ancaster of No. 617 Squadron, R.A.F., commanded by an R.C.A.F. officer, Group Captain John E. Fauquier, scores
t on an enemy bridge with a 22,000-pound "Grand Slam" bomb during the spring of 1945.

R.C.A.F. heavy-bomber squadrons frequently attacked railways in the occupied countries in preparation for D Day. These railway repair shops in Nantes, France, testify to the effectiveness of their bombing.

and Spitfires were carried out with little loss. One of No. 6 Group's last operations, a raid on Heligoland, was perhaps the most spectacular of all, for the Group's objective, an airfield on the adjacent island of Dune, was completely obliterated under a carpet of bomb bursts. During its 28 months of operations with Bomber Command, No. 6 Group flew 271,981 hours on 40,822 sorties and dropped 126,122 tons of bombs and mines.

Aircrews in Bomber Command needed courage of a very special order. The long dark flights over enemy territory, undertaken night after night in the face of all the lethal defences that German scientific skill could devise, were enough to try the nerve of the boldest. Often many of the big planes failed to return. The toll in blood was tragic — higher, probably, than in any other major component in the Allied forces. A total of 9980 Canadians lost their lives in Bomber Command — almost as many as died in the 11-month campaign of First Canadian Army, a very much larger force, in 1944-1945. The R.C.A.F.'s commitment to Bomber Command was responsible for much more than half its casualties, and for the fact that its deathroll in proportion to its strength was longer than either the Army's or the Navy's.

Coastal Operations

As implied in its slogan, "Find the enemy; strike the enemy; protect our ships", the R.A.F. Coastal Com-

mand's great task from September 1939 to May 1945 was to wage war against the enemy's U-boats, warships and merchant shipping in close cooperation with the Royal Canadian Navy, the Royal Navy and the United States Navy. Coastal Command's other responsibilities included photographic reconnaissance, air-sea rescue, meteorological flights and — in the early months of the war — minelaying. From an organization of five headquarters and 25 subordinate units, the Command developed into a powerful force which finally comprised ten headquarters and 247 units.

The Allies' war at sea had two principal aims — to protect the maritime supply routes to Britain and to strangle the enemy's seaborne commerce. Canada contributed large numbers of aircrew and ground personnel, as well as a small group of scientists, familiarly known as "boffins". From 1941 until VE Day, R.C.A.F. squadrons were active in the Battle of the Atlantic. At one time or another seven R.C.A.F. units served in Coastal Command. Three squadrons, Nos. 404, 407 and 415, were equipped with landplanes — Blenheims, Beaufighters, Mosquitoes, Hudsons, Wellingtons, Hampdens and Albacores. Three more, Nos. 413, 422 and 423, flew Catalina and Sunderland flying boats. The war records of the Canadian squadrons illustrate the versatility of Coastal Command's operations.

No. 404, which spent most of the war in northern Scotland and the Shetland Isles, began its career as a

photo.)

342 receiving its death blow some 500 miles south-west of Reykjavik, Iceland, 6 April 1944, from an aircraft of No. 162 Squadron, R.C.A.F.

and the Dutch coast. With a record of 83,000 tons of shipping sunk or damaged in a single month, it was acclaimed the most successful strike squadron in Coastal Command during the latter part of 1941 and early 1942. When the Hudson became obsolete for this work, No. 407 was converted to an anti-submarine role, using Wellingtons equipped with powerful Leigh Lights to illuminate targets for night attacks. Four definite kills were credited to the crews of this squadron, in addition to several other U-boats and midget submarines damaged. After a period of service on Hampden torpedo-bombers attacking enemy shipping, No. 415 Squadron was re-equipped with Wellingtons and Albacores and won many successes in night attacks on flakships, motor torpedo boats and merchant vessels in the North Sea and English Channel before it was transferred to Bomber Command in the summer of 1944. Nos. 422 and 423 Squadrons were continuously employed in the campaign against the U-boats, escorting convoys and searching the seas from Iceland to Gibraltar. Six submarines were sent to the bottom by crews of these squadrons. Early in 1944, No. 162 Squadron flew its Cansos from Nova Scotia to Iceland to join Coastal Command's forces in the Battle of the Atlantic. Its crews also killed six U-boats, five of them in a period of less than a month.

South-East Asia

Farther afield, No. 413 Squadron carried out coastal duties over the Indian Ocean and adjacent waters as one of the units of South-East Asia Air Command. Formed in Britain, it had conducted operations over the North Sea late in 1941, but early the following year,

coastal fighter unit, sending its Blenheims on long reconnaissance and escort missions across the North Sea to the coast of Norway. Then, re-equipped with rocket-firing Beaufighters, it became a strike unit, harrying German shipping from the fjords of Norway to the ports of southern France. No. 407 also gained fame as an anti-shipping unit that made daring mast-high attacks on enemy convoys off the Frisian Islands

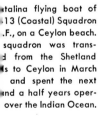

atalina flying boat of
13 (Coastal) Squadron
.F., on a Ceylon beach.
squadron was trans-
d from the Shetland
s to Ceylon in March
and spent the next
nd a half years oper-
over the Indian Ocean.

D.N.D. photo.)

after Japan had declared war, it was hastily transferred to South-East Asia. The Catalinas arrived in Ceylon just in time, for on one of the first sorties flown from the new bases, a Canadian aircraft discovered an approaching Japanese fleet. The Catalina was shot down by enemy fighters, but its warning message enabled the island's defences to be manned and Ceylon to escape disaster. In the months that followed, the squadron sent detachments to work from atolls in the Indian Ocean, from airfields in the Persian Gulf and from the east and west coasts of Africa, until it became the most widely dispersed unit of the R.C.A.F. No. 413 Squadron continued its reconnaissance, convoy escort and air-sea rescue operations until late 1944, when it returned to Britain for conversion to a new role; this was interrupted by the termination of hostilities.

Transport Command

Canada also contributed units to the R.A.F. Transport Command. In the late summer of 1944, three Canadian transport squadrons were formed overseas, two to operate in South-East Asia and one in North-West Europe. The third unit, No. 437, saw action almost immediately, towing gliders for the airborne landing at Arnhem in September 1944. In the months that followed, its Dakotas dropped supplies and ferried troops, equipment, ammunition and gasoline to continental bases, returning loaded with casualties. In March 1945 the squadron again towed gliders for the crossing of the Rhine at Wesel and then resumed its routine ferrying work. After the German surrender, No. 437 Squadron moved to the continent and extended its operations as far afield as Oslo, Vienna, Naples and Athens, bringing home released prisoners of war and displaced civilians, carrying food supplies for the relief of the starving people of Europe and flying mail to Canadians scattered over the continent.

In the South-East Asia theatre the Dakotas of Nos. 435 and 436 Squadrons did similar work in vastly different surroundings. In support of the Fourteenth Army's operations in Burma, the Canadians dropped supplies by parachute on dropping zones, usually small clearings in the jungle which from the air appeared no larger than "geranium pots". In addition to the hazards of the jungle and the storms and diseases of the tropics, the crews often had to run a gauntlet of intense ground fire from Japanese positions close to their dropping zones or landing strips, and on one occasion the unarmed Dakotas were attacked by enemy fighters.

Despite the conditions under which they had to work and the severity of the summer monsoons, Nos. 435 and 436 Squadrons achieved a remarkable record of flying hours and loads lifted. Between March and July 1945, they transported over 35,350 tons of freight, evacuated 1429 casualties and carried more than 16,100 other passengers. In July alone the squadrons logged 4897 hours of operational flying. These two units were the last R.C.A.F. squadrons engaged in operations against the enemy, for their work continued until the Japanese surrender in August 1945. They then returned to the United Kingdom where they joined No. 437 Squadron in ferrying supplies, mail and personnel for the occupation forces.

Tiger Force and Air Forces of Occupation

When the war ended in Europe, the R.C.A.F. proceeded with plans to send a contingent of eight heavy bomber squadrons to the Pacific theatre for operations with "Tiger Force", a Commonwealth formation which was also to include ten R.A.F. and two R.A.A.F. bomber squadrons. The eight squadrons of No. 6 Group flew their Lancasters home to Canada in June, but the war in the Far East ended before they had been re-formed and re-equipped.

After the defeat of Germany, the R.C.A.F. contributed a disarmament wing, a fighter wing of four squadrons and one A.O.P. unit to the Air Forces of Occupation. Four bomber squadrons were also retained overseas for a time as part of Bomber Command's Striking Force and were employed on troop-transport flights between Britain and Italy. Another bomber squadron was transferred to Transport Command and for some months was engaged in flying troops to India.

Other R.C.A.F. Contributions to Victory

The work of Royal Canadian Air Force squadrons at home and overseas, outstanding as it was, was only part of the Force's total war effort. In July 1941, a Women's Auxiliary Air Force (subsequently renamed the Women's Division) was formed to release men for combat duties. Canadian women were enlisted and trained in some 40 trades, ranging from clerks to airframe, aero-engine, radar and wireless mechanics. Many served overseas at R.C.A.F. Headquarters and on stations of No. 6 Bomber Group. In November 1941 the Air Cadet League was formed as a voluntary civilian organization but was incorporated into the R.C.A.F. in April 1943. In its 380 squadrons more than 30,000 schoolboys between 12 and 18 years of age received preliminary instruction during the war. Training was also given in University Air Training Squadrons, the air force equivalent of the Canadian Officers' Training Corps. Many trainees under these two schemes later served with distinction in operational squadrons.

Some 60 per cent of R.C.A.F. aircrew overseas served in Royal Air Force units. In August 1944, for instance, after the policy of Canadianization had been in effect for more than two years, 17,111 R.C.A.F. aircrew were serving with the R.A.F., but only 9993 were in Canadian units. Many R.C.A.F. fighter pilots distinguished themselves in Royal Air Force squadrons in North Africa and the Mediterranean. It has been estimated that at least one pilot in every four who served in the Battle of Malta came from Canada. Flying Officer F. G. Beurling, a Canadian, was credited with 28 aerial victories over Malta.

Canada was also well represented by R.C.A.F. personnel serving in Royal Air Force bomber squadrons outside No. 6 Group, having, at the end of the war, some 1250 pilots, 1300 navigators, 1000 air bombers, 1600 air gunners and 750 wireless operators with R.A.F. bomber squadrons. When Wing Commander Guy Gibson led No. 617 Squadron to breach the Möhne and Eder dams on 16-17 May 1943, 29 of his 133 aircrew were members of the R.C.A.F. Canadians shared too in the sinking of the *Tirpitz* and in the many other achievements of this famous squadron. In No. 8 Pathfinder Group and all other groups of Bomber Command, "Canada" badges were conspicuous.

About one-fifth of the aircrew in Coastal Command units were Canadians. One of them, Flying Officer K.O. Moore, sank two U-boats in 22 minutes in the early hours of 8 June 1944, a feat unequalled in the annals of anti-submarine warfare. Finally, tribute should be paid to the approximately 6000 Canadian radar mechanics who served with the R.A.F. Although there were no R.C.A.F. radar units overseas, many R.A.F. units were almost wholly Canadian in personnel.

Before the outbreak of war, several hundred Canadians had joined the Royal Air Force in Britain. Many were killed in action; others transferred to the R.C.A.F.; a few remained in the R.A.F. after the war. Canadians were in action during the Battle of France in 1940, flying fighters and bombers. During the Battle of Britain, Canadians in the R.A.F. destroyed approximately 90 enemy aircraft.

The services of the R.C.A.F. in the British Commonwealth Air Training Plan, in home defence and in overseas operations were recognized in the long list of awards conferred upon its personnel. The R.C.A.F.'s Roll of Honour for the Second World War contains the names of 17,100 men and women who gave their lives in the service and who are buried from Iceland to Burma, in Canada, Britain, France, Germany, Poland, Italy and other lands. Almost 5200 of these gallant men and women have no known grave.

THE CANADIAN WAR AT SEA 1939-1945

On 31 August 1939 the four destroyers H.M.C. Ships *Ottawa* (Senior Officer), *St. Laurent, Fraser* and *Restigouche* lay quietly at anchor in Vancouver harbour on view to an admiring public, which had come to town for the annual Pacific Exhibition. That forenoon a grand parade had marched through the streets, and seamen landing parties were returning by boat from shore when the Commanding Officers of *Fraser* and *St. Laurent* were summoned to report on board *Ottawa*. Here they were shown a secret message from Naval Service Headquarters ordering their ships to sail for Halifax forthwith. The next day the Royal Canadian Navy was placed on active service, and on 10 September the King, on behalf of Canada, declared war on Germany.

The navy's immediate tasks were to organize auxiliary forces to give protection to shipping against mine and submarine attacks in home waters and to assist the Royal Navy in keeping sea communications clear of enemy warships. To meet these requirements, the R.C.N. requisitioned all suitable government and civilian vessels and arranged for the purchase of 14 private yachts in the United States. The available destroyers were concentrated on the East Coast to provide protection for merchantmen arriving and departing. The latter were organized into convoys, a process that was hastened by the sinking of the British liner *Athenia* on 3 September. Ships were given anti-submarine protection only in terminal areas, a battleship or cruiser guarding the more important convoys against surface raider attack on the high seas.

In the next few months an ambitious three-year building programme was begun to provide the navy with new destroyers, escort vessels, "Bangor" Class minesweepers, "Fairmile" motor launches and three armed merchant cruisers converted from former liners.

The escorts were to be of a "whaler-type" developed by the British Admiralty and classified as "corvettes", a name since immortalized in the Battle of the Atlantic. In January and February 1940, the Cabinet authorized contracts for 64 corvettes to be built by 12 shipbuilding firms situated on the East Coast, the St. Lawrence, the Great Lakes and the West Coast. Ten of these escorts were for the Royal Navy, whose home dockyards were to lay down four "Tribal" Class destroyers for the R.C.N. The construction of ships for each other's navies was to become standard practice for Canada and Britain as the war progressed.

The first "HX" (Halifax-United Kingdom) convoy headed out across the Atlantic on 16 September. By Christmas 1939 the Canadian destroyers, now based on Halifax, could look back on three exceptional convoys. Twice they had been sent to meet and escort into harbour R.N. warships bringing over British gold consigned to the Bank of Canada, and on 10 December five liners carrying men of the 1st Canadian Division had been led to sea by Canadian destroyers and turned over to a strong R.N. force. In March 1940 H.M.C.S. *Assiniboine* joined the British cruiser *Dunedin* in the capture of the blockade-running German merchant ship *Hannover*. Fitted out as an auxiliary aircraft carrier and renamed H.M.S. *Audacity,* this prize was to prove a valuable weapon against U-boats.

On 22 May, when German armies were driving triumphantly into France, the Cabinet War Committee, in response to an urgent British plea for help, agreed to send four destroyers — the whole disposable Canadian force — to the English Channel. The *Restigouche, Skeena* and *St. Laurent* steamed into Plymouth Sound on 1 June. For the next month the Canadian destroyers, joined by *Fraser* from the West Indies on 3 June, formed part of a large force of miscellaneous warships

H.M.C. Ships *Assiniboine* and *Saguenay* steam out of Halifax in line ahead on a routine convoy mission, September 1940.

desperately trying to salvage something from the wreckage of the Allied front in Europe. As the Germans swept down the French west coast, troops had to be evacuated; other military units were landed to engage the enemy briefly or carry out important demolitions; and refugees were brought on board. On 9 June *Restigouche* and *St. Laurent* saw the flames rising over Le Havre 30 miles away and two days later they were off St. Valéry-en-Caux. Before long the destroyers' 4.7-inch guns were barking in anger for the first time, as they returned the fire of a German battery on the cliffs behind the town.

France surrendered on 22 June, the same day that *Fraser* joined a group of R.N. ships off St. Jean-de-Luz near the Franco-Spanish border, one of the last boltholes out of occupied France. Off Arcachon she picked up a party of escaping Commonwealth diplomats, including the Canadian Minister to France, Lt.-Col. Georges Vanier, who had left harbour in a small fishing boat. The "refugees" were quickly helped over the side and *Fraser* transferred them to the cruiser H.M.S. *Galatea* off St. Jean-de-Luz. For the next 48 hours dejected soldiers and fleeing civilians were ferried out

to waiting merchant ships, which were dispatched to England.

However, by 25 June the end was in sight. The Germans were fast approaching, and the Vichy-controlled authorities ashore had indicated that they meant to implement the terms of the recently signed Armistice. The cruiser H.M.S. *Calcutta,* with *Restigouche* and *Fraser* under her orders, made for Bordeaux to investigate a report of enemy shipping there. Their patrol proving fruitless, the three ships then hauled round for Plymouth. Shortly after darkness fell, *Calcutta* sliced through *Fraser* as they were manoeuvring into line ahead. The destroyer's bow quickly sank, and as salvage was impossible, her after part had to be scuttled. *Calcutta* and *Restigouche* steamed sadly away, the former still bearing *Fraser's* bridge perched on her forecastle.

Disaster was heaped on disaster at the end of June 1940. France was out of the war; Italy, sensing quick profit, was in on the side of Germany, who now controlled the western coast of Europe from the North Cape to the Bay of Biscay; and the more pessimistic New York papers predicted that Britain too would succumb within a week. Against this sombre background, R.C.N. units in United Kingdom waters prepared with the Royal Navy for the coming onslaught.

The Battle of the Atlantic

As the enemy prepared to launch a seaborne assault against the British Isles, German submarines vigorously pressed their attacks against convoys and independently-routed ships. In September, for the first time, U-boats began to attack in groups at night, using the so-called "wolf pack" tactics. German naval commanders later referred to the period July-September 1940 as "the happy time". The R.N., whose anti-submarine strength had been seriously depleted by losses in the Channel, was compelled to concentrate most of its forces against invasion. When possible, it released ships to combat the growing threat to the convoys, which were re-routed around the north of Ireland, leaving only coastal traffic in the South-Western Approaches and the English Channel itself. *St. Laurent, Skeena* and *Restigouche* remained under the orders of the Commander-in-Chief Plymouth until the end of July, when they were transferred to the Northern Escort Force based on Rosyth in Scotland. The destroyers later moved to Greenock, Liverpool and ultimately Londonderry.

The Canadian ships' duties consisted of routine escort patrols, anti-submarine sweeps in coastal waters and the rescue of survivors from torpedoed merchantmen. On 2 July *St. Laurent,* now part of a striking force supporting convoys between the Scilly Isles and Ireland, was sent to pick up survivors from the liner S.S. *Arandora Star,* which had been torpedoed some 90 miles off the north-west coast of Ireland. *St. Laurent* arrived on the scene to find a Sunderland flying boat circling overhead. Hours of exhausting work followed, and when *St. Laurent* finally steamed away, she had 857 oil-soaked passengers crowded on her messdecks.

By the third week of September 1940 the embattled R.A.F. had won a clear-cut victory in the skies over Britain; equinoctial gales were whipping up the Channel; and an invasion that year was now unlikely. *St. Laurent, Skeena* and *Ottawa* (replacing *Restigouche* who had returned home for refit) settled down to the steady routine of escorting an outward-bound convoy for a two-day period and then, if schedules and fuel permitted, escorting an inward-bound convoy through the dangerous Western Approaches to the British Isles.

On the other side of the Atlantic the fighting strength of the R.C.N. was increasing. The first of the armed merchant cruisers, H.M.C.S. *Prince Robert,* arrived at Esquimalt and was sent south to join British warships keeping a watch on several German merchantmen lying in various ports on the west coast of the North American continent. *Prince Robert's* particular charge was the *Weser* in Manzanillo Bay, Mexico. A week of patrolling to seaward by day and closing the land at night passed without incident, but on the night of 25 September *Prince Robert* sighted *Weser* under way. The Canadian ship quietly moved nearer the shore and followed her quarry out of territorial waters. Then, with guncrews at action stations, the *Prince Robert* raced up on the port quarter of *Weser,* who surrendered to the boarding party without a struggle. *Weser,* the most important Canadian prize of the war, was sent into Esquimalt wearing the White Ensign above the swastika flag. She sailed again as the M.V. *Vancouver Island* and was ultimately sunk by a German torpedo.

(D.N.D. photo.)

H.M.C.S. *Ottawa's* company rescuing survivors of the British cargo vessel *Eurymedon,* torpedoed in the Atlantic, September 1940.

Other increases to the fleet resulted from the agreement between the United States and United Kingdom Governments to transfer to the R.N. 50 "over-age" American destroyers in exchange for leases on bases in the British West Indies and British Guiana. Canada agreed to man six of these vessels, which were delivered to Halifax by the U.S.N., and on 24 September Canadian sailors streamed up the gangways of H.M.C. Ships *Annapolis, Columbia, Niagara, St. Clair, St. Croix* and

Arriving at Halifax after a gruelling 370-mile tow in January 1943, H.M.C.S. *Columbia,* an ex-U.S.N. "four stacker", brings in the damaged British destroyer *Caldwell.*

(D.N.D. photo.)

St. Francis. A seventh ship, *Hamilton,* at this time being manned by the R.N., was later transferred to the R.C.N. These "Town" Class destroyers left much to be desired as escorts but at this critical stage of the war any anti-submarine vessel was invaluable.

Since the loss of *Fraser,* the former British destroyer H.M.S. *Diana* had been purchased by Canada and was commissioned on 6 September as H.M.C.S. *Margaree.* This ship was destined to be as unlucky as *Fraser* had been. She was rammed and sunk by the M.V. *Port Fairy* en route to Halifax with a small convoy on 21 October. Three days previously the elderly trawler H.M.C.S. *Bras d'Or* had foundered with all hands while shadowing a neutral Romanian steamship in the Gulf of St. Lawrence. These losses were offset by the commissioning of the *Windflower* and the *Trillium* on 20 and 31 October 1940, the first of a steady stream of Canadian-built corvettes now coming into service. In December the second and third armed merchant cruisers, *Prince Henry* and *Prince David,* hoisted the White Ensign.

In November and December 1940 anti-submarine measures and bad weather brought an appreciable decline in sinkings. Three of the "Town" Class destroyers, *St. Clair, St. Croix* and *Niagara,* headed eastward, where there was still a desperate shortage of escorts. Beset by gales and mountainous seas, *St. Croix* was forced to return to Halifax, but *St. Clair* and *Niagara* reached Greenock on 11 December. There were now six Canadian destroyers in United Kingdom waters, but one of them was temporarily out of the fray. *Saguenay* had been torpedoed by the Italian submarine *Argo* on 1 December with a loss of 21 men but managed to reach Barrow-in-Furness five days later after a hazardous voyage that had required outstanding seamanship and navigational skill. Towards the end of January 1941, another four Canadian destroyers, *Assiniboine, Restigouche, Columbia* and *St. Francis,* reached Britain.

By the beginning of 1941 the Royal Canadian Navy had grown to a force of approximately 15,000 men. Halifax was still the major East Coast base, but six other bases had been established — Montreal, Quebec and Saint John, which ministered to the needs of merchant ships and naval units before they became operational, and Sydney, Shelburne and Gaspé Bay, which supported operational warships. Sydney was particularly important in early 1941, as it had become a convoy assembly port.

On the West Coast, base facilities had also been ex-

H.M.C.S. *Battleford,* a typical wartime corvette, in station on the port side of a transatlantic convoy, November 1941. (D.N.D. photo.)

Seamen on the quarter-deck of a Canadian anti-submarine frigate reload as the depth-charge pattern just dropped explodes in the ship's wake.

panded, although not to the same extent as in the East. Esquimalt, Vancouver and Prince Rupert were reorganized, but by October 1940 the only naval force of any size on the West Coast was the Fishermen's Reserve of 17 vessels and 150 officers and men drawn from the British Columbia fishing community. The navy's first success in 1941 came in the Pacific, where *Prince Henry* had for several weeks been keeping four German merchant ships under surveillance in Callao, Peru. When two of the group, *Hermonthis* and *München,* attempted a breakout, *Prince Henry* caught them in the open sea, but both ships were destroyed by their crews.

In the Atlantic, U-boats, supported by long-range aircraft, were being forced by R.A.F. Coastal Command and a growing force of naval surface escorts to probe farther and farther west for their prey. The British countered by setting up bases in Iceland, which had been occupied the previous year, and by mid-April 1941 protection for convoys on the northern route was extended from about 18° to 35° West Longitude. This arrangement was to be only temporary, for the Admiralty and the R.C.N. were already planning complete east-west coverage.

As the war at sea crystallized into a widespread struggle with the enemy's U-boats, the Royal Canadian Navy began to accept greater responsibilities as a separate force. The Admiralty decided that the strategically-placed port of St. John's, Newfoundland, close to and approximately a third of the way along the Great Circle route to and from North America, was well suited for an anti-submarine base. On 20 May the R.C.N. agreed to escort convoys in the Newfoundland area, using, as far as possible, its own resources of destroyers and corvettes with an R.C.N. officer in overall command. On 31 May 1941 Commodore L. W. Murray, R.C.N., was appointed Commodore Commanding Newfoundland Force, which was to include both R.C.N. and R.N. units.

A group of seven recently-commissioned corvettes reached St. John's on 25 May to form the Newfoundland Escort Force and five days later they were joined by two R.N. destroyers. During June the Canadian destroyers in United Kingdom waters were withdrawn for service in the western ocean. In the first week of June the Newfoundland Escort Force was designated a separate command, although still coming under the general authority of the C.-in-C. Western Approaches, who now directed the whole Atlantic battle from his headquarters at Liverpool. St. John's was developed as a joint British-Canadian undertaking, with the R.C.N. responsible for administration and maintenance. By July 1941 there were 900 Canadian naval personnel at St. John's; three years later the figure stood at 5000.

From early June eastbound convoys were escorted by ships of the Halifax or Sydney Escort Forces to a western rendezvous (known later as the Western Ocean Meeting Points or WESTOMPS) where they were taken over by the Newfoundland Escort Force to 35° West, known as the Mid-Ocean Meeting Points (MOMPS). There ships of the Iceland Escort joined to give protection to roughly 18° West. From this locality (Eastern

185

CANADIAN DESTROYERS
by E. H. Holgate (1892-   )
H.M.C.S. *St. Laurent* and another "River" Class destroyer alongside a Halifax jetty, 1941.

Ocean Meeting Points), the Western Approaches Force escorted the merchantmen to their destinations in the United Kingdom. By July 1941 there were sufficient escorts to give westbound convoys complete coverage, and the Newfoundland Escort Force totalled 12 groups. R.A.F. Coastal Command and R.C.A.F. aircraft, flying from both sides of the Atlantic and from Iceland, patrolled the entire route except for a gap of about 300 miles in mid-ocean. To deal with shadowing German bombers, Catapult Aircraft Merchant ships were attached to convoys. These were cargo vessels equipped with a single, short-range Hurricane fighter, which, once

it had been shot off, had to be abandoned when its fuel ran out. On 23 May, during the crucial period when the escort forces were regrouping, the German battleship *Bismarck* suddenly broke out into the North Atlantic. After destroying the battlecruiser H.M.S. *Hood* in the waters between Greenland and Iceland, she was finally sunk by the Home Fleet. *Saguenay, Assiniboine* and *Columbia* were among the ships that took part in supporting operations as *Bismarck* was being harried to her death.

Meanwhile, the United States had become increasingly involved in the war at sea. One of the results of the

Atlantic Conference in August 1941 between Prime Minister Churchill and President Roosevelt was that from September the United States Navy began to escort convoys of vessels of non-American registry. A Western Atlantic Area, comprising that section of the ocean west of 30° West, was made an American strategic responsibility, with a U.S.N. Commander at Argentia controlling the northern part. Canada remained responsible for a Canadian Coastal Zone, but the Newfoundland Escort Force was absorbed into the new task force and passed under the command of the still-neutral United States. The Royal Navy's Third Battle Squadron, whose battleships and armed merchant cruisers had guarded Atlantic convoys against surface raiders since 1939, was withdrawn from Halifax.

In the early hours of 10 September 1941, a slow-moving convoy of 64 vessels in 12 columns was being guarded by *Skeena, Alberni, Kenogami* and *Orillia* a few miles to the south-east of Greenland when it fell foul of a wolf pack of at least eight U-boats. A vicious running battle began. In the morning *Orillia* left the scene with a disabled tanker in tow, but two more corvettes, *Chambly* and *Moose Jaw,* arrived late that evening. *Chambly*

and *Moose Jaw* sank a U-boat, but the convoy lost 15 merchantmen and had two more damaged before the arrival of the local British escort group forced the submarines to break off the fight. Two important lessons were learned from this "Battle of Cape Farewell" — first, that stronger escorts were required for North Atlantic convoys, and secondly, that more emphasis had to be placed on group training. A reorganization took place, but before it could become effective, H.M.C.S. *Levis* had been sunk while with a thinly-escorted convoy on 19 September. As winter storms began to batter the convoys, marine casualties from causes other than enemy action rose steadily. A victim in December was *Windflower,* who collided with S.S. *Zypenberg* in dense fog off the Newfoundland banks.

More sophisticated vessels than the "Flower" Class corvettes were required to fight the improved U-boats now being deployed. The Canadian Government therefore placed orders for frigates (twin-screw corvettes) and for improved versions of the original design. In future, "Flower" Class ships would be relegated to coastal service. More motor launches were also laid down, as were larger minesweepers of the "Algerine"

Green seas break over the corvette H.M.C.S. *Barrie,* as she struggles out of the trough of a mid-Atlantic swell.
(D.N.D. photo.)

H.M.C.S. *Brantford* at St. John's, Newfoundland, after an arduous winter convoy mission.

Class, 16 of which were to be exchanged with the Admiralty for four new corvettes and 12 large "Castle" Class corvettes. The shipbuilding programme was only one aspect of the growing complexity of a 28,000-man navy. The time had come for changes at headquarters in Ottawa. Since 12 July 1940, the R.C.N. had had its own Minister of National Defence for Naval Services. On 22 January 1942, an advisory Naval Board, headed by the Chief of the Naval Staff, Vice Admiral P. W. Nelles, was established, and the previously informal Naval Staff organization was officially constituted to submit proposals and plans to the Naval Board.

Early in 1942 escorts were regrouped into a Mid-Ocean Escort Force (which included the Newfoundland Escort Force) and a Western Local Escort Force. Later in the war the Western Local Escort Force was re-named the Western Escort Force. The position of WESTOMPS was moved eastward to 45° West and the Western Local Escort Force became responsible for convoys to and from that area. From WESTOMPS they were guarded by the Mid-Ocean Escort Force which shuttled between St. John's and Londonderry,

thereby avoiding the Iceland lay-over. On 10 February H.M.C.S. *Spikenard*, the senior ship of her group, was fatally hit by a torpedo while guarding a convoy. Unfortunately, the entry of the United States into the war in December 1941 weakened the Atlantic anti-submarine defences since the U.S. Fleet had to move most of its ships to the Pacific. Enemy submarines extended their patrols close to the North American coast, where they wreaked havoc during the opening months of 1942 before a coastal convoy system could be set up. U-boats were bound to enter the St. Lawrence as soon as the ice was clear, but apart from planning, little could be done to prepare for the attack, which opened with the sinking of two ships during the night of 11-12 May. The R.C.N. instituted local convoys and drew on its meagre resources to form a small St. Lawrence Escort Force of "Bangors", armed yachts and motor launches.

U-boat depredations continued in the St. Lawrence, the final total for the year being two warships, H.M.C. Ships *Charlottetown* and *Raccoon,* and 14 Allied merchant vessels destroyed in the river and gulf. Submarines came again later in the war but the defences were then much stronger; the only casualties, the frigate H.M.C.S. *Magog* and an independently-routed freighter, were both brought safely into port.

By July 1942 new tactics and better team-work in escort groups were paying dividends. *St. Croix,* one of the old four-stackers, heavily depth-charged a contact on 24 July and had the satisfaction of collecting an assortment of wreckage and grisly remnants from *U-90.* A week later *Skeena* and *Wetaskiwin* disposed of the submerged *U-588* after a long, deliberate hunt. The next sinking was far more spectacular. *Assiniboine* chased *U-210* in and out of fog patches until the enemy turned to fight on the surface. For about an hour the destroyer and submarine manoeuvred desperately to

outwit one another, with *U-210* trying to get within the destroyer's turning circle as *Assiniboine* swung around to ram. Close-range weapons blazed away and occasionally the destroyer managed to get off a round from one of her 4.7-inch guns. *Assiniboine* finally succeeded in twice ramming her foe and then finished her off with a pattern of depth-charges.

Shortly after these successful engagements in the North Atlantic, another victory was reported from the U-boats' new hunting ground between the West Indies and the United States' coast. H.M.C.S. *Oakville,* one of six Canadian corvettes on loan to the U.S.N. for duty with Caribbean convoys, rammed and sank *U-94;* six of the corvette's company were decorated for their skill

H.M.C.S. *ASSINIBOINE* VERSUS U-BOAT *U-210*, 6 AUGUST 1942.
by Harold Beament (1898-   )

and determination in the action.

These successes were offset by a severe loss on 14 September. *Ottawa,* investigating an asdic contact ahead of a westbound convoy, had her bows blown off, and a quarter of an hour later a second torpedo finished the damaged destroyer. Both ship's boats, still at the davit head, went down with her and only two or three overcrowded rafts floated clear. The result was that many of those flung into the water died from exposure. By the time help arrived, five officers and 109 men had perished. This convoy was severely mauled, and a subsequent inquiry emphasized the point that none of the escorts was fitted with adequate radar. This handicap of Canadian ships' not having up-to-date equipment was to become more serious in succeeding months.

As the struggle entered its grimmest phase in the fall of 1942, New York replaced Halifax and Sydney as the main convoy port. Shipping losses rose as the German Naval High Command established patrol lines to cut the supply arteries. In November alone, 119 Allied vessels of 729,160 gross tons were lost. Even more ominous for the escorts, which were often seriously depleted in numbers by weather damage and refits, was the increase in the numbers of U-boats pitted against them. During the year, the operational German submarine strength grew from 91 to 212. For the R.C.N. the most hotly-contested action occurred between Christmas and New Year's Eve 1942, when an outward-bound convoy was fiercely attacked in the North Atlantic. The escort group had no apparent success, but post-war analysis has credited *St. Laurent, Chilliwack, Battleford* and *Napanee* with sinking *U-356.*

British and American heavy bombers pounded the Biscay submarine bases in the first few months of 1943, but this had no discernible effect on the U-boat offensive. Shipping losses declined during the tempestuous weather of January, but in February they shot up again to 63 ships of 359,328 tons. The Battle of the Atlantic reached its climax in March 1943; in that month the U-boats sent 108 Allied ships – 627,377 tons of vital shipping – to the bottom. These figures were lower than in November 1942, but what was so shocking to Allied naval leaders was that 85 of the ships lost had been in convoy or straggling and most had been sunk in the North Atlantic. The only glimmer of hope lay in the success of the air and naval escorts in exacting a toll of 16 U-boats, one of which, *U-87,* had been sunk by H.M.C. Ships *Shediac* and *St. Croix.*

In March worried senior officers of the R.N., R.C.N. and U.S.N. assembled in Washington for the Atlantic Convoy Conference. One important result of this meeting was that Britain and Canada were placed in complete charge of trade convoys on the northern routes, for which they were now providing 50 per cent and 48 per cent of the escorts respectively. A new command, to which Rear Admiral Murray was appointed with the title of Commander-in-Chief Canadian Northwest Atlantic, was created to replace the U.S. Commander Task Force 24, most of whose U.S.N. ships had long since been withdrawn for other duties. Admiral Murray was given operational control of convoys west of the so-called "Change of Operational Control (CHOP) Line", which, north of 29° North, was based on the meridian of 47° West; to the eastward of CHOP the C.-in-C. Western Approaches retained control of movements. No other event in the Second World War illustrates more dramatically the new stature and growing effectiveness of the Royal Canadian Navy than the appointment of one of its officers to this key post. The new arrangement also meant that Newfoundland again became a sub-command and the Canadian escort groups were no longer known by American designations.

It may be said that it was in April 1943 that the Allied navies began to win the battle. A number of factors combined to defeat the U-boat menace. There were now sufficient escorts to form Support Groups, which could range the ocean independently and be available to help a threatened convoy; small escort aircraft carriers were attached to Support Groups; and Merchant Aircraft Carriers, which were oil or grain-carrying vessels fitted with a flight-deck and equipped with three or four Swordfish aircraft, were beginning to sail with transatlantic convoys. Finally, the dreaded "Greenland Gap" had been closed by very-long-range Liberator bombers, which now brought the areas through which convoys passed under total aerial surveillance. The combination of these powerful new forces was too much for the U-boats, and in May no less than 41 of them failed to return to their bases. One of these, *U-456,* was sunk through the combined efforts of H.M.C.S. *Drumheller,* a British frigate and No. 423 Squadron R.C.A.F. However, the enemy sprang one surprise at the end of the month by sending a submarine to mine the approaches to Halifax. The local minesweepers, including some old coal-burners which had been steaming in and out of the harbour for years on their tedious but vitally necessary task, were at last given the opportunity to show their skill, and did so most capably.

During June, July and August the destruction of merchantmen markedly declined. The R.C.N. continued to hunt U-boats in the deep waters and also joined the R.N. and Coastal Command on offensive sweeps into the Bay of Biscay to catch submarines

(D.N.D. photos.)

Top—A Very Long Range Liberator on an anti-submarine patrol over a North Atlantic convoy.

Left—Refuelling in mid-ocean. An escort approaches a tanker in convoy to fire over a line by Coston gun.

191

bound to or from their bases. Among the ships that took part in these forays were the corvettes *Edmundston*, *Calgary* and *Snowberry*. On 25 August they were part of a Support Group patrolling close to the towering cliffs of Cape Ortegal, where U-boats were suspected of taking advantage of territorial waters to sneak in and out of the bay at night. Halfway through a sunny afternoon, as the group was quietly steaming along in line abreast out from the Spanish coast, 17 Dornier bombers escorted by fighters approached from the north-east. In a moment the ships were desperately trying to dodge revolutionary new missiles which were being directed on to them by the distant aircraft. This was the first use of radio-controlled glider bombs, promptly nicknamed by an apprehensive onlooker "Chase-me-Charlies". On this occasion only one British sloop was damaged, but two days later in the same area glider bombs sank H.M.S. *Egret* and severely damaged the destroyer H.M.C.S. *Athabaskan*.

In the summer of 1943 Canada arranged with the British Admiralty to take over a variety of warships, including escort carriers, frigates, landing craft, fleet destroyers and, ultimately, light fleet carriers. These Canadian commitments were helpful to the Royal Navy, whose manpower resources had become very strained as the war progressed. Now, too, measures were taken to overcome the equipment deficiencies of Canadian escorts. The Minister of National Defence for Naval Services sent his personal assistant to England to investigate the R.C.N. shortages, and the technical liaison staff in London was greatly increased. Vice Admiral G. C. Jones became Chief of the Naval Staff, succeeding Vice Admiral Nelles who was appointed Senior Canadian Flag Officer (Overseas) to head the enlarged organization. Henceforth new radar and asdic sets and other vital technical equipment were made available on a more equitable basis to the R.C.N.

On 20 September the Canadian destroyer *St. Croix* was struck in the North Atlantic by an acoustic torpedo, a new weapon which homed on the sound of a ship's propellers. Hurrying to her aid, a British corvette, *Polyanthus*, met a similar fate, and it was left to H.M.S. *Itchen* to pick up the 81 men who had survived the sinking of the Canadian vessel. Two nights later a great mushroom of flame was seen in the area of *Itchen's* night station. Rescue ships converged on the spot but were able to save only three persons, one from *St. Croix* and two from *Itchen*.

Scientists quickly developed an answer to the acoustic torpedo in the form of a noise-making device towed astern of each escort; the version used by the R.C.N. was known as Canadian Anti-Acoustic Torpedo Gear, or "CAT" for short. Frustrated again in the north, the U-boats shifted to the Gibraltar and southern routes but here also they were rebuffed. On 20 November *Calgary* and *Snowberry* and the British frigate *Nene* sank *U-536* some 460 miles west of Cape Finisterre. In all parts of the ocean anti-submarine air and sea forces were now on the offensive, forcing the Germans to abandon their wolf-pack tactics which had been so successful earlier in the war.

Redispositions for the long-expected invasion of Europe began early in 1944 as escort groups were withdrawn and convoy schedules changed. In the first three months of the year the enemy sank only three merchant vessels out of 3360 convoyed, but he lost 36 of his submarines. H.M.C.S. *Camrose* cooperated with H.M.S. *Bayntun* in sinking *U-757*. New Canadian

(D.N.D. photo.)

H.M.C.S. *Chilliwack's* boarding party secures a whaler alongside the sinking *U-744*. The White Ensign is draped over the conning tower ready to hoist over the prize.

frigates were commissioning and one of them, H.M.C.S. *Waskesiu,* sank *U-257* on 24 February. On 6 March, *U-744* fought a long evasive action until she was finally destroyed by a group of five Canadian and two British escorts. A week later, the Canadian frigate *Prince Rupert* assisted in the destruction of *U-575.* The frigate H.M.C.S. *Swansea,* fresh from sinking *U-845* in company with *St. Laurent, Owen Sound* and H.M.S. *Forester* on 10 March, joined H.M.S. *Pelican* the following month in sinking *U-448.* Early in April H.M.C.S. *Valleyfield* was torpedoed and sunk off Newfoundland with the loss of 125 of her company.

The end of April 1944 marked the first anniversary of Canadian operational control in the Northwest Atlantic. It had been a period of impressive growth and consolidation. For the moment, the North Atlantic had been practically swept clear of U-boats, and during the year the R.C.N. had reached a personnel total of 78,486 officers and men and 4335 members of the Women's Royal Canadian Naval Service, which had been established on 31 July 1942.

Dieppe

By 1942 a total of 500 R.C.N.V.R. officers were on loan to the Royal Navy and by the end of the war some 4000 Canadians had served with the R.N. in various branches, from the Fleet Air Arm to the submarine service. As early as October 1941, the Admiralty had asked for help in manning landing craft, and a party of 350 officers and ratings had been sent to the Combined Operations base in Scotland. By the time of the raid on Dieppe in August 1942 a few R.C.N. personnel, 70 in all, were distributed amongst the 179 British landing craft involved.

For the Canadian sailors in the landing craft, the Dieppe raid was a brief, action-packed period of triumph and disaster. Typical of their adventures was the experience of two young sub-lieutenants who brought their landing craft through heavy fire to land troops a little to the east of Dieppe. Later, as they approached another beach for re-embarkation, they found a group of Canadian soldiers clinging to a capsized landing craft. By this time the area was a veritable inferno and it was possible to take off only a few before retiring. These craft were among the lucky ones, for several others were sunk or wrecked and their crews taken prisoner.

North Africa and the Mediterranean

As the experience of Dieppe was being studied by tri-service planners, more Canadian sailors arrived at Inveraray, where they helped man six of the landing craft flotillas that were being readied for the forthcoming landings in North Africa. Eleven Canadian corvettes were released from Canadian Atlantic waters for this operation and five more were obtained by bringing round the entire corvette force from the West Coast. The initial objectives were Algiers and Oran on the Mediterranean and Casablanca on the Atlantic coast of North Africa. The Royal Navy, to which the Canadian landing craft flotillas were attached, was responsible for convoying and supporting the troops bound for the first two ports. Off Madeira ten U-boats harried a Sierra Leone-United Kingdom convoy but failed to detect the military convoys passing in adjacent waters. The landings on 8 November were entirely successful, and the Canadian flotillas ferrying American and British troops at Algiers suffered only minor casualties.

After the initial landings, enemy aircraft and sub-

(D.N.D. photo.)

H.M.C.S. *Prince David's* assault craft race toward the beach during large-scale invasion exercises off the South Coast of England in May 1944.

ATLANTIC CONVOY
by Leonard Brooks (1911-)

marines concentrated on the supply line along which the material and reinforcements for the Allied armies in Tunisia had to pass. On 13 January 1943, H.M.C.S. *Ville de Québec* sank *U-224* off the North African coast, and six days later H.M.C.S. *Port Arthur,* steaming toward Gibraltar with a slow homeward-bound convoy, destroyed the Italian submarine *Tritone.* North African convoys were hammered constantly in February. H.M.C.S. *Louisburg* was sunk by an aerial torpedo on the 6th, but on 8 February, H.M.C.S. *Regina* destroyed an Italian submarine. Towards the end of the month, H.M.C.S. *Weyburn* struck a mine and went down off Cape Spartel.

By March 1943 a few escorts could be spared from the North African run to return to the North Atlantic, but while some R.C.N. vessels were withdrawing from the western end of the Mediterranean, others were entering it by way of the Red Sea and Suez Canal. Two landing craft assault (L.C.A.) flotillas, the 55th and 61st, and two landing craft mechanized (L.C.M.) flotillas, the 80th and 81st, manned by Canadian personnel, were among the nearly 2600 Allied naval vessels preparing for the invasion of Sicily. The operation would

be launched by an American Western Task Force and a British Eastern Task Force, the army component of which consisted of the Eighth Army, including the 1st Canadian Division and the 1st Canadian Army Tank Brigade. The R.C.N. flotillas were also in the Eastern Task Force but would not be working directly with Canadian military units.

On 10 July the 55th and 61st Flotillas, each of their landing craft loaded with a platoon of British soldiers, were slipped from the landing ships *Strathnaver* and *Otranto* seven miles offshore. Less than 12 hours later the Canadian flotillas had completed their task, having landed two-thirds of a brigade of troops and their equipment. Four hours after the initial assault, L.C.M. of the 80th and 81st Flotillas started to ferry ashore mechanized vehicles and heavy equipment. The two flotillas returned to Malta on 5 August to refit machinery which was showing the strain of constant use. On 2 September the 80th Flotilla embarked personnel of the Royal 22ᵉ Régiment, The West Nova Scotia Regiment and The Carleton and York Regiment near Messina, Sicily, and at dawn on the 3rd landed them on the Italian mainland. For the next few weeks

194

the 80th Flotilla was occupied with the build-up of supplies. The last Canadian combined operations unit to return from the Sicily and Italy landings reached England at the end of October 1943.

In European Waters

As the Allied invasion of Europe drew nearer, the navy struck at the enemy's warships and waterborne traffic with increasing intensity. The German battleship *Tirpitz* was immobilized in April 1944, an operation in which two recently-acquired "Fleet" Class destroyers, H.M.C. Ships *Algonquin* and *Sioux,* took part. Five months later *Algonquin* and *Sioux* formed part of the destroyer screen for a powerful British force which bombed *Tirpitz* in Alten Fjord and put her out of action for three months.

Meanwhile, the "Tribal" Class destroyers *Haida, Athabaskan* and *Huron,* attached to the 10th Destroyer Flotilla at Plymouth, were engaged in shipping-interdiction missions and in supporting minelaying sorties across the English Channel. On one routine anti-shipping patrol on the evening of 25 April, Force 26, consisting of the cruiser H.M.S. *Black Prince,* the Canadian destroyers and H.M.S. *Ashanti,* surprised three German "Elbing" Class destroyers off St. Malo. As the fleeing German ships gradually altered course to the southward to hug the coastline, one "Elbing" became separated from the others. Disregarding a British-laid minefield in their track, *Athabaskan* and *Haida* pursued and their heavy fire soon caused explosions and flames to leap up from the enemy destroyer. She stopped, ablaze from end to end. Her companions had escaped, and since dawn was near, *Athabaskan* and *Haida* had to leave. Shortly afterwards the German warship rolled over and sank.

On 28 April *Haida* and *Athabaskan* intercepted two "Elbings" moving westward between St. Malo and Roches Douvres. The enemy warships fled, but a torpedo from one of them sank *Athabaskan.* *Haida* continued the chase and repeatedly hit one of the "Elbings" which ran on the rocks. Returning to *Athabaskan*'s last position, *Haida*'s company worked desperately until daybreak to save their comrades. After sunrise three small German vessels came on the scene and hauled out those still struggling in the water.

Two new Canadian Motor Torpedo Boat Flotillas, the 29th and 65th, formed in the early months of 1944 from Canadian veterans of R.N. flotillas, were among those making frequent sorties from their bases in the south of England to intercept the enemy's inshore convoys. The Germans, knowing that an invasion was probable, had concentrated their small craft in such places as Cherbourg and Le Havre. Boats of both the 29th and 65th Flotillas fought several sharp night engagements with their counterparts.

The Invasion of North-West Europe

As the invasion of the Continent drew nearer, *Prince David* and *Prince Henry* were converted from armed merchant cruisers to landing ships infantry and had attached to them, respectively, the 529th and 528th L.C.A. flotillas. In addition, the R.C.N. acquired from the R.N. and U.S.N. 30 landing craft infantry large (L.C.I.(L)) — craft capable of crossing the Channel under their own power — and formed them into the 260th, 262nd and 264th Flotillas.

Allied grand strategy had decided upon June 1944 as the most suitable period to invade. At the end of May corvettes began to bring slow convoys of tows and blockships south from Scottish ports. The next week naval units took up stations to counter any moves by the approximately 200 surface vessels and 50 U-boats that the German Navy could readily deploy against the invasion forces. The Home Fleet, operating from Scapa Flow in the Orkney Islands, was poised to the north-east of the British Isles, while farther south forces were prepared to counter any movement towards the Strait of Dover from the North Sea. In the South-West Approaches to the English Channel, the area of greatest threat, three guard lines were established. On the periphery were 40 anti-submarine vessels, supported by escort carriers, watching over 56,000 square miles of ocean from a point south of Ireland, across to the French Ile de Vierge, and thence southward to include a large section of the Bay of Biscay. Two of the escort groups, E.G. 6 and E.G. 9, were composed of six R.C.N. frigates apiece. Inside the Channel were destroyer groups, including the Canadian Escort Groups 11 and 12. The innermost defence line, ready to intercept any enemy vessel that managed to penetrate the barrier, included the Canadian "Tribals" and M.T.B. flotillas.

All along the south coast of England tens of thousands of men waited in sealed camps for the signal to invade. Also waiting, to transport and cover this great Allied army, were two main naval forces: the British Eastern Task Force responsible for the divisional sectors of "Sword", "Juno" and "Gold" and the American Western Task Force responsible for sectors "Omaha" and "Utah". A total of 5339 vessels were to reach the focal area, "Piccadilly Circus", off the Isle of Wight and then cross on a 20-mile front until they reached the first obstacle, a German minefield forming a barrier in depth from Cap de la Hague to Boulogne. Passage

View over the stern smoke floats of a landing craft assault (L.C.A.) as she heads away with four others from H.M.C.S. *Prince Henry* during operations in the English Channel, 1944. The invasion ships in the background fly barrage balloons to discourage enemy aircraft.

(D.N.D. photos.)

H.M.C.S. *Prince David* sends her 529th L.C.A. Flotilla carrying troops of Le Régiment de la Chaudière and the British Army, to shore on D Day.

through the mined belt and the final approaches to the landing sectors would be confined to ten channels, each of which had to be previously swept and buoyed by a fleet minesweeping flotilla. This task was mainly an R.N. commitment and six Canadian "Bangors" were allocated to British flotillas in the Western Task Force. The ten-ship Canadian 31st Minesweeping Flotilla was also responsible for a channel leading to an American sector.

On 4 June a summer gale, driving big breakers against the Normandy beaches, forced a postponement of the invasion. The minesweepers, which were already on their way, returned to Weymouth Bay. Early the next morning, although the weather was still unsettled, the Supreme Allied Commander decided to proceed with Operation "Neptune". The 31st Minesweeping Flotilla shortened in cables and struggled eastward in a short, choppy sea towards "Piccadilly Circus". By eight o'clock in the evening it had swept through the minefield and shortly after midnight had reached the terminal point of Assault Channel No. 3 to "Omaha", completely ignored by the enemy. Ahead, the sky was lit by the brilliant flashes of exploding shells as Allied bombers were engaged by anti-aircraft fire. The minesweepers now altered course to sweep closer to the land and at 3 a.m. on 6 June were within one and a half miles of the shore, where they swung to port and headed north, meeting battleships and cruisers streaming in to their bombardment positions. The 31st Flotilla's final assignment was to clear the waters from the transport area to the "Omaha" beaches between St. Laurent and Port-en-Bessin.

In the British sector 30 "Fleet" Class destroyers, including *Algonquin* and *Sioux,* opened fire as the landing craft, carrying part of the 3rd Canadian Infantry Division, moved away from *Prince David* and *Prince Henry.* The landing craft found themselves among mines and deadly hidden defences, which could tear the bottom out of a boat in seconds. Few escaped some damage. After the assault troops had seized their immediate objectives, a second wave began to arrive from England in the L.C.I. In the forefront were the 260th, 262nd and 264th Flotillas carrying 4617 soldiers, mostly from the 3rd Canadian Division. Naval losses had been incredibly light. The Canadian L.C.I. returned to England on the afternoon of 6 June, as corvettes escorted the follow-up convoys of men and equipment into the Baie de la Seine.

On 8 June three German destroyers and a fleet torpedo boat put to sea from Brest to strike at the western Normandy flank. Off Ile de Batz they encountered eight of the 10th Destroyer Flotilla's "Tribals", four British, two Canadian and two Polish. During the first confused phase of the ensuing fight, the German destroyer *Z.H.1* was sunk. *Haida* and *Huron,* pursuing the remainder, temporarily lost contact, but then de-

L.C.A. of the 528th Flotilla from H.M.C.S. *Prince Henry* steam past a sunken freighter towards the Normandy beaches, July 1944. (D.N.D. photo.)

tected one destroyer steering for Cherbourg. The German ship suddenly altered course back to the south-west and the three ships raced towards the Ile de Batz on parallel courses. Hit time after time, the German ran aground and concentrated fire rapidly reduced her to a blazing hulk.

The destruction of two of his destroyers thwarted the enemy's plans for surface action in the assault areas, and the moment was therefore propitious for "Tribals", destroyer escort groups and M.T.Bs. to close in on the German coastal convoys. On one of these missions on 27 June, H.M.C.S. *Huron* and H.M.S. *Eskimo* sank a minesweeper and a trawler, and on 5 July Escort Group 12, consisting of *Qu'Appelle, Saskatchewan, Skeena* and *Restigouche,* stalked three German "M" Class minesweepers ten miles south of Brest. The destroyers ran down the enemy line, each picking her own target. When the guns finally ceased firing, all three 'sweepers were gone, but both *Qu'Appelle* and *Saskatchewan* had suffered casualties and been scarred by their opponents. In the second week of July, *Haida* and two other "Tribals", *Tartar* and *Blyskawica,* accounted for a convoy of two merchantmen and a trawler.

The U-boats' attempts to penetrate the screens around the Baie de la Seine failed, but the enemy submarines now presented their hunters with a new challenge in the form of the "Schnorkel", a breathing pipe which the boat could raise while submerged. As it no longer needed to come up for battery recharging, a Schnorkel-equipped U-boat could remain beneath the water for as long as the crew could stand the strain. Nevertheless, by the end of June the navy and Coastal Command aircraft had destroyed ten submarines and *Haida* had added to her impressive list of "kills" by joining with H.M.S. *Eskimo* and a Czech-manned Liberator to sink *U-971.*

Meanwhile, the build-up in the bridgehead continued. Cherbourg fell to the Allies on 26 June, and within ten days the Naval Commanders of the Eastern and Western Task Forces had withdrawn from the Baie de la Seine. The duties of the seaborne forces would henceforth consist of routine sweeping, escort and supply duties and some bombardment of land targets.

The Final Phase of the European War

The Royal Canadian Navy faced the last nine months of the war against Germany in a mood of confident optimism. Manned overwhelmingly by amateurs, it had nevertheless become a highly professional force. With only about 50 officer cadets being accepted yearly at H.M.C.S. *Royal Roads,* the regular force training college at Esquimalt, the vast majority of executive officers

were being commissioned into the R.C.N.V.R. from the lower deck and trained at H.M.C.S. *Kings* at Halifax.

Following an initial period at Naval Divisions, whose facilities had been considerably expanded, new ratings were sent to H.M.C.S. *Cornwallis* at Deep Brook, Nova Scotia. This establishment provided shore instruction in schools and departments formerly located at Halifax and practical sea training in a miscellaneous flotilla of armed yachts and venerable four-stacker destroyers. Having qualified at *Cornwallis,* a young sailor would probably join a newly-commissioned ship. Groups of destroyers and escorts were sent to Bermuda, where the staff of H.M.C.S. *Somers Isles* exercised them with the help of the depot ship H.M.C.S. *Provider* and her two flotillas of motor launches. In addition, from late 1944 officers and ratings were sent to England to train with the Fleet Air Arm.

Further additions to the fleet were the escort carriers *Nabob* and *Puncher,* which the Cabinet in January 1944 had approved manning. These vessels, built in the United States, had been transferred to Britain under Lend-Lease. Since the Canadian government would not accept vessels under Lend-Lease arrangements, *Nabob* and *Puncher,* although they had Canadian officers in command, remained H.M. Ships and operated R.N. air squadrons.

As the navy increased in size and capability, the Naval Control Service and the Naval Trade Division in Ottawa took a firm grip on the organization and routeing of convoys. The Defensively Equipped Merchant Ships (DEMS) Branch provided the Merchant Navy with trained personnel and equipment to defend itself against attack from submarines and aircraft. Schools qualified both merchant seamen and naval ratings, who at peak strength numbered 1631. Canadian DEMS gunners served in ships that sailed the oceans of the world and contributed to many a successful convoy action.

The principal task for most R.C.N. ships was still to guard the North Atlantic convoy routes. The naval force assembled for D Day was reduced by paying off the L.C.I., by sending *Prince David* and *Prince Henry* with their landing craft to the Mediterranean and by attaching *Algonquin* and *Sioux* to the Home Fleet. The remaining ships stayed in the general area of the English Channel for a few more months and, in the case of the corvettes, minesweepers and M.T.Bs., until the last stages of the war. "Tribals" and the destroyer escort groups continued to wreak havoc among coastal convoys. *Iroquois, Haida, Qu'Appelle, Assiniboine, Skeena* and *Restigouche* all took a hand in destroying armed trawlers, minesweepers, coasters and flak ships

Left—H.M.C.S. *Kootenay* pitches a pattern of hedgehog bombs into the sea ahead during the successful attack on *U–621* in the Bay of Biscay, August 1944.

Below —Torpedo hit. A large armed trawler off the French coast is hit by a torpedo from H.M.C.S. *Iroquois*, 23 August 1944.

Bottom—Grey day in the North Atlantic. The "Castle" Class corvette H.M.C.S. *Hespeler* of the Mid-Ocean Escort Force, with other ships of her group.

(D.N.D. photos.)

199

in the Bay of Biscay. The annihilation of seven enemy vessels by *Iroquois* and H.M. Ships *Mauritius* and *Ursa* in Audierne Bay on 23 August helped end any organized attempts to move supplies by convoy. This was *Iroquois'* third such engagement during August; in this one month she assisted in the destruction of seven merchantmen, four minesweepers, six armed trawlers, two flak ships, one escort ship and a coaster. Other destroyers, on anti-submarine patrols, added to the enemy's discomfiture. *Ottawa* (the second of that name), *Kootenay* and *Chaudière* sank *U-621* in the Bay on 18 August, and two days later accounted for *U-984* off Ushant. For *Ottawa* and *Kootenay* it was the third successful attack in six weeks, for they and H.M.S. *Statice* had sunk *U-678* in July. At the end of August, H.M.C. frigates *Saint John* and *Swansea* destroyed *U-247*, and early next month *Dunver* and *Hespeler* cooperated with No. 423 Squadron R.C.A.F. in disposing of *U-484*. Canadian corvettes on convoy duty in British waters were less fortunate. *Regina* and *Alberni* went down in August, the victims of torpedo attacks.

Since advancing Allied forces were rendering the Biscay ports useless as submarine bases, the U-boat Command was forced to divert its boats to Norway. This meant that Allied convoys could again use the South-Western Approaches to the United Kingdom which had been abandoned in 1940. *Nabob* joined the Home Fleet in August and for her first operation sailed with other carriers for a large-scale aerial minelaying sortie in the channels between the Norwegian coast and outlying islands. *Nabob*'s next, and last, operation was another massive Fleet Air Arm raid on the *Tirpitz*, still lying in Alten Fjord. On the late afternoon of 22 August, as the squadron began to withdraw, *Nabob* and a British frigate were hit by acoustic torpedoes fired by *U-354*. The carrier, with a huge hole in her starboard quarter, settled fast by the stern, but there seemed to be a chance that her after engine-room athwartship bulkhead might hold against the sea. For the next four hours *Nabob* lay inert, a "sitting duck", while parties below worked desperately to place shores and restore services. At last she slowly worked up to ten knots for the 1100-mile voyage home. On 27 August she steamed slowly into the Scapa Flow anchorage, having been saved by the determination and energy of her company. Uneconomical to repair at the time, *Nabob* paid off at the end of September.

The "Fleet" destroyers *Algonquin* and *Sioux* continued as the R.C.N.'s only representatives in the Home Fleet. During September they had their first introduction to the North Russia convoy run, a Home Fleet commitment made particularly hazardous by icefields to the north and west and the close proximity of German air and naval bases. In the autumn and winter of 1944-1945 both destroyers were frequently used to screen carriers on anti-shipping and minelaying sorties. In mid-November two cruisers and four destroyers, one of which was *Algonquin*, destroyed two ships out of a convoy of four and five of the six accompanying escorts in the vicinity of Lister Light, on the south-west coast of Norway.

On 15 August *Prince David* and *Prince Henry* took part in Operation "Dragoon", the code name for the invasion of southern France. *Prince Henry* carried the Canadian-American First Special Service Force and *Prince David* a French Commando. The landings on a 15-mile stretch of the Riviera were entirely successful. Toulon fell on 26 August; Marseilles two days later; and the Allies fanned out to link up with the divisions advancing from Normandy.

On 15 September *Prince David* put a British Commando unit ashore on the Greek island of Kithera, which had been evacuated by its German garrison. At dawn on 14 October 1944 Canadian craft landed British and Greek soldiers at the Piraeus, the port of Athens. Meanwhile, *Prince David* had hurried back to Taranto to transport M. Papandreou, the Prime Minister of the Greek Government-in-Exile, to Athens. Off Poros, M. Papandreou transferred from *Prince David* to the old Greek cruiser *Averoff* for his formal return to the capital.

While Canadian sailors in the Mediterranean were enjoying the first taste of victory, those in the Atlantic were still being strongly challenged. The Germans had completed the first U-boats of two improved classes and had constructed concrete protection pens at the new Norwegian bases of Bergen and Trondheim. The Type XXI and Type XXIII submarines, which were faster than their predecessors and had a greater range while submerged, had been laid down as an interim measure until certain technical problems of the even more revolutionary "Walter" type could be solved. Work on the "Walter" submarine, which was driven by hydrogen peroxide, had been going on for some time, but — luckily for the Allies — none became operational during the Second World War. However, the Schnorkel had given the enemy considerable advantage and he was returning in strength to the shipping lanes near the United Kingdom.

Support Groups were shifted to meet the changing situation, and on 16 October H.M.C.S. *Annan* with Escort Group 6 destroyed *U-1006* south of the Faeroe Islands. This success and the sinking of *U-877* by H.M.C.S. *St. Thomas* at the end of December were the only highlights in a generally depressing period. In October the frigate H.M.C.S. *Chebogue* was torpedoed in the Atlantic and the "Bangor" H.M.C.S. *Mulgrave* hit a mine while sweeping off Le Havre. Both were brought back to harbour but had to be scrapped. Next, the veteran destroyer *Skeena* dragged her anchors in a howling blizzard and was thrown on a jagged reef near Videy, Iceland. Another loss was the corvette H.M.C.S. *Shawinigan,* torpedoed with all hands in Cabot Strait in November. The minesweeper *Clayoquot* was torpedoed near Halifax on Christmas Eve, but most of the crew were rescued.

By the beginning of 1945 the anti-submarine campaign had again reached stalemate. In spite of more sensitive radar and better weapons, escorts were not driving the enemy from British inshore waters. No less than 37 groups, 14 of them Canadian, each of six to eight vessels, had been allocated to Western Approaches Command to combat the new threat. On the other hand, the Germans were not causing much damage to Allied shipping. Although only a few Type XXI and Type XXIII submarines managed to get out on patrol, the German underwater fleet reached its greatest strength, 463 boats of all types, in March 1945. The majority stayed close to their bases, but a small number scattered abroad, some as far as the Eastern seaboard of Canada. It was in the main combat area that frigates achieved the last "kills" for the R.C.N. — *U-309* by H.M.C.S. *Saint John* on 16 February, *U-1302* by H.M.C. Ships *Strathadam, La Hulloise* and *Thetford Mines* on 7 March, and *U-1003* by H.M.C.S. *New Glasgow* on 20 March. However, the Canadian submarine-hunters did not go unscathed, for on 22 February the corvette H.M.C.S. *Trentonian* was torpedoed and sunk in the Channel.

Elsewhere in the closing months of the war the Home Fleet hammered away at the remnant of the German mercantile marine creeping in and out of the Norwegian fjords. The second Canadian-manned escort carrier, the *Puncher,* which since commissioning had been ferrying aircraft across the Atlantic, reached Scapa Flow in February. During the next two months she flew her Barracudas and Wildcats on several successful missions to disrupt sea traffic and blast shore installations. Other newcomers with the Home Fleet, *Haida, Huron* and *Iroquois,* also became familiar with the rugged coast of Norway, usually on carrier screening duty. *Sioux* made two more trips to North Russia,

H.M.C.S. *Iroquois* fires a salvo to starboard.

(D.N.D. photo.)

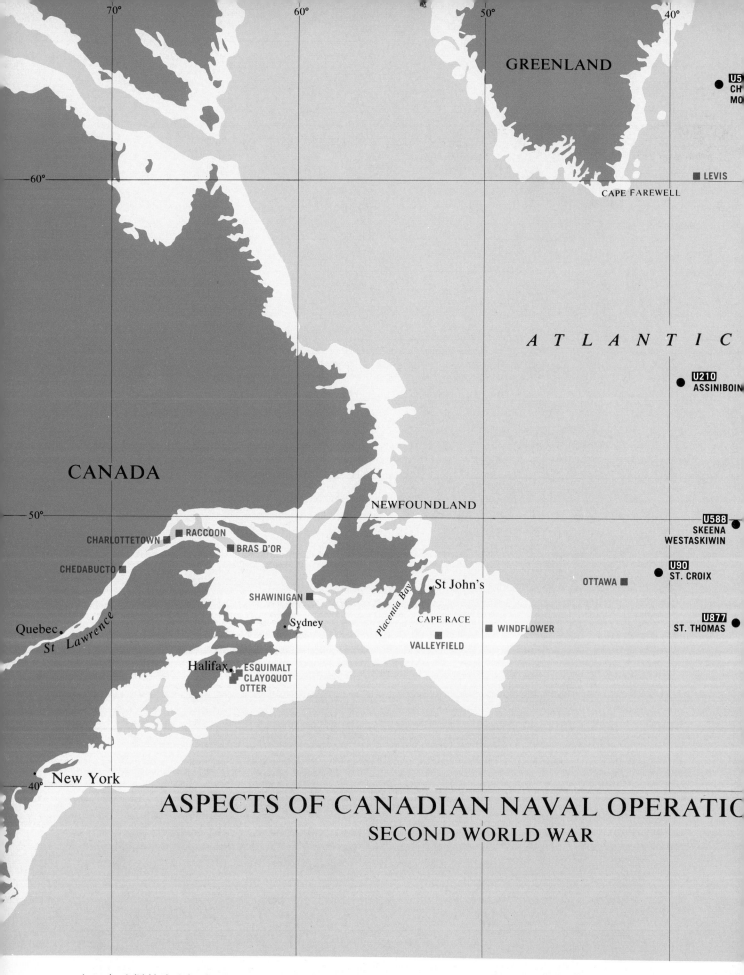

ASPECTS OF CANADIAN NAVAL OPERATIONS
SECOND WORLD WAR

GREENLAND

ATLANTIC

CANADA

NEWFOUNDLAND

CAPE FAREWELL

■ LEVIS

● U5
CH
MO

● U210
ASSINIBOINE

■ U588
SKEENA
WESTASKIWIN

● U90
ST. CROIX

■ U877
ST. THOMAS

OTTAWA ■

CHARLOTTETOWN ■   RACCOON ■
■ BRAS D'OR

CHEDABUCTO ■

SHAWINIGAN ■

Quebec •
St Lawrence

• Sydney

St John's •

Placentia Bay

CAPE RACE
■ WINDFLOWER

VALLEYFIELD

Halifax •   ESQUIMALT
■ CLAYOQUOT
OTTER

New York •

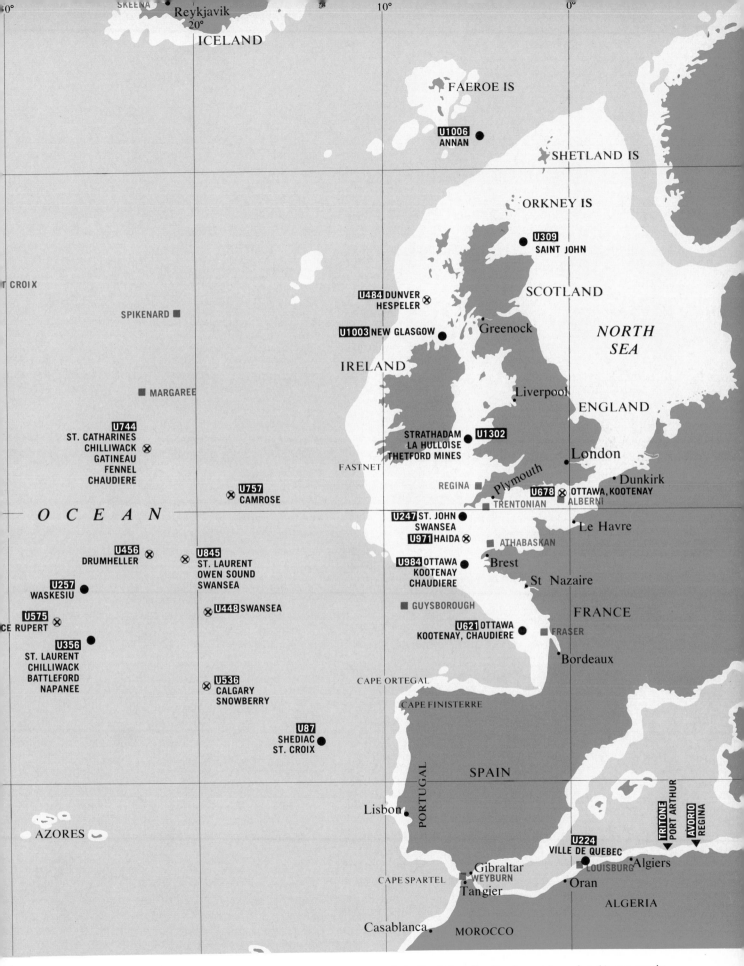

ICELAND
Reykjavik
20°
SKEENA

10°

0°

FAEROE IS
U1006 ANNAN

SHETLAND IS

ORKNEY IS

U309 SAINT JOHN

SCOTLAND

NORTH SEA

ST CROIX

SPIKENARD ■

U484 DUNVER
HESPELER ⊗

U1003 NEW GLASGOW

Greenock

MARGAREE ■

IRELAND

Liverpool

ENGLAND

U744
ST. CATHARINES
CHILLIWACK ⊗
GATINEAU
FENNEL
CHAUDIERE

STRATHADAM
LA HULLOISE
THETFORD MINES

U1302

London

FASTNET

REGINA

Plymouth

Dunkirk

U678 ⊗ OTTAWA, KOOTENAY
ALBERI

O C E A N

⊗ U757
CAMROSE

TRENTONIAN ■

U247 ST. JOHN
SWANSEA

Le Havre

U456 ⊗
DRUMHELLER

⊗ U845
ST. LAURENT
OWEN SOUND
SWANSEA

U971 HAIDA ⊗

ATHABASKAN ■

U984 OTTAWA
KOOTENAY
CHAUDIERE

Brest

U257
WASKESIU

St Nazaire

⊗ U448 SWANSEA

U575 ⊗
CE RUPERT

GUYSBOROUGH ■

FRANCE

U356
ST. LAURENT
CHILLIWACK
BATTLEFORD
NAPANEE

U621 OTTAWA
KOOTENAY, CHAUDIERE

FRASER ■

⊗ U536
CALGARY
SNOWBERRY

CAPE ORTEGAL

Bordeaux

CAPE FINISTERRE

U87
SHEDIAC
ST. CROIX

PORTUGAL

SPAIN

AZORES

Lisbon

TRITONE PORT ARTHUR ▼

AVORIO REGINA ▼

U224
VILLE DE QUEBEC

LOUISBURG ■

Algiers

Gibraltar
WEYBURN ■

CAPE SPARTEL

Tangier

Oran

ALGERIA

Casablanca

MOROCCO

map of the North Atlantic Ocean and adjacent sea areas, shows an important aspect of the Royal Canadian Navy's war at sea; but this was not the
▼ one. The text tells of the exploits of Canadian ships on the high seas and of actions and operations around the world.

Survivors from H.M.C.S. *Clayoquot* cluster around the Carley rafts after *U-206* had torpedoed their ship off Halifax on Christmas Eve, 1944. H.M.C.S. *Fennel* picked up all but eight of the minesweeper's company.

braving the usual stormy weather and frequent attacks by U-boats and Junkers 88 torpedo bombers.

The 29th and 65th Canadian M.T.B. Flotillas were now based at Ostend, their task being to protect Thames-Antwerp convoys from E-boats and the enemy's new midget submarines. On 14 February there was a tragic accident. Gasoline ignited on the surface of Ostend harbour and flames quickly spread among the packed ranks of small craft. The 29th Flotilla was almost wiped out; five of its eight boats were destroyed, and 26 Canadian sailors were among those burned to death.

The 31st Minesweeping Flotilla had been working steadily for months clearing channels to the French coast. A few of the "Bangors" had been "rotated" to Canada, and on 17 March the returning H.M.C.S. *Guysborough* went down with heavy loss of life after a double torpedoing on a passage to Plymouth. In mid-April the flotilla swept in ahead of a strong French naval force on the last large combined operation of the war in Europe; the object was to force the surrender of garrisons between the mouth of the Gironde River and Bordeaux, by-passed in the earlier advance. On the way back, the 'sweepers captured a German naval trawler, which was steamed to England by a prize crew

from H.M.C.S. *Thunder*.

Haida, Huron and *Iroquois* dropped anchor in Scapa Flow on 6 May after an arduous voyage from Murmansk. Forty-eight hours later came the official word that the war in Europe had come to an end with the unconditional surrender of all German forces. The electrifying news had little immediate impact at sea but tangible proof was not long in coming. Strict wartime regulations were still in force as convoy ON 300 steamed quietly westward on 11 May. In the forenoon the frigate H.M.C.S. *Victoriaville* and a corvette, H.M.C.S. *Thorlock,* were detached to close a submarine, which had reported its position in accordance with instructions transmitted by German naval control. The corvette sighted a single white navigation light ahead, and shortly after midnight the White Ensign was flying over *U-190,* which on 16 April had sunk the "Bangor" minesweeper H.M.C.S. *Esquimalt* near Halifax. Everywhere now the detested U-boats were rising to the surface and hoisting black flags in token of surrender.

In the ensuing weeks the "Tribals" paid a final, happier visit to Norway. *Iroquois* took part in the triumphal return of Crown Prince Olaf to Oslo on 13 May and *Haida* and *Huron* toured the northern fjords,

204

CANADIAN MOTOR TORPEDO BOATS GOING INTO ACTION
by Anthony Law (1916-   )
The 29th Canadian M.T.B. Flotilla leaves the British assault area in Normandy to patrol off Le Havre. The artist commanded M.T.B. 459 at the time and was Senior Officer of the flotilla.

distributing relief supplies and greeting the thousands of Norwegians who swarmed aboard. The remaining destroyers, frigates and corvettes headed for home. The Admiralty lent *Puncher* to the Canadian Government for trooping, and until the end of the year she was employed in bringing back army, navy and air force personnel. By July the R.C.N. had gathered in most of its scattered units, except for the minesweepers which remained in the English Channel for a few more months.

The Pacific War

By May 1945 considerable planning had been done for the diversion of naval strength to the Pacific, but this theatre had had very low priority while Germany remained undefeated. In October-November 1941 a force of some 2000 Canadian soldiers had been carried to Hong Kong by *Prince Robert* and S.S. *Awatea* to augment the British garrison there. The Japanese entry into the war on 7 December 1941 had meant that Canada's western seaboard immediately became more vulnerable, but on the other hand, the United States would now help in its defence. One immediate R.C.N. commitment was to protect sea communications in the coastal zone. By January 1942 two of the armed merchant cruisers, *Prince David* and *Prince Robert,* three corvettes, five minesweepers, three armed yachts and patrol craft of the Fishermen's Reserve were carrying out regular patrols. Only one action was fought, when S.S. *Fort Camosun* was torpedoed and shelled 70 miles off Cape Flattery on the night of 19-20 June 1942. Warships rushed to the scene, scattering depth-charges in their wake, but made no contact. The next night a Japanese submarine surfaced and shelled the lighthouse and radio station at Estevan Point, B.C.

In the north during June the Japanese were more active. They seized the Aleutian islands of Attu and Kiska and bombed the nearest United States base at Dutch Harbor. Canadian assistance was requested and the "Princes" and two corvettes, H.M.C. Ships *Dawson* and *Vancouver,* spent two and a half months on convoy escort duty from Kodiak and Dutch Harbor. The corvettes returned to Dutch Harbor in the spring of 1943 and passed another three months helping the Americans concentrate military forces against Attu, which was retaken in May without Canadian naval participation. *Dawson* made a final trip to Alaska when she escorted a troop convoy in July for the assault on Kiska. No Canadian warship was present on 15 August 1942 as a joint American-Canadian force made an amphibious landing on the island only to find that the Japanese had evacuated it.

"A" and "B" turrets' gun crews aboard the cruiser H.M.C.S. *Uganda* clear decks after bombarding Sukuma airfield in the East China Sea on 4 May 1945.

(D.N.D. photo.)

Plans for eventual full-scale participation in the Far East and for the post-war period began to be clarified during the ensuing 18 months. The two problems became closely inter-related and also connected with the efforts to develop naval aviation. At the second Quebec Conference in September 1944, Allied strategy against Japan was determined. A month later the Cabinet War Committee decided that Canada would send to the Pacific two light fleet carriers, two cruisers, *Prince Robert* re-armed as an anti-aircraft ship, ten fleet destroyers and some 50 frigates and "Castle" Class corvettes. This force would be manned by a total complement of 13,412 all ranks. The Canadian ships were to be employed only in the Pacific and not in the Indian Ocean. This condition ruled out the participation of *Prince David* and *Prince Henry* in operations in South-East Asia for which they had been requested. Therefore the Landing Ships Infantry were recalled from the Mediterranean, paid off and lent to the R.N. Of the approved Canadian Pacific fleet, only *Prince Robert* and the cruisers actually reached the theatre.

The 8000-ton former Royal Navy cruiser *Uganda* was commissioned into the R.C.N. in October 1944. Six months later she joined British Task Force 57 which was operating in intimate cooperation with the large U.S. Third Fleet's Fast Carrier Force. By now the Japanese were steadily being dislodged from outlying island bases and driven inexorably back on their homeland. *Uganda* became part of the anti-aircraft guard for the British carriers as they flew strikes against Formosa and the Sakishima Islands, neutralizing Japanese airpower and shielding the American invasion of Okinawa. For a few hours on 4 May *Uganda* was detached with the battleships and other vessels to bombard enemy installations on Miyako Island in the Sakishima group.

Uganda's next detached operation the following month was an aerial strike and cruiser bombardment against Truk in the Caroline Islands. Meanwhile, on 21 June, after 82 days of bitter fighting, enemy resistance ended on Okinawa and the Allied fleet closed in on the Japanese main islands. Between 17 and 25 July the Canadian cruiser performed her customary duty of anti-aircraft screen or picket guard, as naval aircraft raided Tokyo, Nagoya, Kure and Kobe. On 28 July, because of the government's policy that only those who volunteered would be required to serve in the Pacific war, *Uganda* sailed for home where she would recommission with an all-volunteer crew, then return to the Pacific theatre. But events moved too rapidly; when *Uganda* secured in Esquimalt on 10 August very few days were left of the Second World War.

After nuclear bombs had been dropped on Hiroshima and Nagasaki, Japan capitulated on 14 August 1945. The second Canadian cruiser, H.M.C.S. *Ontario,* received the news as she was steaming across the Indian Ocean. *Prince Robert,* a recent arrival from Canada, celebrated VJ Day in Sydney, Australia. She was then detailed for the Hong Kong relief squadron. She reached Hong Kong on 30 August, and men of her crew entered Shamshuipo Camp and liberated 1500 prisoners of war, including 400 Canadian soldiers. *Ontario* anchored in the harbour with another relief convoy. On 16 September the Japanese in Hong Kong formally surrendered to high-ranking Allied officers.

Ontario, the last of the Pacific contingent to return, secured alongside at the R.C.N.'s West Coast base in November 1945. By now the R.C.N. was already greatly reduced. Many of its ships had been turned over to War Assets Corporation for disposal, and a steady stream of sailors was happily returning to "Civvy Street".

During the Second World War, R.C.N. enlistments totalled 99,688 men and some 6500 members of the Women's Royal Canadian Naval Service. Canadian ships, alone or in company with other ships and aircraft, had sunk 29 German and Italian submarines. And 1990 Royal Canadian Navy personnel gave their lives for their country. Excluding unarmed craft on harbour or coastal duty, the R.C.N. had deployed 471 ships during the war, and had evolved into a self-sustaining, multi-purpose fleet. Perhaps most important of all was the fact that the war brought home to Canada that she was a nation with oceans on three sides of her territory and that her first line of defence lay on the tumbling grey waves of the sea.

An Otter of No. 115 Air Transport Unit, R.C.A.F., and a Canadian reconnaissance patrol in the Sinai desert.

Since its establishment in 1949, the Field Service has continually supported U.N. operations around the world. However, the fact that there was a need for such a force was perhaps the final admission that the wartime hopes for collective security had collapsed. The disagreements of the Great Powers had apparently ended the prospects of planned security under the aegis of the United Nations. All that remained was the desire of men like the Secretary-General to use the United Nations to prevent the Cold War from spreading or from turning into a major conflict. The Field Service was a pragmatic attempt to reach this goal. Indeed, from that time to the present, the history of the United Nations attempts at peace-keeping is a record of pragmatism. The second Secretary-General of the organization, Dag Hammarskjold, made this pragmatism his policy: "The basic policy line for this organization", he said in 1959, "is that the United Nations simply must respond to those demands which may be made of it." This it has done.

United Nations peace-keeping forces have carried out many tasks since the collapse of the Organization's early plans for collective security. In some way each force has expanded the concept of peace-keeping and has contributed to the large body of precedent now available to guide the actions of the Secretary-General and the nations that contribute to his forces. Generally, U.N. forces have not operated in a fighting role. The one great exception, the Korean War, is usually seen by both historians and planners as a response to a unique situation. Peace forces have normally been used in a supervisory capacity to check on truces, armistices or cease-fires, to patrol disputed borders, cordon off areas of possible disturbance, or maintain internal security in areas in which law and order have collapsed.

No two forces have been the same, for every force has been organized under different conditions. Of course, only the attitude of the Great Powers really determines the success or failure of U.N. intervention in a crisis. Similarly, the reaction of countries bordering on the area of hostilities is vital, as is the character of the Secretary-General and the structure and abilities of the Secretariat. The lessons of the past, then, provide a guide for dealing with current problems, but a guide that must be used with care. At the time of the first U.N. attempts to create a "presence" in 1948, however, there were no precedents for anyone to follow.

Palestine

The outbreak of war between the newly-formed state of Israel and her Arab neighbours in May 1948 was the culmination of long-smouldering hostility. The United Nations had first become involved in the Palestine problem in April 1947 and for over a year had attempted without much effect to check the drift towards insecurity and war. The proclamation of the state of Israel in May 1948 was the signal for the outbreak of hostilities, and with this, U.N. efforts turned to attempts to establish a truce. Two appeals by the Security Council for a cease-fire were ignored, but

243

a third succeeded, and a period of uneasy quiet lasted for four weeks. To police the truce, Belgium, France and the United States were to supply equipment, technical personnel and 93 military observers. The first observers arrived on the scene within three days, but despite their efforts, hostilities were resumed when the truce expired. The Security Council then invoked Articles 39 and 40 of the Charter, relating to threats to the peace, and imposed a cease-fire of its own. Implementation of this and subsequent directives was the responsibility of the United Nations Truce Supervision Board, or Truce Supervision Organization, as it soon came to be called.

In 1949 UNTSO assumed the responsibilities it still carries out. Each of the armistice agreements concluded that year between Israel and the four neighbouring Arab states of Egypt, Lebanon, Syria and Jordan provided for the supervision of a Mixed Armistice Commission, composed of the representatives of the two parties, under a Chairman who was to be either the Chief of Staff of UNTSO or an officer designated by him.

Canada did not become involved in UNTSO until 1954, when renewed fighting along the Israel-Jordan border necessitated a larger observer force. Since that time Canada has supplied approximately 17 army officers each year for duty in Palestine. From 1954 to 1956 the Chief of Staff of UNTSO was Major-General Burns.

The officers who supervise the fulfilment of the armistice provisions live and work in trying circumstances. The terrain is inhospitable, the climate uninviting and the dangers considerable. The story is told of a Canadian officer who returned to his quarters after being pinned down alone in his observation post by mortar fire for four hours only to be bitten by a poisonous snake when he took his boots off. Usually an officer spends at least half his one-year posting working from outposts or permanent observation posts. The rest of his time is taken up with radio duty, investigations, special tasks and administration.

On the whole, the Israelis and Arabs have appreciated the efforts of UNTSO to preserve the peace, but numerous obstacles have impeded the observers' work. Occasionally, observers have been fired at, and one Canadian officer, Lt.-Col. George A. Flint, was killed in 1957 while trying to effect a cease-fire on the slopes of Mount Scopus, Jerusalem. Sometimes, too, UNTSO observers have been denied access to certain sectors. But, despite the difficulties, UNTSO has usually succeeded in curbing the tensions of this turbulent area. Even at the time of the Egyptian-Israeli war in 1956,

when passions were at their peak, UNTSO managed to safeguard peace on the other three frontiers over which it had charge.

Kashmir

In Palestine, although the political issues are as far as ever from settlement, the U.N. did succeed in getting the states involved to consent to a cease-fire and then to armistice agreements. In the dispute between India and Pakistan over the State of Jammu and Kashmir, the United Nations likewise found itself unable to bring the parties to political agreement. Nevertheless, except for sporadic outbursts of fighting, the situation remained under control until August 1965, when more serious clashes occurred, and even then the U.N. played an important role in stabilizing the situation.

Hostilities first broke out in Kashmir with the end of British rule in 1947 and the founding of the successor states of India and Pakistan. In January 1948 the Security Council created the United Nations Commission for India and Pakistan to investigate the situation in Kashmir, and three months later authorized the employment of military observers. In fact, however, it was not until January 1949, after much fighting and a subsequent cease-fire, that the first military observers arrived.

The first intimation that Canada would be asked to join in the work of the Military Observer Group for India and Pakistan came early in December 1948, and a formal request for four to six officers was received the next month. The Cabinet agreed to the U.N. request, and four officers from the Canadian Army Reserve Force were selected for duty in Kashmir. Four more officers arrived in the fall of 1949, and shortly thereafter officers of the regular army began to fill the Canadian posts in UNMOGIP. Continuing efforts to resolve the crisis, including a lengthy attempt by General A. G. L. McNaughton of Canada, President of the Security Council in 1949-1950, met with no success. After a marked increase in tension in 1963, the number of observers was increased from 34 to 40, and the Canadian contribution was raised to nine officers. In addition, in 1964 Canada supplied a Caribou aircraft and three officers and five technicians of the Royal Canadian Air Force, bringing the Canadian contribution to 17, the largest national group in UNMOGIP.

Military observers in Kashmir find life exceedingly rigorous and have described their tasks as "the toughest military assignments in the world". For instance, one observer team reported that an officer had been hospitalized for lack of oxygen at 18,380 feet elevation, that they had all been sick five times because of bad food and that they were all afflicted with fleas, ticks and saddle-sores. The observers' normal duties were often hazardous as well as uncomfortable. Brigadier H. H. Angle, a Canadian and the Chief Military Observer of UNMOGIP, was killed in an air crash in 1950. Other officers risked their lives in attempts to keep the peace. One observer who had witnessed a confrontation between an Indian and a Pakistani patrol jumped into his U.N.-marked jeep as the two groups started firing at each other and drove into the path of fire with the U.N. flag flying from his vehicle. Both patrols ceased firing, and with the arrival of more observers the fighting stopped.

The original task of the Military Observer Group was to mark the cease-fire line between the contending parties, and this was accomplished in 1949. Then the observers took up their posts on both sides of the line and began the routine tasks which they carried out until 1965. They reported on troop movements, kept count of the military supplies and personnel in their areas, and assisted local commanders in resolving minor disputes. As in Palestine, the observers had no power to enforce the cease-fire but could only report violations to their headquarters. As a result, they were helpless in the face of the large-scale fighting that flared along the borders in August and September 1965. A new U.N. force with a wider mandate was a necessity, and after the cease-fire of mid-September the United Nations India-Pakistan Observer Mission was created. Major-General Bruce F. Macdonald, a Canadian officer who had been serving with the U.N. in Cyprus, was appointed commander of the UNIPOM, and the Canadian government also provided an R.C.A.F. Air Transport unit with three Caribou and three Otter aircraft and a number of observers from the navy, army and air force.

Korea and the "Uniting for Peace" Resolution

The work done in Palestine and Kashmir illustrates the achievements of the United Nations in stabilizing, if not resolving, troublesome situations. A growing awareness that disputes on far-off frontiers might lead to Great Power involvement and to an uncontrollable spread of fighting made most nations willing to use U.N. machinery to extinguish brushfire wars. The pattern of these developments changed drastically in 1950 with the invasion of South Korea.

In Korea, for the first time, the U.N. had to deal with a major military conflict in which the Great Powers were vitally concerned. The previous methods of conciliation and persuasion, of mediation and observation, were useless in the face of open, purpose aggression.

(D.N.D. photo)
A Canadian Provost Corps sergeant on UNEF patrol passes one of the great Egyptian pyramids.

Therefore the U.N. was forced to organize and use collective military action against the aggressors. In so doing, the organization broke new and significant ground. Until 1950 it had been assumed that the Charter's provisions for collective security could never be implemented, largely because of Soviet intransigence. The initial actions of the Security Council, the only body with authority to act, were effective in the Korean crisis only because the Soviet Union fortuitously happened to be boycotting the Council in protest against the continued representation there of the Nationalist Republic of China. There was no reason to believe that such good fortune would be repeated in any other crisis, and, indeed, the special circumstances of June and July 1950 merely emphasized the limited reliance that could be placed on the Security Council as an effective instrument of security. The result was the passage of the "Uniting for Peace" proposals, introduced by the United States and co-sponsored by Canada and six other nations.

The Uniting for Peace resolution provided a method of evading the paralysing effect of the unprincipled use of the veto. In essence, in cases where the veto blocked action, the resolution transferred the responsibility for peace and security from the Security Council to the General Assembly. Speaking in the debate, Mr. Pearson, the Secretary of State for External Affairs, told the General Assembly:

> We are not going to repeat the mistakes of the thirties when collective security was betrayed.... and when states fell one by one.... Nor are we going to repeat the mistakes of June 1950 when we were not organized to carry out quickly the collective security obligations we had undertaken when we signed the Charter.

The resolution also asked member states to maintain, within their own forces, elements trained, organized and equipped for prompt service at the call of the U.N. The Canadian Government had anticipated this by authorizing on 7 August 1950 "the recruitment of an additional Army brigade . . . specially trained and equipped for . . . the United Nations. . . ."

Unfortunately, however, although virtually all non-Communist states were prepared to assert the Assembly's authority on security matters, they were not yet ready to provide the physical means necessary to make it effective. Canada's offer of a special force for the United Nations remained a pioneer venture that failed to stimulate any general emulation. This lack of response was disappointing, but it did not deter the Canadian Government from regarding its stand-by force as essential to its foreign and defence policy.

Indo-China

The first and only peace-keeping operation in which Canada has participated outside the United Nations resulted from a conference held in Geneva in the summer of 1954 on the war between the French and the Viet Minh in Indo-China. In an effort to prevent the conflict from expanding, the Conference drew up three agreements, one for each of the successor states of the former French Indo-China. Each agreement provided for an International Commission to supervise and control its implementation, and Canada, India and Poland were asked to staff these Commissions. The United Nations could not deal with this problem, primarily because Communist China, one of the parties principally concerned, was not a member.

Canada had not participated in the Geneva Conference on Indo-China, and the request that she assist in staffing the International Commissions came as a complete surprise. On 28 July 1954, after careful investigation had disclosed what was felt to be a reasonable chance of success, the Canadian Government accepted this new peace-keeping role. Within a few days diplomats and senior military officers from the three states forming the Commissions met in New Delhi and drafted the terms upon which they would operate. The Commissions for Laos, Cambodia and Viet Nam were established on 11 August 1954, and within a month approximately 140 Canadian servicemen and members of the Department of External Affairs were on duty in Indo-China.

The immediate military functions of the Commissions were carried out fairly successfully. The first task in Viet Nam was to ensure that the cease-fire was obeyed,

Troopers of the Canadian reconnaissance squadron with UNEF meet a solitary traveller in the Sinai desert.

(D.N.D. photo)

246

order restored and the military forces of the disputants transferred to their respective zones. In Cambodia and Laos similar tasks were carried out with equal success. But this was the part of the armistice, the end of fighting, on which there was mutual agreement. In carrying out its long-term role of controlling the entry of military personnel and war materiel, the record has been less satisfactory.

The Geneva Agreement on Viet Nam outlined the steps to be taken to prevent the importation of arms. Points of entry were established, inspection teams formed and patrols sent out. The Canadian and Indian members of the Commission made vigorous efforts to ensure that appropriate control was achieved, but they were soon involved in an endless series of procedural disputes with the Communist Poles. The result, wrote an experienced Canadian diplomat,

was that in the North the I[nternational] C[ontrol] C[ommission] was unable to observe violations of the arms control stipulation but never able to maintain adequate inspection to be assured that no violations were taking place. In the South the struggle was with the indifference and reluctance of the authorities and the persistent effort of the Americans to press the terms of the Agreement farther than they could properly be stretched. The violations in the South were, needless to say, observable, and the attitude of the Americans was negative but decent. The Commission was in a position to prove Southern but not Northern violations. The Southerners and Americans inevitably complained and increasingly insisted that the known if not proved disregard of the arms control provisions by the Communists not only justified but made essential their doing likewise.

For similar reasons the Commission was unable to control infiltration from North Viet Nam to the south. The dilemma is clear. The existence of an ineffective inspection system can serve to conceal Communist violations and expose those who act more openly. On the other hand, to abandon the inspection system totally or to resign from the Commission might jeopardize what remains of the Geneva accords and make an already critical situation more serious.

In Cambodia and Laos the International Commissions were more successful. The Cambodian Commission in particular accomplished its tasks quickly and has existed only in token form since 1956. The reunification of Laos in 1958 under a coalition government apparently ended the work of the Commission there, but unfortunately the coalition collapsed in 1961. A new Geneva Conference was then called, and the International Commission was revived.* The situation in Laos continues to be a troublesome one.

----
*Technically, the Laos Commission now operates under the "Protocol to the Declaration on the Neutrality of Laos, July 1962," and not under the Geneva accords of 1954.

The frustrations of coping with Communist intransigence make life trying for the Canadians in Indo-China, and the conditions of service are onerous. The climate is appalling, and the all-pervading dampness produces spectacular effects. At some places in Laos, one officer reported, boots and shoes fill to the top with blue mold overnight; another officer told of clothing being ruined in two or three days. Often stationed at remote jungle outposts, observers are thrown on their own resources. An officer with no taste for contemplative study and intellectual pursuits could find his Indo-China tour un-

(D.N.D. photo)

A Sinai desert patrol of the Reconnaissance Squadron, The Fort Garry Horse, with UNEF pauses to report progress by radio.

pleasant, for there is scant relief from the frustrating task of attempting to maintain the peace in the midst of near-war.

Why, then, does Canada not declare the whole structure raised at Geneva a farce and go home? The answer, states one authority,

is that [the Geneva Agreement] remains as a tacit recognition of the anxiety of the powers to limit and control the situation in Indo-China, to recognize some mutuality of interest in avoiding all-out conflict, to respect the Geneva disposition to bargain even without observing all the provisions of a bargain once made. It is significant that neither the Communist powers nor the United States call for a repudiation of the Geneva Agreements. Each demands rather that the other side live up to their terms. There are demands for a renegotiation . . . not for . . . denunciation.

"It seems, therefore", concludes this account, "to be the often humiliating duty of the I[nternational] C[ontrol] C[ommission] to stay in place, acting as a presence, a reminder of the involvement of the great powers."

The United Nations Emergency Force

By 1956 the United Nations and several of its member states, including Canada, had accumulated a sizeable body of experience relating to peace-keeping operations. Observer groups were functioning in Kashmir and Palestine, a large and growing number of officers from many countries had gained valuable experience in dealing both with the United Nations and with obdurate nationalities, and throughout most of the world a climate of opinion was developing which accepted the value of U.N. forces.

The Suez Crisis of October and November 1956 brought the world to the brink of nuclear war. The fighting in the Middle East, which began with the Israeli invasion of Egypt on 29 October and which was followed by an Anglo-French combined operation to seize the Suez Canal, faced the world organization with its most severe test. In grappling with this terrible crisis, which threatened to involve the Soviet Union and the United States, the United Nations created an international police force to separate the combatants and police the border between them. The Canadian role in the fall of 1956 was a vital one and undoubtedly the most valuable contribution Canada has ever made to world peace.

The idea of a United Nations police force in the Middle East was not a new one — as early as 1953 Canadian spokesmen had broached the idea in discussions with interested parties — but these attempts had failed, and similar efforts in 1955 and 1956 had also been unsuccessful. A full-scale crisis, however, reawakened interest in the idea, and fortunately the U.N. was in a position to act. Thanks to the Uniting for Peace resolution of 1950, a veto in the Security Council did not eliminate the possibility of action to restore peace. This resolution was invoked for the first time, overriding the vetoes of France and the United Kingdom, co-sponsors of the proposals in 1950, and a special emergency session of the General Assembly met on 1 November 1956.

The delegates to the Assembly session were in an angry mood. The seemingly successful Hungarian revolution had raised hopes for an early end to Soviet colonialism, but now Britain and France, the old colonial powers, had intervened in the Middle East. Early in the morning of 2 November, the aroused Assembly quickly passed a resolution calling for an immediate cease-fire, a withdrawal behind the armistice lines established in 1949 and a ban on the introduction of military supplies into the area.

The Canadian Government abstained on this resolution, and it was only after the vote had been taken that

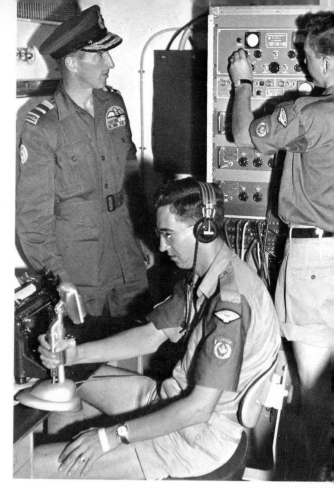

(D.N.D. photo)
Air Commodore C.G.W. Chapman, R.C.A.F., Air Commander in the Congo, w[ith] two R.C.A.F. radio technicians at work in his Leopoldville headquarters.

Mr. L. B. Pearson was able to state Canada's position.

> I regret the use of military force [he said] . . . but I regret also that there was not more time, before a vote had to be taken, for consideration of the best way to bring about that kind of cease-fire which would have enduring and beneficial results. . . . We need action, then, not only to end the fighting but to make the peace. . . . I therefore would have liked to see a provision in this resolution . . . authorising the Secretary-General to bargain to make arrangements . . . for a United Nations force large enough to keep these borders at peace while a political settlement is being worked out. . . . My own government would be glad to recommend Canadian participation in such a United Nations force, a truly international peace and police force.

The Canadian suggestion met with quick acceptance from delegates seeking to avoid catastrophe, and after consultations with Secretary-General Dag Hammarskjold, friendly governments and the Cabinet in Ottawa, Mr. Pearson produced a resolution calling for a study of the possibility of such a force. This resolution was passed by the General Assembly on 4 November by a vote of 57 to 0, with 19 abstentions.

Later that same day, the Secretary-General met informally with Mr. Pearson and several other delegates and improvised the plan requested in the Canadian resolution. Taking advantage of the presence of UNTSO in the area, the Secretary-General appointed Major-

General Burns, its Chief of Staff, head of a United Nations Command. Burns would be provided with a staff, and soon thereafter troops would be sent. The General Assembly subsequently approved this plan, but the British and French nevertheless persisted with their military operations. A ceasefire was not agreed to until the Secretary-General presented his final proposals for the force to the General Assembly on 6 November.

Hammarskjold's report, delineating the principles and procedures upon which the peace force would operate, was a vitally important document, not only for the immediate crisis but also for all future U.N. peace-keeping operations. The most important of his provisions was that barring permanent members of the Security Council from participation in the force within the war zone. Political control was vested in the Secretary-General alone, although an advisory committee was established to assist him. The force, soon to be christened the United Nations Emergency Force, would be "more than an observer's corps, but in no way a military force temporarily controlling the territory in which it is stationed." UNEF was to be a political neuter, and it was not intended to impose the will of the world body on the combatants; its sole purpose was to assist in the restoration of peace. The entire action of the United Nations, the report continued, was based on the "recognition by the General Assembly of the unlimited sovereign rights of Egypt." With the acceptance of this report, UNEF was created on paper. The difficult task of shaping an effective force yet remained. In these efforts, too, Canada was to play a role of the first magnitude.

The Canadian Government was proceeding with planning for its pledged contribution to UNEF. Discussions were held in Ottawa to consider such questions as supplies, the possibility of using Naples as a forward base for the force, the attachment of a military adviser to the Canadian delegation at U.N. Headquarters, and the choice of the infantry battalion to be sent to Egypt.

A Royal Canadian Medical Corps corporal attached to No. 57 Canadian Signal Unit in Leopoldville administers penicillin to a sick Congolese baby.
(D.N.D. photo)

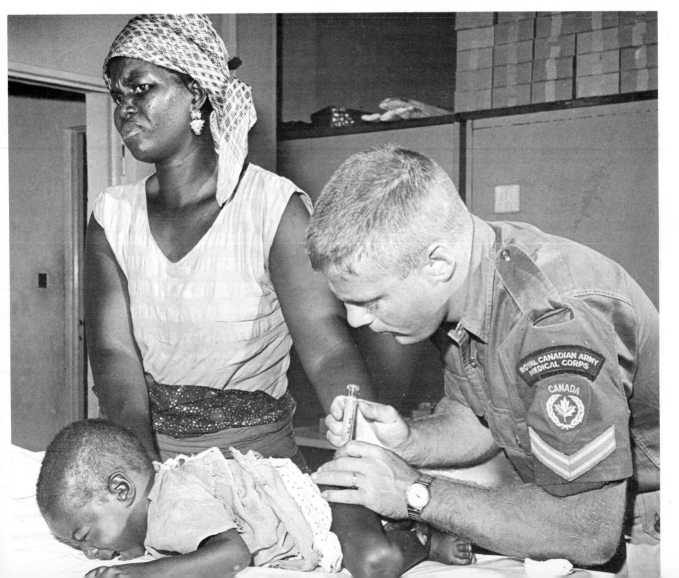

The tenor of the discussions, with their emphasis on logistics, was to set the tone of the Army's role in UNEF. Alone among the contributors to the international force Canada evinced a realistic interest in the prosaic details of administration and supply. When, therefore, Prime Minister St. Laurent announced the Canadian contribution of a unit of "battalion size", he was able to add the key phrase "augmented by ordnance, army service, medical and dental detachments". As far as possible the Canadian contingent would be self-contained. The Prime Minister also announced the Government's willingness to fly the troops to the Middle East in R.C.A.F. aircraft and to ship supplies and equipment on board the aircraft carrier H.M.C.S. *Magnificent*. The carrier would also be used to accommodate a small hospital and force headquarters, and to provide a communications link to Canada.

Simultaneously, planning was proceeding in New York. Three senior Canadian officers, representing the three army staff branches — operations, personnel and supply, or "G", "A" and "Q" — had joined the group of military men advising the Secretary-General. These able, experienced officers, fully in touch with the capabilities and resources of their branches, made a contribution to joint planning that was valuable out of all proportion to Canada's numerical representation on the Military Advisory Group. As had been foreseen in Ottawa, the problems facing UNEF's organizers were primarily logistical. How could UNEF be maintained? How could it be efficiently administered? Offers of troops were pouring in from countries as varied as Colombia, Denmark and India. An additional complicating factor, later noted by General Burns, was that "nearly all offers were of infantry, practically no administrative units being proposed in the first instance." Some countries offering troops, it soon became clear, would not even be able to supply the initial equipment, and especially the vehicles, necessary to support their contingents. In a paper presented to the Military Advisory Group on 10 November, the Canadian liaison officers took a large step toward overcoming these problems.

The first point in their presentation, which established the principles of supply and command for UNEF, dealt with the location, responsibilities and functions of the main base. The Canadians suggested that the United States be asked to supply the base from its extensive Mediterranean resources. This, they maintained, would

(D.N.D. photo)
A Canadian Provost Corps sergeant talks with a trooper of the 2nd Armoured Car Squadron, Irish Army, during a training patrol in the Congo.

ensure adequate supplies of military equipment for the peace force and, as the base would be in Naples, would not violate the Secretary-General's prohibition of Great Power participation in the war zone. Their second point recommended the consolidation of headquarters and support units and urged that, as the command structure was largely English-speaking, these units be English-speaking. As their last point, the Canadian officers suggested that the size of the force be fixed. These proposals received unanimous support and subsequently were largely carried out. The organization of UNEF was now well in hand.

Suddenly, but perhaps not unexpectedly, Egypt raised difficulties over Canadian participation in the force. Secretary-General Hammarskjold had attempted to anticipate Egyptian objections by immediately accepting offers of troops only from "non-controversial" nations, and he had included Canada in this group. The Egyptian complaints were first revealed in Cairo to the Commander of UNEF. General Burns later recalled that, while readily acknowledging Canada's independ-

Opposite page — IN THE DESERT. A Royal Canadian Corps of Signals officer, accompanied by an Indonesian Army sentry, watches the Israeli frontier from an outpost in the eastern Sinai desert. (D.N.D. photo.)

251

ence in foreign policy, the Egyptian foreign minister said "the trouble was that Canadian soldiers were dressed just like the British soldiers, they were subjects of the same Queen — the ordinary Egyptian would not understand the difference, and there might be unfortunate incidents." The difficulty over uniforms was further compounded when it became known that the Canadian infantry unit selected was a battalion of The Queen's Own Rifles of Canada. "There is no regiment in the Canadian forces that I respect more than the Queen's Own", General Burns wrote, "but it did seem an unlucky choice, in view of the Egyptian argument." On the advice of the U.N. Secretariat that these difficulties were only temporary, the government decided there was as yet no need to change the form of the Canadian contribution. But after several days of fruitless wrangling, the Canadian position hardened, and Mr. Pearson emphatically informed the Secretary-General

> that we felt it absolutely essential to the success of this effort that neither Egypt nor any other country should impose conditions regarding the composition of the force. I told him that on this matter we would negotiate only with him ... although we recognized ... that he should discuss these matters with Egypt. ...

Hammarskjold was in Egypt discussing the composition and duties of the force with President Nasser. On November 17 he informed Pearson that, while Canada was welcome as a state from which elements of UNEF could be drawn, the most important contribution at present would be air support. The Secretary-General believed that the question of ground troops could best

be settled later. "The present situation seems to be one where it is not a lack of troops for the immediate task but of possibilities to bring them over and maintain their lines of communication." As a result of this message and of the growing realization of the need for administrative personnel, the departure of The Queen's Own Rifles was postponed and finally cancelled. Instead, the 300 service troops originally intended to support the infantry battalion were flown to Egypt to administer the whole force until other arrangements could be made. The first Canadian troops landed at Abu Suweir, Egypt, on 24 November, ten days after the arrival of the first UNEF personnel.

The Canadian strength in UNEF was soon increased. Early in December General Burns decided that more administrative personnel were urgently needed, and he suggested to the Secretary-General that Canada be asked to provide these troops "instead of the infantry battalion originally proposed". The Canadian Government agreed to send a signals squadron, an R.C.E.M.E. infantry workshop, two transport platoons and an R.C.A.F. communications squadron. An armoured reconnaissance squadron was also prepared for UNEF service but was not dispatched until March 1957. With the arrival of the additional Canadian servicemen on 12 January 1957, the Canadian strength in Egypt exceeded 1000, fully one-sixth of the force. Since then almost 9000 Canadian soldiers and airmen have served in UNEF.

The Canadian servicemen in UNEF, apart from those

Lieut. Terry Liston of the Canadian Army and machine-gunners of the Armée Nationale Congolaise to which he was attached as U.N. Liaison Officer.
(D.N.D. photo)

"BETWEEN ARAB AND ISRAELI"

(D.N.D. photo)

A ferret scout car of the Reconnaissance Squadron, Royal Canadian Dragoons, patrolling the Egyptian-Israeli border.

in the reconnaissance squadron engaged in patrolling the armistice line, perform functions not essentially different from the ones they undertake at home. Their prosaic tasks of administration, however, must be done by someone, and both U.N. and Canadian officials believe that UNEF could not operate without the Canadian contribution. The morale of the troops is high, but, understandably enough, rotation back to Canada is the high point of the soldier's service.

The value of UNEF should not be underestimated. Although its creation has not led to a permanent solution of the political problems in the area, UNEF did prove that in certain circumstances the United Nations could react quickly and in some strength to halt fighting and prevent its resumption. Both the Egyptians and the Israelis are fully aware of the services to peace pro-

vided by the force. For the United Nations itself, UNEF was no less important. It was the first major peace-keeping force, the first strong exercise of power by the Secretary-General in a peace-keeping role, and the first enunciation of principles clearly applicable to the future. The worth of the knowledge gained at Suez was to be clearly demonstrated before much time had passed.

Lebanon

Although UNEF was successful in its task of stabilizing the border between Egypt and Israel, this was not the only trouble spot in the Middle East. Early in June 1958, the tiny half-Moslem, half-Christian nation of Lebanon came to the Security Council of the United Nations with charges that the United Arab Republic was aiding Lebanese rebels. The situation was confused, with local politics inextricably entangled with oil interests and the policies of the Great Powers. The one certainty was that the situation was potentially dangerous, and therefore the Security Council authorized the formation of a new observer force, the United Nations Observation Group in Lebanon.

Because of the need for haste, Secretary-General Hammarskjold turned first to UNTSO in Palestine and drew ten officers from that body to act as the nucleus of the new force. This first group included one Canadian officer. Shortly thereafter Ottawa received and quickly approved a request for ten officers. During the months of June and July 1958, UNOGIL's strength rose to approximately 130 observers, equipped with jeeps and light aircraft. Observer teams patrolled all accessible roads in the border areas both by night and by day; a system of permanent observer posts was established at key locations; and a reserve of observers was established to cope with emergencies. Lebanon appeared to be well on the way to stabilization until a new crisis wracked the area.

On 14 July 1958 a revolution in nearby Iraq overthrew the monarchy and government. The King and prominent pro-Western political figures were killed and their bodies dragged through the streets by mobs. Fearing for its survival, the Lebanese Government appealed to the United States for aid, and the following day American marines landed on the beaches near Beirut. A few days later British troops flew into Jordan to assist the government of that country. The Anglo-American operations were designed to protect Jordan's flank and deter outside intervention on behalf of the

A Caribou of No. 115 Air Transport Unit, R.C.A.F., serving in Yemen.
(D.N.D. photo)

254

Lebanese rebels.

Predictably, American intervention in Lebanon produced Soviet charges of aggression, but as a result of the ensuing debate at the United Nations, Secretary-General Hammarskjold flew to the Middle East to investigate. His decision was to strengthen UNOGIL further, and Canada was invited to contribute an additional 50 officers to the observation group. Eventually the observer force in UNOGIL reached a strength of 591 and the Canadian contribution totalled 77 officers and men. The increased force contributed to the pacification of the Lebanese borders and the United States troops withdrew early in November. On 17 November UNOGIL reported that its task was completed, and by 9 December 1958 the main body of the force had departed.

The Congo

The United Nations had satisfactorily resolved the Lebanese political crisis despite the interest of the Great Powers in the area. That the result was satisfactory was a tribute to the perseverance and skill of the Secretary-General and to the willingness of the Middle Powers to continue the peace-keeping functions they had assumed in 1956 with UNEF. Both the Secretary-General and the Middle Powers were soon to be tested again in a new theatre, the Congo.

Long before the Congo lapsed into anarchy in the summer of 1960, Secretary-General Hammarskjold had begun to increase the U.N. "presence" in the area, hoping thereby to insulate the emerging nations of the African continent from the pressures of the Cold War. The onset of the crisis of July 1960 was almost wel-

The Caribou and the camel serve in Yenne.
(D.N.D. photo)

comed by the U.N. Secretariat, who saw it as a chance to expand the positive functions of the Organization. Almost before the world was aware of it, a peace-keeping operation of unprecedented magnitude and complexity was in being. An international military force of 19,000 troops, a United Nations political team, and an extensive civilian administrative organization were all in the field. Financial difficulties plagued the U.N. throughout the operation and problems were increased with the death of Secretary-General Hammarskjold in an air crash in September 1961. In many ways the U.N. emerged from the Congo crisis in 1964 weaker than it had been in 1960, but the effort had had to be made.

The Canadian contribution in the Congo was small in numbers but of vital importance. The first request was for the secondment of two officers from UNTSO for duties in Leopoldville. This was followed by requests for three more officers and then for five specialist officers from UNEF. On 28 July, after a U.N. appeal for signals personnel, and despite a serious shortage of qualified technicians, the Government authorized the provision of a maximum of 500 personnel, including 200 signallers, for UNOC. The R.C.A.F. also participated in the operation. Four North Star aircraft transported a Canadian contribution of 40,000 lbs. of food to the Congo and were then used in logistical support of UNOC. The internal airlift was under the command of a Canadian officer and the R.C.A.F. also supplied some ground crew and technicians.

The signals role was the main Canadian commitment. The officers and men of No. 57 Canadian Signal Squadron had been concentrated at Barriefield Camp, Ontario, in early August 1960. There they had been documented, immunized and equipped for their tropical posting, while technicians had prepared the signals equipment for tropical conditions by varnishing every wire in the radio sets as a precaution against fungus. The first signallers arrived in the Congo on 19 August, and within a short time the entire squadron was in place. The Canadians manned the Leopoldville message centre for UNOC headquarters and staffed seven regional centres scattered throughout the interior. The signallers worked solely through and for the United Nations and had nothing to do with Congolese radio traffic. Their work was dull but essential. However, some other Canadians had hair-raising experiences.

In 1964 Lt.-Col. P. A. Mayer, a Canadian officer attached to UNOC headquarters, helped rescue a number of missionaries held prisoner in Kwilu Province. When he landed by helicopter in the town of Kisandji on 27 January:

There was much waving of arms, yelling and jabbing and spitting at me but I kept insisting that we go to the Mission to carry on the talks. The Chief then suddenly demanded to know what the ring on my right hand represented. As one of the Jeunesse indicated that he wanted it and was motioning that he would cut it off, I explained it was a wedding ring. The Chief then began to ask a series of questions about my family.... The result.... was that the Chief suddenly embraced me whereup the Jeunesse tried to pull us apart. It was during this moment that [I was hit] from behind with the flat of [a] machete.... The Jeunesse were now arguing as to who was to kill me.... The man put [my] pistol against my stomach, thumbed back the hammer and pressed the trigger but the pistol did not fire since I had forgotten to put a round up the chamber....

Eventually, Lt.-Col. Mayer escaped and rescued the missionaries. In all, more than 100 were saved in a series of similar operations. Mayer's heroism, and that of Sgt. J. A. L. Lessard of the Royal 22ᵉ Régiment who had worked with him on the rescue operations, was recognized by the award of the George Medal.

UNOC terminated its duties on 30 June 1964. The force withdrew before full stability was achieved because of continuing difficulties in financing the operation. But although the international peace-keeping force had encountered many frustrations, on balance it had succeeded in facilitating the re-integration of secessionist Katanga province and in maintaining a reasonable state of security within the Congo. Most important for the future was that UNOC was the first explicit development of U.N. military power entirely within a sovereign state.

West New Guinea and Yemen

While the Congo operation was still in progress, the United Nations launched two more peace-keeping ventures, both of which set new precedents. In West New Guinea (West Irian), the United Nations Temporary Executive Administration (UNTEA) assumed the entire administration of the former Dutch colony from 1 October 1962 until control was transferred to Indonesia on 1 May 1963. In Yemen, the United Nations Yemen Observer Mission (UNYOM) was charged with supervising the cease-fire and disengagement agreements between Saudi Arabia and the United Arab Republic. The Mission performed its task from 11 June 1963 until 4 September 1964. In each of these operations the U.N. provided the umbrella under which disengagement could take place. This was a service to world peace, of course, but it was even more of a service to the disputants. As a result, Indonesia and the Netherlands shared all the costs of UNTEA, and Saudi Arabia and the United Arab Republic divided the expenses incurred in the operation of UNYOM.

In these two operations Canada was represented primarily by officers and men of the Royal Canadian

(D.N.D. photos)

dian airmen in Yemen
he outer walls of San'a,
apital.

goslav soldier with the
d Nations Yemen Ob-
Mission mounts guard
R.C.A.F. aircraft at
an.

Governor General Georges Vanier says farewell to men of the Royal 22ᵉ Régiment leaving Quebec City for U.N. duty in Cyprus, March 1964.

Air Force. In West New Guinea, where the main military force was a battalion of Pakistani infantry, the R.C.A.F. provided five officers and eight ground crew, along with two float-equipped Otter aircraft. The usual task of the Canadians was to operate a regular flight from Biak over the jungle to Fak Fak carrying U.N. officials and freight. The Yemen Observer Mission was first staffed by Military Observers including five Canadian Army officers, seconded from UNTSO, and by two Canadian aircraft borrowed from UNEF. A Yugoslav reconnaissance squadron soon took up ground patrol duties in the desert country and it was joined by a Canadian air unit, which at its peak strength numbered approximately 50 officers and men. These two operations got little attention from the world press, but their contributions to peace were nonetheless real. Both UNTEA and UNYOM prevented any escalation

of the disputes and both helped to create an atmosphere conducive to political settlement.

Cyprus

Even in the jet-age 1960s the crises in Yemen and New Guinea had seemed far away. The situation in Cyprus, on the other hand, was much closer to the Canadian consciousness. Cyprus was a fellow Commonwealth country, torn asunder by fighting between its Greek and Turkish inhabitants. Both Turkey and Greece were NATO partners of Canada, as was the United Kingdom which had been trying to keep the peace in Cyprus since the beginning of fighting in 1955. As tension increased in 1963 and early 1964, the *New York Times* commented editorially that this island of 3750 square miles and 580,000 inhabitants "threatens to embroil Europe, the United States and even the whole world in its petty communal strife. . . . The Cyprus issue could become the classic example of how international conflicts become world conflicts." In these circumstances, an international force to keep the peace while negotiations were carried on was a necessity. Canada was to play a key role in its establishment.

The first attempts to establish a peace force were made under the auspices of NATO and the Commonwealth. These efforts collapsed, largely because the Greek Cypriots insisted that the only acceptable force would be a United Nations one. However, the situation deteriorated until on 11 March 1964 Turkey issued an ultimatum that it would intervene in defence of the Turkish Cypriots unless a United Nations force was on the island within a few days. "It is generally conceded", wrote a former U.N. official,

> [that] it was Canada's Secretary of State for External Affairs, Mr. Paul Martin, who saved the peace. Mr. Martin flew down to New York on March 12 and had lengthy discussions with [Secretary-General] U Thant . . . The following day, Friday 13, Mr. Martin, back in Ottawa, made a series of telephone calls — to Ankara, to Stockholm, to Helsinki, to Dublin, to Washington, and to New York. At 6 p.m. U Thant announced that a U.N. Force made up of troops from Canada, Ireland, Sweden and some of the British troops already in Cyprus would be constituted . . . And on the same fateful day, Turkey issued a statement welcoming the establishment of the Force. The danger of war had been averted — but by a narrow margin.

Parliament authorized Canadian participation in an evening session on 13 March. Addressing the House of Commons, Prime Minister Pearson announced that the Canadian contribution would consist of the 1st

H.M.C.S. *Bonaventure*, which transported men and material for the Canadian U.N. force in Cyprus, unloads an armoured vehicle at Famagusta.

(D.N.D. photo

260   Ferret scout cars of a Canadian reconnaissance squadron patrol a Cypriot village in the Nicosia zone.

(D.N.D. p

Battalion, Royal 22e Régiment, and a reconnaissance squadron of The Royal Canadian Dragoons. The force would be air-lifted to Cyprus by the R.C.A.F.'s Transport Command, and vehicles and materiel would be shipped on board the aircraft carrier H.M.C.S. *Bonaventure*. A reconnaissance party for the contingent arrived in Nicosia on 15 March and the first flight of the main body landed the following day. The Canadian High Commissioner in Nicosia reported to Ottawa that the prompt arrival of the Canadian troops was "the

turning point in the Cyprus crisis", and indeed the situation did ease perceptibly for a time. With the arrival of the *Bonaventure* on 30 March and with the Government's decision on 10 April 1964 to authorize the provision of a brigade headquarters for Cyprus,* the Canadian contribution was complete.

The Canadian Government had agreed to bear all

----
*The brigade headquarters was withdrawn on September 1965 in what was described as a U.N. "economy measure".

A soldier of the 1st Battalion, The Canadian Guards, on lookout duty in the Kyrenia Mountains, Cyprus.

(D.N.D. photo)

the costs involved in transporting the contingent to Cyprus and maintaining it there, although this was a departure from the long-standing Canadian position that all U.N. members should bear the costs involved in peace forces. However, Canada recognized that the deployment of the United Nations Force in Cyprus could not wait for the resolution of lengthy financial negotiations. It should be noted, too, that Britain also pays the expenses of her contingent, and that some 35 U.N. members contribute to the $2 million monthly cost of the force.

The Canadian troops in UNFICYP are disposed along the strategic Kyrenia Road, linking Nicosia to the north coast of the island and are responsible for maintaining a convoy system on it. In December 1964

other U.N. troops relieved the Canadians of the task of patrolling the "green line" dividing the Greek- and Turkish-Cypriot quarters of Nicosia. This had been a frustrating task, but their relief did not free the Canadians of danger. Patrols were often fired at from the hills along the country roads, and there were some near misses. "One bullet hit 45A Car and went through the rear jerri-can, back deck, tarp and ricocheted off the turret, missing the car commander . . . by inches", the War Diary of The Royal Canadian Dragoons recorded on one typical day. "No fire was returned." The situation in Cyprus required a high degree of discipline from every officer and man. One senior Indian officer with the force told the Canadian High Commissioner that "he was very much impressed with the Canadians

Men of the 1st Battalion, The Canadian Guards, on outpost duty in the Kyrenia Mountains, Cyprus.

(D.N.D. photo)

Ferret scout cars of a Canadian reconnaissance squadron patrol a Cypriot village in the Nicosia zone.

here . . ." He added that he was particularly impressed with the junior officers who knew their jobs and stayed cheerful in trying circumstances.

Canada has participated in ten peace-keeping operations – all there have been. What seems to have made her participation a virtual *sine qua non* for these forces? The answer is complex, but perhaps the most important factor has been the willingness of Canadian governments, regardless of their political complexion, to participate in joint efforts to keep the peace. Providing United Nations forces is irksome; they involve casualties, expense and political and military difficulties; they can be embarrassing; and not every nation is interested in participating. Another factor of vital importance is the Canadian reputation for impartiality. Canada belongs to NATO and the Commonwealth, and is linked with the United States in defence pacts. Despite this, Canadians have managed to project an image of objectivity, and there is no blemish of colonialism on the nation's record. However, all this would be of little value in peace-keeping were it not for the capabilities of the defence forces of the Dominion. Unlike most other middle and small powers, Canada has had – since the Second World War – a military organization capable of providing, transporting and maintaining troops anywhere and anytime. This is a great asset, the result of the willingness of the Canadian taxpayer to foot the bill.

But why should Canada involve herself in all the world's squabbles? Why should Canada spend money on peace-keeping? The obvious answer, and one no

263

Left—KEEPING THE PEACE IN CYPRUS. A section commander of The Queen's Own Rifles of Canada scans the terrain from a hill near Nicosia, Cyprus.

Delegates to the Ottawa Peace-keeping Conference, 1964, watch a demonstration by a detachment of the 1st Battalion, The Canadian Guards. In the background is an R.C.A.F. Yukon.

less true for being obvious, is that peace is every nation's business. The Suez crisis, the Cyprus situation and the India-Pakistan War posed clear threats to world peace, and other conflicts could easily have "escalated" into full-scale conflagrations. And yet peace still prevails, albeit shakily. It may not have been the United Nations that preserved the peace, but even its most virulent critics would have to admit that it helped. Surely this is reason enough. Furthermore, Canadian prestige and influence at the United Nations can be attributed in part to our role as a peace-keeper. Suez and Cyprus are battle honours on the flag of Canadian diplomacy. Finally, on a more practical level, Canada's U.N. commitments provide independent sources of information on world trouble spots. All these factors play their part in maintaining Canadian interest in peace-keeping.

Canadian leadership in the field was demonstrated at the Ottawa Peace-Keeping Conference of November 1964, called on Canada's initiative. Representatives from 23 countries which had either contributed substantially to U.N. operations or had placed stand-by units at the call of the Organization met to review their experiences and discuss informally ways of improving peace-keeping operations. The Canadian Government

had no preconceived ideas on what might emerge from the discussions, and it looked on an exchange of views as valuable in itself. Although no immediate decisions were taken, the informal contacts made should be invaluable in any future operation. A general recognition of the value of stand-by forces and preparatory planning was also noted, and this could also be helpful.

No one in the 1930s could have foreseen the Canadian role in the years since 1945. Canadian isolationism is dead, and its resurrection seems most unlikely. The shrinking of the world has given new responsibilities to every nation, but not many are willing to take up the burden. If another world war and a nuclear holocaust are averted, the credit may well go to those nations that have been willing to take what active steps they could to keep the peace. And Canada has a good claim to be numbered among them.

During the century we have surveyed, Canada's armed forces, as we have remarked before, have been the primary instrument by which she has exerted influence abroad. They played a distinguished part in the South African War; they fought as part of the forces of international alliances in two world wars, and in doing so helped to halt aggression and incidentally to advance Canada's own status; they served the United Nations under fire in Korea. It is suitable and satisfactory that they should be serving now in a variety of distant lands, still making their country's name and flag known and respected, but contributing not to the making of war but to the keeping of peace.

288